Computer Hardware Diagnostics for Engineers

Computer Engineering Series

PERRY • *VHDL*, Second Edition 0-07-049434-7

ROSENSTARK• *Transmission Lines in Computer Engineering*
0-07-053953-7

PICK • *VHDL Techniques, Experiments, and Caveats* 0-07-049906-3

CHEN • *Computer Engineering Handbook* 0-07-010924-9

DEVADAS, DEUTZER, GHASH • *Logic Synthesis* 0-07-016500-9

LEISS • *Parallel and Vector Computing* 0-07-037692-1

HOWLAND • *Computer Hardware Diagnostics for Engineers*
0-07-030561-7

Related Titles of Interest:

KIELKOWSKI • *SPICE Practical Parameter Modeling* 0-07-911524-1

KIELOWSKI • *Inside SPICE* 0-07-911525-X

MASSABRIO, ANTOGNETTI • *Semiconductor Device Modeling with
SPICE,* Second Edition 0-07-002469-3

Computer Hardware Diagnostics for Engineers

Ronald E. Howland

McGraw-Hill, Inc.

New York   San Francisco   Washington, D.C.   Auckland   Bogotá
Caracas   Lisbon   London   Madrid   Mexico City   Milan
Montreal   New Delhi   San Juan   Singapore
Sydney   Tokyo   Toronto

Library of Congress Cataloging-in-Publication Data

Howland, Ronald E.
  Computer hardware diagnostics for engineers / Ronald E. Howland.
     p.   cm. — (Computer engineering series)
  Includes index.
  ISBN 0-07-030561-7
     1. Electronic digital computers—Testing.   2. Electronic digital com-
puters—Circuits—Testing.   3. Electric circuit analysis.
  I. Title. II. Series.
  TK7888.3.H69   1995
  621.39'16'0287—dc20   94-48891
                                                                 CIP

1   2   3   4   5   6   7   8   9   0   DOC/DOC   9   0   0   9   8   7   6   5

ISBN 0-07-030561-7

*The sponsoring editor for this book was Stephen S. Chapman and
the production supervisor was Suzanne W. B. Rapcavage. It was set
in New Century Schoolbook by J. K. Eckert & Company, Inc.*

Printed and bound by R. R. Donnelley & Sons Company.

Contents

Foreword

Well, it's finally here! A text for design engineers, software developers, quality assurance engineers, and production test engineers alike. I have been encouraging Ron to write this book for almost ten years, and here it is. This isn't the kind of book that you snuggle up with by the fireplace with your favorite drink and read into the wee hours of the morning but, rather, a book that will help you make your product better—a book that will be a well used reference. Engineers, production staff, and quality assurance people will see the fundamental techniques for testing memory, I/O, and so forth, and at the same time get a working test executive that can be used to run diagnostic test routines. This offers a powerful testing tool that can be added to and modified during the life of the product. The needs of development engineering, production, quality assurance, and test are all addressed here. The techniques outlined within this book, in combination with your unique requirements, will afford you a superior product.

From an engineering perspective, when diagnostics are complete, prototype construction errors, bugs, and design flaws are identified quickly. Most people think of testing as a technique for the isolation of wiring and production errors, but in reality the very first thing that diagnostics do with new products is confirm their design algorithms. Hardware and software engineers should be using diagnostic techniques every bit as much as quality assurance, test, and manufacturing personnel. Its easy to verify wiring errors; stuck bits; faulty parts; faulty security mechanisms, communication protocols, and parsers; and other design flaws when a properly designed diagnostic is in place.

Quality assurance people can use diagnostic test suites to verify that the functional specification is in fact being met. Ron outlines the importance of this, and quality assurance personnel should take advantage of this book to make testing support available to supplement what the design engineers offer. Remember, it is difficult for engineers to cover all of the bases because of their unique perspective: They are the creators who have preconceived notions about the design and implementation, and this influences any diagnostics they produce. That's why we have quality assurance and test engineering personnel.

Test engineering organizations will benefit from this book by gaining understanding of what the real *guts* of a diagnostic are composed of. Since they write and modify many of the diagnostics used by production, it is imperative that test personnel understand the concepts of diagnostic engineering techniques.

Production organizations can take advantage of the diagnostics produced by the quality assurance, manufacturing engineering, and development organizations. Using Ron's executive will make the work of both production testing and production repair more reliable and reproducible.

The end goal of a good diagnostic is a great product. Seldom is such a claim made, and that's with good reason. There are hundreds of texts on design, using specific design techniques, and using CAD/CAM systems. There are even texts that emphasize the importance of testing, but nowhere is there a text on *how to do it*—nowhere is there a compilation of years of practical day-to-day diagnostic techniques. Not until now.

If you are a hardware engineer, software developer, quality assurance engineer, or test engineer, your technical resources, along with those described within this book, will assist you in delivering a better product. This book will offer an important insight into the *guts* of a diagnostic. If you are part of a production test or troubleshooting organization, you can also gain by having a deeper understanding of diagnostics.

In a single book, Ron has covered years of professional, practical, real-world experience in the area of diagnostics. There is no other single source that I am aware of that provides such detailed information on the interior workings of diagnostics. Remember, a great design + great quality assurance + great testing + great diagnostics = great product. The effect that a great diagnostic will have on customer acceptance is second only to offering that customer an appropriate solution to a problem. No matter how great your design is, if your customers experience problems because of bugs or design flaws, they will not be happy campers. We have all heard the horror stories, and some of them have come from some very experienced manufacturers. They lost sight, even if just for a moment, of the importance of diagnostics. When done properly, diagnostics are not done *after* the design but, as Ron points out, in parallel, and they should influence the final product design.

Give your customers a great design in combination with a bug-free product, and your customers will have a positive experience.

Henry (Hank) Sousa
Senior Corporate Consulting Engineer

Preface

The purpose of this book is to present the tools, techniques, and test methods for developing computer hardware diagnostics. It is acknowledged that testing is expensive, and major efforts are in place to increase testing while decreasing its cost.

The tools, techniques, test methods, and diagnostic executives described in this book should aid diagnostic programmers in developing their diagnostics faster and with better tests.

About the Book

The first chapter introduces the topic of computer diagnostics, the need for and types of diagnostics, and test mythology. The overall conclusion is that there is a great need for diagnostic programs.

Chapter 2 presents the process of developing good diagnostic test. Also, the concept of design for test-ability is introduced. The reader is introduced to fault modeling, simulation, and built-in test. The development process proceeds through fault insertion and code release.

Chapter 3 provides an overview of testing the complete CPU mother board. All systems, from intelligent gauges to complete full-blown computer systems, have processors, memory, and a number of devices that need to be tested.

Chapter 4 introduces the memory array and the different types of memories. A basic RAM board is used as the basis for developing several well known memory diagnostic tests.

Chapters 5, 6, and 7 describe generic diagnostic tests for communication systems, mass storage, and video subsystems.

Finally, in Chapter 8, three diagnostic executives are presented. Each of these provides a powerful and friendly user interface. The code for these executives is provided in the appendices.

As a technical writer, I must thank those who have provided help, inspiration, and encouragement to the completion of this book.

I would like to thank a very close friend and co-worker Henry (Hank) Sousa for convincing me that there is a need for a book describing diagnostic testing. Many thanks also goes to Philip LaPlant who spent many hours in helping with the format and organization of this book. Without their help this book would never have made it.

Ronald E. Howland

Abbreviations

ATE	automatic test equipment
BON	bed of nails tester
BIST	built-in self test
CAE	computer aided engineering
CPU	central processing unit
DFT	design for test
DMA	direct memory access
EPROM	erasable programmable read-only memory
FIFO	first in, first out (memory)
FRU	field replaceable unit
ICT	in-circuit tester
I/O	input/output
ISR	interrupt service routine
LAN	local area network
LED	light emitting diode
LFSR	linear feedback shift register
LSB	least significant bit
LSI	large scale integration
MUX	multiplexer
MSB	most significant bit
MTBF	mean time between failure
MTFF	mean time to first failure
NMI	non-maskable interrupts
NV-RAM	nonvolatile RAM
OS	operating system
PAL	programmable array logic
PROM	programmable read-only memory

PWB   printed wire board
RAM   random access memory
ROM   read-only memory
SAM   sequential address memories
s-a-1   stuck at 1 fault
s-a-0   stuck at 0 fault
SA   signature analysis
UART   universal asynchronous receiver transmitter
VLSI   very large scale integration

The Hardware Diagnostic

1.0 Introduction

In recent years, system testing and hardware diagnosis for computers has been given more attention. There are four primary reasons for this:

1. Board designs are becoming more complicated and difficult to test.
2. There is a greater drive to push products to market quickly.
3. The cost of repairing design errors increases as the hardware enters latter stages of its life cycle.
4. Computer down time is very expensive.

The purpose of this book is to present test algorithms and procedures for the development of computer diagnostic programs to the novice diagnostic programmer. This book will also serve as a reference to the seasoned diagnostic programmer and perhaps contains some new ideas on testing boards. The book also presents three different types of diagnostic executive, which is the human interface to the diagnostic test. Many hours have been spent in the design of these executives. Hopefully, these executives will serve as a guide and help you to get started with developing your own diagnostics.

1.1 What are Diagnostics?

A *diagnostic* is a computer program that checks programmable computer hardware and determines whether that hardware is working as specified. There are two basic purposes to diagnostic testing.

The first is fault detection, which may be met simplistically by operating the unit under test in such a way as to exercise all functional blocks. A failure of the proper operation is the detection of a fault.

The second purpose of testing, and the more difficult to achieve, is *fault isolation*. That is, to reasonably isolate a failure to the lowest common functional block or component. Chapter 2 provides greater detail on fault isolation.

1.2   The Life Cycle of Hardware

A brief look into the life cycle of a computer circuit board provides an understanding of how diagnostics are used over time.

Diagnostics are used as soon as the engineer has built a prototype of the hardware to determine that the hardware works as specified. Next, the hardware goes through a series of tests to verify that the design is durable and reliable. Generally, the hardware is placed in environmental chambers which varying the temperature and humidity.

As the board enters its productivity stage, the manufacturing group enters its start-up operation and must prepare to receive the first group of boards. Manufacturing requires some means of testing the boards before shipping them. The manufacturing test provides fault isolation so that the technicians may repair boards that fail.

Finally, when the hardware enters the field, the customers need diagnostic programs to verify that the hardware continues to work correctly. These tests can be simple "go, no-go" tests, a power on start up test, or a very complicated set of on-line diagnostics.

As you can, see many different diagnostics are needed throughout the life cycle of the hardware. Occasionally, a single diagnostic might be used for all cases, but this is very uncommon.

1.3   Board Testing

Although the functionality of VLSI chips is increasing, these chips must still be connected in a circuit via a *printed wiring board (PWB)*. Technological advances are not only confined to the device packages. Improvements may also be found in the design of the PWB. These improvements, which further complicate testing, include:

1. many layers pressed together (multilayer boards)
2. finer lines (traces)
3. improved routing techniques
4. plotted through-holes

There a four test techniques used by manufacturing to verify a printed wire board. These techniques are:

1. bare-board testing
2. pre-screening
3. in-circuit testing
4. functional testing

The sequencing of these tests is depicted in Fig. 1.1.

1.3.1 Bare-board testing

A *bare-board test* is used to check boards before components are placed on them. The purpose of this test is to check for continuity, leakage, shorts, and open circuits. Bare-board test systems can cost from $30,000 to $500,000.

1.3.2 Pre-screening testing

A *pre-screening test* is used to determine the quality of assembly for simple PWB components such as resistors, diodes, and other semi-passive discrete components. A *bed of nails* (BON) tester (so called because it contains a large number of spring-loaded test pins on a flat test fixture) is generally used to access points on the PWB. This tester verifies the correct value, orientation, existence, and proper connection of the components.

1.3.3 In-circuit testing

This test determines whether a component has been inserted properly and will operate within tolerances. In-circuit automatic test equipment (ATE) employs drivers and receivers that operate through switching circuits that are connected to the BON fixture. The *in circuit test* (ICT) can perform more than just simple truth table checks.

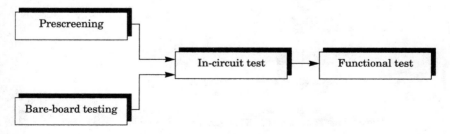

Figure 1.1 Typical manufacturing test sequence.

For example, newer in-circuit testers can test programmable gate arrays, intelligent chips, and microprocessors. Some employ backdriving techniques to effectively isolate complex devices on the board. They cannot, however, verify that the powered-up board will function as intended.

1.4   Functional Test

The *functional test* checks the functionality of the circuit in its true environment. For each set of inputs to the circuit, there are outputs. The functional test presents sets of inputs to the circuit and compares the outputs to those that are expected. If a comparison fails, the test fails.

In more sophisticated functional testers, the ATE is specifically programmed to emulate the system environment of the board under test. The board is connected to the ATE via a connector, and intelligent probes are positioned automatically to determine fault locations.

1.5   The Economics of Good Diagnostics

As systems become more complex, the cost of testing becomes a larger part of the overall system cost. Hence, there is greater emphasis on reducing the cost of testing by improving test techniques and procedures. Moreover, it is becoming more important to detect problems early. The problems that appear during system integration and after the product is in the field become very expensive to diagnose and repair. In fact, the cost of repairing these problems will increase at each stage of the development process (see Fig. 1.2).

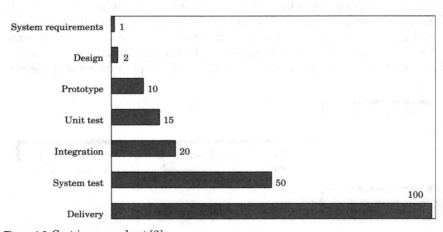

Figure 1.2 Cost increase chart [2].

1.6   Test Principles

The following is a set of important testing principles or guidelines that can help in the development of a diagnostic program.

1.6.1   Know the expected result

If the expected results are not known, then the chances of getting erroneous ones are increased. One way to combat this is to define all the expected outputs in advance. Each test case must consist of two components: a description of the test and a description of the correct output.

1.6.2   Avoid testing your own design

The development diagnostic is designed to find faults with the design of the hardware. Therefore, in a sense, it is destructive testing. Imagine, that you, as an engineer who is being creative, have to write a program that finds faults. It may be difficult for you to change your frame of mind quickly from being creative to being destructive.

Furthermore, imagine that you have just finished what you think is a very good design. You have invested many hours in it, and you feel very good about the design. Now you are told that you must find faults with it. This design is your creation and you subconsciously want it to be perfect. If you write the diagnostic, you will have to change your mental attitude to one of wanting to expose errors.

Finally, the design may have errors attributable to your misunderstanding of the design specification. In this case, it is very likely that any diagnostic you write will carry the same misunderstanding and thereby mask the fault.

1.6.3   Invalid testing

There is a tendency when testing to concentrate on the valid and expected condition at the expense of the invalid and unexpected ones. For instance, we always want to read and seek to valid tracks of a disk subsystem. What happens when seeking or reading invalid tracks?

What happens when a communication device receives one more characters than expected? We must test for these and other unexpected occurrences.

1.6.4   Your attitude: "Errors will be found"

The diagnostic is a destructive program designed to find faults and design errors. Enter the diagnostic effort with the attitude that you are going to find faults. If you execute your program and no faults are found, it proves only that the program executed correctly.

1.6.5 Testing requires creativity

Many programming engineers frown upon testing because they believe that there is little challenge or creativity involved. This is not true. Testing can be both creative and challenging because:

1. In many cases, the hardware under test is a new design using the latest technology.
2. When a problem is found during testing, the tester must determine if the problem is hardware or software.
3. The diagnostic programmer can influence the design of the hardware and/or software.
4. The test diagnostic must provide full test coverage of the board.
5. The diagnostic must have a friendly interface.
6. The diagnostic must isolate, to the lowest level, the component that is failing.

1.7 Types of Diagnostics

This section defines different types of diagnostics and provides a brief explanation of their purposes. A more detailed explanation of each is provided later in this chapter.

Engineering This diagnostic is used by the diagnostic engineer to verify that the hardware design is correct. The diagnostic is developed as soon as possible in the design stage. In many cases, the diagnostic engineer may have to work with a simulation model and develop the code on a simulator. The diagnostic is generally the first code that exercises the board under development.

Design certification This diagnostic is used by the engineering group to test the new or modified hardware for durability and reliability, and to verify that the hardware is functioning in accordance with the intended design.

Manufacturing This diagnostic is used in the manufacturing environment to verify that there are no faults in the hardware. This test must isolate faults to the component level so that the test technician can repair the board.

Power up (self-test) This diagnostic is used when power is applied to the system as a quick test before the system is allowed to be used. In many cases, the power up sequence must be fast, and therefore not all of the hardware is tested during the power-up diagnostic.

Field service   This diagnostic test is used in the field to check that the hardware works. This diagnostic must isolate faults to the *field replaceable unit (FRU)* (usually at the board level). Once the unit is replaced, the faulty unit can be returned to the shop for repair.

On-line   This diagnostic is developed so that it executes while the system is operating. The diagnostic cannot hinder, in any way, proper operation of the system. The on-line diagnostic will reduce system performance, but the reduction in performance must be within acceptable levels. It is used to detect the trend of a component that might indicate that a subsystem is going bad.

Remote diagnostic   This test uses a remote station to implement diagnostic procedures and determine what is wrong before the field service technician is sent to the site.

1.8   Development Diagnostics

When a computer or PWB is designed, the engineer designing the board must verify that it works as defined in the functional specifications. Generally, on more complicated boards, the engineer needs a program that can be used as an aid in the development of the board.

As an example, assume that the board being developed is a communications PCB as shown in Fig. 1.3. On the board there is a block of memory, a serial communications port, a clock chip, and a parallel I/O port.

When power is first applied to the prototype wire wrap board, it is called a *smoke test*. If the board passes the original smoke test, then the engineer must verify that different sections of the board work as expected.

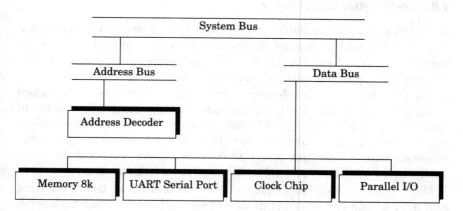

Figure 1.3 Typical computer board.

In the case of our board, the engineer probably would like to verify that the CPU is able to read and write to the memory. In this case, he might use a debugger program and attempt to write to the memory on the board and then read from the memory. A *debugger* or *monitor* program is a system program, usually in ROM, that allows the engineer to access memory and I/O directly. In many cases, it can be used to write simple assembly language programs directly into memory.

A more sophisticated test must be developed to check that the address lines are not crossed, shorted, opened, or otherwise improperly wired or designed. Here is where the engineer needs a program specifically developed to verify that the CPU is able to read from and write to memory, and check out all possible problems with the associated circuitry.

After checking the memory block, the engineer would move on to testing the parallel logic I/O. Once again, the engineer might use a debug program here.

Next, the engineer might want to check the communications chip. Using a debugger again, the engineer is able to create small programs to verify that the bus logic to the communication port works.

Finally, a more complicated program must be developed to transfer and receive data via the communication port. If the port has the ability to communicate at different baud rates, then it must be checked out at those rates.

As you can see, the engineer needs diagnostic test programs as soon as the prototype becomes available. It is also evident that the diagnostics must be developed and tested at the same time that the board is being developed (or, if possible, before development begins).

1.9   Certification Diagnostics

A *Certification test*, or *design verification test,* is used to demonstrate that the product has met all functionality goals as stated in the engineering functional specifications, and to determine if the design is stable enough to proceed to the next stage.

For example, most developers require that a new system be tested in an environmental chamber to be sure that the system is capable of functioning in a wide range of environments. The humidity is raised and lowered, as is the temperature. The environmental conditions are recorded, along with any errors that occur. There may also be pressure, shock, vibration, and other kinds of environment stress.

Many systems may undergo certification testing at the same time and over a long period. During these tests, all errors must be logged, and each error must be evaluated for fault determination. All errors that are assessed against a board contribute to the calculation of the mean time between failure (MTBF) for that board.

MTBF is a ratio of operating time to the number of observed failures. A second statistic that is usually calculated during certification testing is the mean time to the first failure (MTFF).

1.10 Manufacturing Diagnostics

A manufacturing diagnostic may be completely different from the development diagnostic used to verify the design. The manufacturing test team might use a test bed, a special test fixture, simulated peripherals, or ATE. Because manufacturing diagnostics must accomplish fault isolation in these special environments, they are difficult to write.

1.10.1 Test bed

A *test bed* consists of a computer and specialized hardware that are designed to exercise the board. A diagnostic program is loaded into the test bed computer and then executed to simulate the true operating environment. Figure 1.4 depicts a typical test-bed system layout.

If the manufacturing test process uses a test bed, the development diagnostic could be modified not only to detect faults, but to isolate the faulty component and report that it is faulty.

1.10.2 Special fixtures

The board under test may require special fixtures that provide signals normally generated from an external source. These fixtures provide some form of simulation that "fools" the diagnostic program into thinking that it is connected to the system.

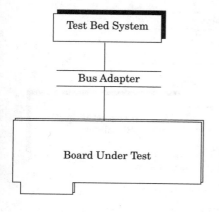

Figure 1.4 Typical test bed configuration.

For example, consider having an automatic test program that must check the reliability of a keyboard. To test a keyboard, many keys must be pressed in some sequence. Suppose the diagnostic could communicate with a special controller that was able to activate solenoids that were positioned to depress keys of the keyboard. The diagnostic would no longer require humans to press the keys, and the key board test could be performed automatically.

1.10.3 Simulated peripherals

To functionally test a controller board that uses a peripheral, you must have that peripheral connected or use a simulator. If the manufacturing department has ten test positions, each connected to the peripheral, and the peripherals costs $20,000 each, it would be very costly to set up the test station. Instead, a simulation device could be designed that takes the place of the peripheral during manufacturing test. Figure 1.5 provides a block diagram of a simulated peripheral. Notice that the CPU has the ability to communicate directly with the simulator via the I/O bus or through a communications port.

For example, assume that the simulated peripheral is a disk drive. The controller would send the proper commands to seek to a track. The simulator would then respond to the controller in the same fashion that the disk drive itself would.

Now two tests can be made to verify that the controller is working as expected. The first test would send a legal seek command and have the simulator respond correctly. A second test would make the simulator respond incorrectly.

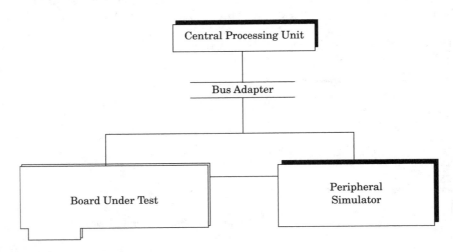

Figure 1.5 Peripheral simulation.

When a read operation takes place through the controller, the diagnostic would transfer the data directly to the simulator prior to issuing the read command. When a write operation takes place, the simulator retains the data, and the CPU is able to directly read the data in the simulator. This type of test determines whether the read or the write operation is faulty.

1.10.4   ATE

As printed wiring board sizes and functionality increase, there are more circuit nodes that need to be tested. In many cases, ATE can be used to provide more sophisticated functional testing. The newest types of ATE can place the board under test through a rigorous testing in a simulated environment. Using the ATE greatly increases the test coverage and reduces the test technician's time to repair the board.

1.11   Field Service Diagnostics

The field service or maintenance diagnostic provides the customer with three types of maintenance: preventive, corrective, and predictive. Field service diagnostics can identify *field replaceable parts (FRPs)* that are at fault. The technician then can replace these parts and get the system back up and running quickly.

Remote diagnostics and performance testing are used to assist the field service engineer in predicting latent problems. This allows the field service engineer to correct such problems before they become critical and cause system downtime.

1.12   Power-Up Diagnostics

Power-up diagnostics test the system before it is available for use. The power-up diagnostics verify that the system has at least a minimal amount of hardware working properly before allowing the user to operate the system.

Power-up diagnostics are used over the life of the product to keep track of required maintenance. For example, these are widely used in the automotive industry—when a particular milestone has been reached, such as a car passing 12,000 miles, the diagnostic reports that maintenance is required. After the maintenance has been performed, the technician resets the diagnostic flag.

Generally, the order of test in a power-up diagnostic is as follows:

1.   ROM test
2.   system memory test

3. test communication ports
4. test storage device media
5. test control panels
6. test printer interface

1.13 On-Line Diagnostics

On-line diagnostics execute under the control of the operating system (OS) during normal computer operation. Their purpose is to detect trends in the hardware that may indicate deterioration. For example, during normal operating mode, the operating system may be able to detect that the disk subsystem is experiencing more soft errors than expected. The operating system can then schedule the disk diagnostic.

On-line diagnostics should not hinder or corrupt normal operation of the operating system. However, these diagnostics do require a small slice of OS time to execute, and they may affect performance slightly.

1.14 Remote Diagnostics

Remote diagnostics are a different type of field service diagnostic. Rather than the field service technician arriving at the site and executing the diagnostic to determine what is wrong with the system, a central site may take control of the computer in question and execute the diagnostic program, as shown in Fig. 1.6. This gives the central site a much better assessment, if not an absolute definition, of the problem before a technician is dispatched. Once the problem has been isolated remotely, the central site informs the field technician that a particular plug-in board is needed. The technician then arrives on site with the replacement board.

The remote diagnostic reduces the amount of downtime for the customer and increases productivity for both the customer and the field service technician. The remote diagnostic, along with monitoring tools, can be a tremendous aid to the field service engineer—particularly when it comes to troubleshooting intermittent faults.

1.15 Summary

This chapter presented an introduction to diagnostics, basic definitions of them, and the reasons they are employed. The types of diagnostics described are summarized in Table 1.1. In addition, this chapter provided an introduction to test principles that should be used in the diagnostic design. Finally, different types of diagnostic tests were described.

Figure 1.6 Remote diagnostics.

TABLE 1.1 Summary of Diagnostics over the System Life Cycle

Diagnostic	When run	Purpose
Engineering	Design stage	Used by design engineer to verify board functionality
Certifications	Late design test	Verify the reliability of the design
Manufacturing	Test	Verify that the board has no faults
Power-up	Power applied	Checks minimum functionality
Field service	Field test	Identifies part of system that needs service or that is failing
On-line	Scheduled by operating system	Detects faults and fault trends in subsystem
Remote	In field	Used by field service from a distant site to determine problem with system

1.16 References

1. Myers, G. 1979. *The Art of Software Testing*. New York: John Wiley & Sons.
2. Kaufman, P.A. 1992. Prototyping alternative. *Computer Design* (April).
3. Brock, D. 1990. Reducing the cost of test development. *Evaluation Engineering* (August).

Designing a Diagnostic

2.0 Introduction

This chapter describes the process used in designing a diagnostic program from the time the diagnostic programmer is assigned to the project to the release of the diagnostic program. Topics include:

1. gathering of necessary information
2. reviewing specifications for testability
3. writing a functional specification
4. identifying test cases
5. coding and testing the diagnostic
6. fault insertion
7. release of the code

The concept of adding hardware logic to the PWB as an aid in board testing is also presented in this chapter. This concept in itself could take several volumes to cover thoroughly, but here it is introduced so that the diagnostic engineer is aware of its existence and understands the concept.

2.1 The Kick-Off

It is unfortunate that, in many cases, a diagnostic programmer is not assigned to a project until after the hardware has been designed. As a result, the diagnostic programmer has little influence on the design.

Test engineers who learn that they are being assigned to a particular project, and that the hardware has yet to be designed, should get involved early in the process. They should obtain a copy of the functional specifications and attend any status and project review meetings that take place. In doing so, a test engineer can influence product design and ensure its testability.

Review the specifications to understand the product's functionality, and evaluate how difficult it will be to write the diagnostics. Be ready to request hardware changes that might facilitate circuit board testing or assist you in debugging the diagnostics.

2.2   The Functional Specification

The functional specification, usually created by the design engineer, describes the product that must be tested. Part of a sample hardware specification is shown in the extracted text block below. This specification defines a read/write I/O port with the lower 5 bits defined.

> The control status register is a read/write word register located at hardware I/O address 385 and control the operation of the Status Interface plus other miscellaneous functions.
>
> Control Status Register (0x385)

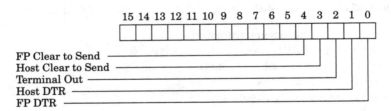

> 0   Data Terminal Ready—This bit controls the flow of incoming characters from the front panel; writing a zero disables incoming data. This bit is zero on power-up.
>
> 1   Host Data Terminal Ready—This bit controls the flow of incoming characters from the host system. Writing a one to this bit enables incoming data from the host; writing a zero disables incoming data. This bit is zero on power-up.
>
> 2   Terminal Output—This bit controls the destination of data through the panel UART. Writing a one to this bit enables the transmit data path between the panel UART and the panel; writing a zero disables the path. This bit is zero on power-up.
>
> 3   Clear to Send—This read-only bit returns a one when the Host is ready to accept a character from the controller. The bit returns a zero when the Host is not ready.

4   Clear to Send—The read-only bit returns a one when the front panel is ready to accept a character from the controller. The bit returns a zero if the front panel is not ready.

Obtain a copy of the functional specification as soon as possible and review it. Review it a second time, jotting down notes on how particular areas of the hardware might be tested. Identify all I/O registers, the memory layout, and hardware interrupts. Encourage the design engineer to place a section of testability into the functional specifications. In doing so, the designer addresses the issue of testability earlier than normal, even if it is only via a statement that "no extra logic will be added to support testing."

2.3   The Schematics

The schematics are the blueprints for the circuit being designed. After the functional specification is written, the engineer starts the hardware design. The design is created by specifying how each logic chip connects into the system. This is defined in the board schematics.

Obtain a set of schematics, and read and understand them. If necessary, spend time with the engineer and ask questions that might help you to understand the circuit better. You are to write a diagnostic that tests the circuit represented by these schematics. If you do not understand the schematics, then it is difficult to write the test. A sample schematic is shown in Fig. 2.1.

Evaluate the initialization process. In many cases, the power-up reset signal is the initialization signal for the components of the board. To ensure the efficiency of a test, the hardware should be placed into a known state before testing. You should insist on a software initialization for all programmable chips.

In reviewing the schematics, attempt to break the logic into functional blocks. Doing so should help in understanding each functional area, its purpose, and how it interfaces with the other functional parts. This also identifies the blocks that must undergo diagnostic testing.

2.4   Design for Testability

The concept of *design for testability* suggests that the test engineer will be included in the design phase and offer concepts that will enhance the product's testability. To have a better understanding of design for testability, the test engineer must understand several important concepts in hardware design and testing. These are:

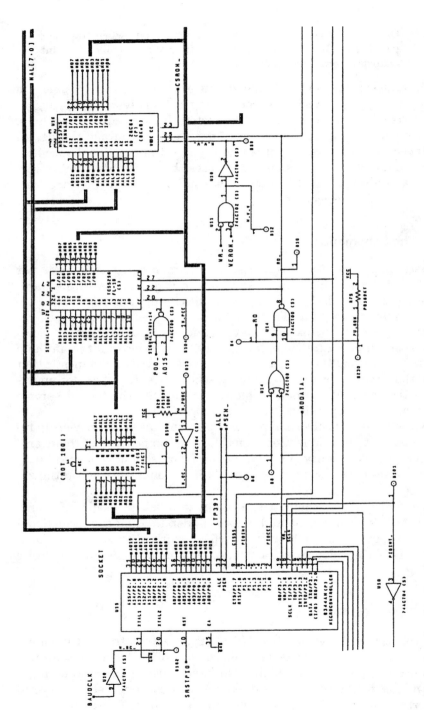

Figure 2.1 Sample schematic.

1. fault modeling
2. fault tables
3. redundant faults
4. simulation
5. built in test logic
    - signature analysis
    - scan pattern
    - built-in self-test

These concepts are described briefly in the following sections to provide the reader with a basic understanding of the subject.

2.5   Fault Modeling

A fault model describes the effect of physical failures within a logic network. The "stuck-at" fault model is used throughout the electronics industry to illustrate a common defect. The stuck-at fault model assumes that a gate input or output is fixed at either logic 0 or logic 1. Figure 2.2a shows a good AND gate, and 2.2b shows a faulty AND gate with an input stuck at 1 (S-A-1).

In Fig. 2.2b, the node A input is stuck at 1. Table 2.1 is the truth table for a good AND gate versus one with input node A stuck at 1. Comparing the truth tables, you can see that the output is incorrect when node B is a 1 and node A is a zero.

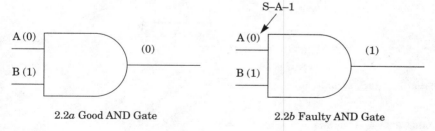

2.2a Good AND Gate   2.2b Faulty AND Gate

Figure 2.2 AND gate.

TABLE 2.1   AND Gate Truth Table

	Good AND Gate		Bad AND Gate	
	B = 0	B = 1	B = 0	B = 1
A = 0	0	0	0	1
A = 1	0	1	0	1

Expanding the idea of the stuck-at fault to a large circuit, as shown in Fig. 2.3, we see that there are three input nodes and a single output node. With this circuit, there is a possibility of having ten stuck-at fault occurrences. Each node can be stuck at 0 or 1. The stuck-at fault model assumes that in the circuit under test there can only be one stuck-at fault at any time.

To completely test the circuit in Fig. 2.3, we must identify all possible test vectors to the circuit. These test vectors are identified in Table 2.2, along with the expected results. After all tests have been defined, we must identify which stuck-at faults can be detected by each test vector (refer to Table 2.3).

Assume test vector $x3 = 0$ $x2 = 1$ and $x1 = 1$ (011) is applied to the input of our circuit. If node A is stuck at 1, the test vector would not detect this as an error. If test vector 010 is applied and node A remains stuck at 1, then the error will be detected. For each test vector applied, evaluate each node to determine if the error can be detected.

2.6   Fault Tables

The basic role of testing is to apply patterns to the circuit under test. Since there is a different response between a good circuit and a faulty

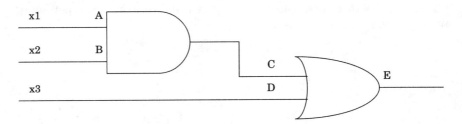

Figure 2.3 Stuck-at fault.

TABLE 2.2   Test Vectors

	Vectors			
D	B	A	C	E
0	0	0	0	0
0	0	1	0	0
0	1	0	0	0
0	1	1	1	1
1	0	0	0	1
1	0	1	0	1
1	1	0	0	1
1	1	1	1	1

TABLE 2.3   Fault Table

Input Combination			Possible Faults									
x1	x2	x3	A/0	A/1	B/0	B/1	C/0	C/1	D/0	D/1	E/0	E/1
0	0	0						x		x		x
0	0	1				x		x		x		x
0	1	0		x				x		x		x
0	1	1	x		x		x			x		
1	0	0							x		x	
1	0	1							x		x	
1	1	0							x		x	
1	1	1							x		x	

circuit, testing boils down to control and observation. *Control* consists of presenting patterns to the input of a circuit, while *observation* consists of evaluating the circuit response.

A fault table identifies all possible controlled inputs and the faults that can be detected with each controlled input. By definition, a complete set of tests for a circuit is the collection of all possible input combinations for that circuit. Table 2.2 provides the complete set of tests for the circuit in Fig. 2.3.

It is always the goal in testing to be able to detect 100 percent of the potential faults. From the fault table, we can identify the minimum test set that must be executed for 100 percent coverage of the circuit.

To identify the minimum test set for 100 percent coverage, select tests that have columns with a single x in Table 2.3. These are tests 001, 010, and 011. Next, identify which stuck at faults are not detected with this set of inputs. In Table 2.3 the only fault not detected with this suite is D/0. By adding test 100, 101, 110, or 111 to the suite, 100 percent of the circuit is tested. This is shown in Table 2.4.

TABLE 2.4   Test Suite for 100 Percent Coverage

Test 1	001	B/1		
Test 2	010	A/1		
Test 3	011	A/0	B/0	C/0
Test 4	1xx	D/0		

2.7   Redundant Faults

Some stuck-at faults are untestable. A fault that cannot be tested is called a *redundant* fault. Do not confuse a redundant fault with a fault that is not detected as a result of insufficient test coverage.

For example, the circuit in Fig. 2.4 shows a simple stuck-at-1 fault that cannot be tested. If node E is S-A-1, there is no way to set signal (F) high without signal (G) also being high. Therefore, there is no test that can verify that node E is in a stuck-at-1 condition.

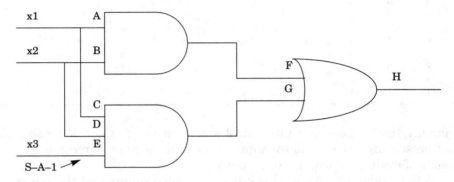

Figure 2.4 Redundant fault.

2.8 Simulation

Computer aided engineering (CAE) programs fall into a category of software that aids the design engineer with logic design, design verification, functional analysis, and change management before the board is committed to prototyping. CAE workstations provide tools for schematic entry, layout, layout verification, circuit simulation, and timing.

In CAE, simulation of the component board is accomplished via software. To perform the simulation, the design engineer creates a *net list* that describes how the parts are connected. Figure 2.5 depicts a simple circuit diagram, and the net list for that circuit appears in Table 2.5.

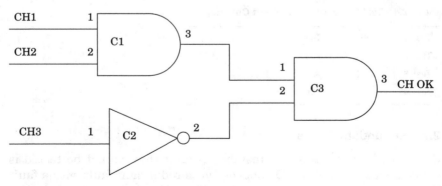

Figure 2.5 Sample circuit.

TABLE 2.5   Net List for the Circuit of Fig. 2.5

Component	Type	Pin/Signal Name
C1:	AND	1/"CH1",2/"CH2",3/C1.3
C2:	NOT	1/"CH3",2/C2.2
C3:	AND	1/C1.3/C2.2,3/CH_OK

Signals with names are generally defined in quotes, and those with no names take the name of the source component and pin number. For example, the inputs to C3 are the source signals from the connected component.

Once the design engineer determines that the simulation is ready for the test engineer, testing the simulated model can start. Since the simulated model demonstrates how the device works, vector patterns representing inputs to the unit under test can be applied, and the actual output can be compared to the expected output.

If the response is incorrect, there is most likely a fault with the board under design. Furthermore, if the test engineer finds a circuit untestable, or discovers a better method of testing, the diagnostic engineer can work with the designer to improve the design.

If the board under test has a CPU and the simulation supports the CPU instruction set, the test engineer can start developing the diagnostic program. The diagnostic can be checked out using the simulator, and a major part can be completed before the board becomes available as a prototype.

If the board does not have a CPU, signals must be supplied to the edge connector to simulate the board under test conditions. The pattern or vectors applied to the edge connector will cause the board to execute a specific function. The results are observed at specific locations on the board. These vectors aid the test engineer in the development of the diagnostic.

2.8.1   Fault simulators

Once the design engineer has produced a good model of the board, fault modeling begins. Fault modeling is the insertion of faults into a good model and evaluation of the results.

By modeling specific faults, the simulator determines the effect and provides a measure of fault coverage and a fault dictionary. In addition, faults that are not covered by a test set can be identified, and new tests can be added to cover those faults. To perform fault modeling, you must establish the following prerequisites:

1. You must have a fault-free network; i.e., a working simulated system that is functionally complete.

2. You must have appropriate test vectors.
3. You must know what model you want to fault; i.e., where the stuck-at faults are to be inserted into the simulation.
4. You must know where to obtain the results; i.e., what is expected to fail with this fault model.

To manually generate new test input vectors, the engineer must look at the results of the fault simulation and pick out any undetected faults. The engineer must then figure out new vectors that test for the undetected faults.

2.9 Built-In Test

PWBs and their associated circuitry can be tested with very expensive in-circuit testers that have access to internal board nodes on the back side of the board. However, with technological advancements in board design (notably, multilayer boards), in-circuit testing has become more difficult. The difficulty in observation and control due to the new board technology and programmable device technology can be overcome if test aids are placed on the board. This new test methodology, *design for test* (DFT), requires that logic be built into the circuit to assist in testing the hardware. In some cases, the built-in hardware provides very extensive tests to the circuit.

The following section provides a brief introduction to three DFT methods that are currently used to test both VLSI and densely populated PWBs. These three methods are:

1. signature analysis
2. scan patterns
3. built-in self-test (BIST)

2.9.1 Signature analysis

Signature analysis is a term coined by Hewlett-Packard to describe a linear feedback shift register (LFSR) used to detect logic faults in hardware. The technique requires planning during in the design stage.

The usefulness of signature analysis is based on the fact that the final values of the LFSR—the signature—depend on the bit pattern that is applied at the input. If a fault causes the output bit sequence to change, this usually results in a different signature.

For example, the 3-bit LFSR in Fig. 2.6 is made up of three linear shift register latches. The shift register has an exclusive-OR gate that takes the output from the output of Q1 and Q3. This output is again OR'ed with the input signal and feed to the first shift register.

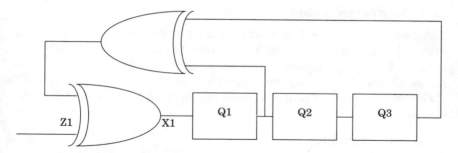

Figure 2.6 Linear feedback shift register.

As the source signal is applied to the input Z1 and clocked through the shift register, the bit pattern in the shift register is modified. The resulting pattern is directly dependent on the input stream that is applied at Z1. The resulting bit pattern is available to be read by the CPU, and it is called the signature. If the signature does not match the expected one, then an error has occurred.

If an input pattern of 01110 is applied to the LFSR shown in Fig. 2.6, we are able to determine the result of the signature. At time t0, all signals are zero. At time t1, a one is applied to the input. The output at the exclusive OR x1 is a 1, and Q1 is now a 1.

Time	Z1	x1	Q1	Q2	Q3
t0	0	0	0	0	0
t1	1	1	1	0	0
t2	1	1	0	1	0
t3	1	1	1	0	1
t4	0	0	0	1	0

A second stream of 1000 produces an output from the LFSR of 011.

The problem with signature analysis that it is possible that bad logic could produce the exact same value as a good network. If this happens, it is called an *alias signature*. For a 16-bit signature register, the probability of an alias is $2^{-16} = 0.0000153$.

Using circuit simulation, faults can be inserted into the logic, and the bad signatures can be collected into a database. The bad signature then can be grouped with the fault inserted via simulation. This database is referred to as the *fault dictionary*. During normal testing, if a fault is detected, a search through the database for the bad signature can help isolate the circuit fault.

2.9.2 Scan pattern testing

The test technique that is described in this section permits access to internal nodes of the circuit. The technique, called *boundary-scan* or *scan-path* testing, provides increased accessibility to the internal nodes, thereby increasing the observable nodes for testing.

Generally, circuitry that was designed for test has two modes of operation:

1. normal operating mode
2. test mode

When the circuit is placed into the test mode, the computer can enter data patterns via an I/O port. Returning the circuit to the normal mode, the signals are allowed to enter the circuit. Placing the circuit in the test mode again allows the scan-path logic to capture the results from the test (see Fig. 2.7).

A large shift register holds test signals from the unit under test. When the unit is placed in test mode, these test signals are shifted through the shift register, which forms a result that can be read via the I/O port. For each test pattern applied, there is an expected reply. Comparing the actual replies with the expected ones determines if the scan test failed.

Boundary-scan testing can provide outstanding results in detecting faults that are responsible for most board failures. Boundary-scan

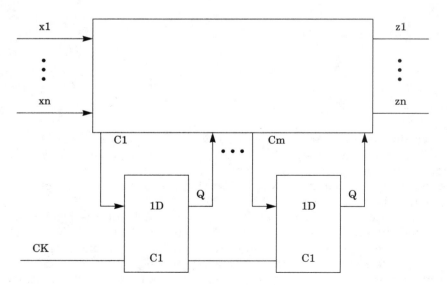

Figure 2.7 Scan pattern block diagram.

tests can be included in the chip design by adding shift register latches to the I/O pins. Boundary-scan technology puts the control and visibility where most faults are located—outside the chip, on the board itself.

Now that the IEEE has defined standards for boundary-scan testing (in IEEE 1149.1), many semiconductor manufacturers are beginning to include boundary-scan testing in standard devices. IEEE 1149.1 defines several test modes. One of these, the external test mode *EX-TEST*, is the most useful for testing boards. Another, *INTEST*, accomplishes an internal test of the chip. The *RUNBIST* test runs built-in tests for the chip. The *BYPASS* test allows the chip circuitry to be bypassed, thereby making the scan ring shorter.

2.9.3   Built-in self-test

As VLSI chip complexity and density increase, it becomes increasingly difficult to access internal nodes for testing. The time and cost associated with testing of these chips also increases. To remedy this problem, logic may be included on the chip or board for the purpose of testing. This technique is called *built-in self-test* (BIST).

Although BIST eliminates or reduces many of the problems associated with testing larger, denser, and more complicated circuits, these benefits do not come without cost. The cost are:

1.   additional *real estate;* i.e., space used on the board or chip
2.   decreased reliability because of increased chip count
3.   possible performance degradation
4.   additional design time and cost

2.9.3.1 Self-test.   Self-test is the ability of a circuit to apply patterns to itself and preserve the results so that they can be observed and compared with the response from a good circuit. For example, in many microprocessor boards, the microprocessor tests the logic block on the board.

However, with the latest technology, many components have been moved from the board level and placed on a single chip. Similarly, the idea of self-test has moved from the board level to the chip level.

Smart chips now have built-in diagnostics. When power is applied or a reset is issued, the chip executes a suite of tests that checks the logic in the chip. At the completion of the diagnostic, the initialization process sets a bit to indicate that the diagnostic is complete. If an error was detected, an error bit is set, along with an error code to indicate the reason for the failure.

2.9.3.2 BIST Using LFSRs.   Another BIST technique uses the scan path and LFSR concepts and integrates them with the signature analysis built into the circuit. While in the test mode, test patterns enter the circuit under test from the LFSR. Data from the output of the circuit is applied to the output LFSR via the output multiplexer (MUX). The signature analyzer has additional logic to match the final signature with the known good result.

There could be several isolated circuits on the board. Each of these circuits could have an associated input and output LFSR and MUXs. When the board is placed into test mode, the tests logic loads the input LFSRs. Next, the input signal is applied to the circuit under test. The output LFSR collects the data. At the end of the test, the test logic compares each of the output LFSRs for the proper pattern.

2.10   Test Case Design

After reviewing the hardware specifications and the schematics, the diagnostic engineer must start to identify and define test cases. As each test case is defined, the engineer writes down the specifics in detail, including the test configuration, inputs, and expected outputs. When defining a test case, expand beyond what might be considered a normal diagnostic. Recommend testing functions that may never be used but nevertheless are present. For example, a communication controller might have unused functions such as:

1.   synchronous communications
2.   variable baud rates
3.   hardware flow control

A rigorous test suite will provide coverage even for these unused functions. In fact, the first pass of selecting and identify test cases should be an overkill. It never hurts to over-test the hardware—later passes might eliminate any inappropriate or redundant test cases. Finally, place each of the test cases into the functional specification. Once this specification is complete, it should be reviewed. During the review, tests may be eliminated and additional ones recommended.

2.11   Design of the Diagnostic

When designing the diagnostic, the test engineer must understand who the final user of the diagnostic will be, because this dictates how the executive and the human interface are presented.

At the start of the project, it is best for the test engineer to meet with all departments that have an interest in the diagnostic. A requirements document should be developed so that these departments and the test engineer know what they have agreed to.

After all departments agree on the requirements document, the test engineer must now write a design and functional specification for the diagnostic. In many cases, the functional specification is written and approved before the design specification. However, since the *functional specification* states what the product will do, and the *design specification* states how the product will do it, the design specification is generally used by test engineers as a guide in the design of tests.

For the purposes of testing, documentation is important. We all realize that, in the real world, specifications are often overlooked because getting the product to market is assigned a higher priority than documentation. Nevertheless, you should make every effort to keep the documentation up to date. Table 2.6 describes the relevant documentation over the life cycle of hardware.

TABLE 2.6   Documentation Process

Requirements	This defines what you are going to do in the diagnostic for each engineering group.
Plan	The diagnostic plan defines planned tasks that must be accomplished and an estimate of when they will be completed.
Functional	The functional specification defines all the functions that the product (diagnostic) is expected to do. This document dos not define *how* to do the programming.
Design	This document defines *how* the programming is to be accomplished. It should describe each function, define all the arguments, and explain how to implement the design.

2.12   Fault Detection vs. Fault Isolation

Many diagnostics (e.g., *field service* or *customer* diagnostics) are used to detect faults. Their purpose is only to identify that the system has a fault and needs to be replaced. Thus, are called *fault detection* tests. Other diagnostic programs attempt to isolate the fault to the replaceable part. These types of tests are called *fault isolation* tests. For example, a manufacturing diagnostic might aid the test technician in isolating faults to the component level. If test program isolates faults on the board quickly, the technician will spend less time repairing the board.

2.13 Fault Insertion

After the diagnostic code has been completed, the diagnostic should be tested to verify that, indeed, it detects faults. After all, if the diagnostic cannot detect faults when they are present, then it cannot performed its job.

There may be electrical points on the board that cannot be tested by a diagnostic. All these points should be identified by the test engineer. Specific test cases then need to be added to insert faults at these points. That is, stuck-at faults need to be inserted for both high and low conditions.

During fault insertion tests, keep an accurate record of all inserted faults that were reported by the diagnostic, as well as those that were not. If a fault was not reported, the hardware design and diagnostic engineers should determine why these faults were not reported as errors.

2.14 Code Review

All code has the potential of having problems and eventually must be maintained by someone other than the original author. For that reason, all diagnostic code should be subjected to a *code review* or *walkthrough*. If done correctly, code reviews will reduce coding errors, improve the quality of the diagnostic, and make it easier to maintain. This also tends to improve the programmer's technique.

A code review is essentially a line-by-line discussion of the diagnostic code by interested parties (e.g., design engineers, test engineers, manufacturing engineers, and management). Code reviews should have a moderator and set of strictly enforced ground rules. The author of the code should neither be placed on the defensive nor forced to make changes. Rather, the purpose of the review is to expose potential problems. No review session should last longer than two hours, and the moderator in all cases may terminate the session for any reason (these sessions can be very stressful). The moderator must not be one of the reviewers. For more specific details on the conduct of code reviews, see the paper by Fagan [16].

2.15 Code Release

Finally, after what may be several grueling months of coding and testing, the diagnostic is complete. The diagnostic code release is the final phase in the life of the diagnostic before it is actually put into use. Most companies have different methods of releasing the code, but generally, the code release requires a sign-off from a quality assurance person and several managers.

Once approved, the source code and assembled results are archived along with the executable program so that, if necessary, the program can be regenerated later. Usually, this requires that two copies of the source, assembly language output, and object files be sent to an archiving agency within the company. If ROMs must be burned, a part number must be obtained for them. The part numbers and two master ROMs must also be sent to the archiving agency along with the files.

2.16 Summary

This chapter examined the steps to be taken when a test engineer is assigned the task of writing a diagnostic program. We discussed the purpose of functional specifications and schematics, since the test engineer must not only know how to write programs but also understand and be able to read schematics. We also discussed the idea of *design for test*. There have been many useful books written on the subject, so this chapter offered just a brief overview.

We discussed the role of simulation in testing. Simulation is advancing to a stage at which the test engineer can write code and test the code on a simulator before the prototype hardware exists. Thus, test engineers no longer have to wait until the hardware is available and working.

We also provided a very brief introduction of signature analysis, scan testing, and BIST. Finally, since the purpose of diagnostics is to test for faults, fault modeling and fault coverage were introduced.

2.17 References

1. Gabay, J. 1990. How much can design-for-test reduce the need for testing? *Computer Design* (September), 94–112.
2. McCluskey, E.J. 1985. Built-in self-test techniques. *IEEE Design & Test* (April), 21–27.
3. Williams, T. and K. Parker. 1982. Design for testability—A survey. *IEEE Transaction on Computers* C-31;1:2–15.
4. Williams, T. 1986. Design for Testability. *VLSI Testing*, 95–160.
5. Sedmale, R. 1985. Built in self-test: Pass or fail. *IEEE Design & Test* (April), 17–19.
6. Brock, D. 1990. Reducing the cost of test development. *Evaluation Engineering* (August) 156–163.
7. Nagvajara, P., M.G. Karpousky, and L.B. Levitin. 1991. Pseudo random testing for boundary design with built in self-test. IEEE *Design & Test* (September), 58–65.
8. McCluskey, E.J. 1986. *Design for Testability—Fault-Tolerant Computing Theory and Techniques*, Vol. I. Englewood Cliffs, N.J.: Prentice-Hall.
9. Bond, J. 1991. Simulation greases test development wheels. *Test & Measurement World* (September), 111–115.
10. Binnendyk, F. 1991. Merging design and test in the 1990s. *Evaluation Engineering* (January), 34–41.
11. Scheiber, S. 1991. DFT in the real world. *Test & Measurement World* (June) 79–84.

12. Bond, J. 1991. Boundary scan simplifies board test. *Test & Measurement World* (January), 41–46.
13. Zurian, Y., and C. Yau. 1991. Linking BIST and boundary scan to testing success. *Test & Measurement World* (May).
14. Bottorff, P.S. 1986. Test generation and fault simulation. *VLSI Testing,* 29–63.
15. Arabian, J. 1986. Fault modeling. *VLSI Testing,* 2–25.
16. Fagan, M.E. 1976. Design and code inspections reduce errors in program development. *IBM Systems Journal,* 15;3:182–211.

3

Microprocessor Board Testing

3.0 Introduction

This chapter introduces the testing of the microprocessor mother board and guides you through its check-out and verification. In addition, two basic concepts are presented that are very important and must be understood by test engineers to effectively write diagnostics. These concepts are the *CPU interrupt* and *direct memory access (DMA)*.

Figure 3.1 provides a block diagram of a typical microprocessor board. Notice that the *central processing unit (CPU)* is depicted as a

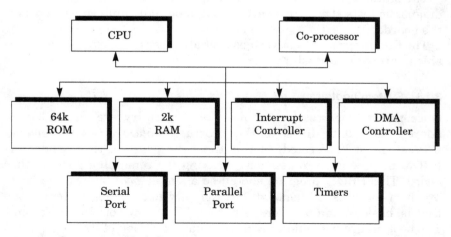

Figure 3.1 Scan pattern block diagram.

single component of the board. This example shows the following components:

1. a CPU
2. a 64k block of *read-only memory (ROM)*
3. a 2k block of *random-access memory (RAM)*
4. a timer device
5. an interrupt controller
6. a floating-point processor
7. serial ports
8. a parallel port
9. a DMA controller

3.1   Check-Out of the Microprocessor Board

In many cases, the diagnostic programmer assigned to develop diagnostics for a microprocessor must also assist the engineer in the check-out of the board. The check-out of the hardware circuit board is accomplished in stages which are as follows:

1. preliminary check-out
2. static test with diagnostic
3. full integration check-out

The preliminary checkout is accomplished by the engineer. This check-out must verify that the minimal portion of the hardware is functional to support a debugger. Generally, the CPU, clock, serial port, and RAM are required.

The static test verifies the remaining part of the board with special diagnostic tests. These tests are executed on individual subsystems of the board.

The full integration test verifies that all subsystems of the board are able to execute successfully together.

3.1.1   System bootstrap

Once the microprocessor and associated circuitry are checked, the address and data lines to the *programmable read-only memory (PROM)* must be verified. At this time, the program that resides in PROM may be used to assist in verifying the remaining parts of the board. This PROM program should be a simple *boot* program. A boot program contains only enough functionality to allow for system boot; that is, basic communication with the CPU and system initialization. The boot program should provide a visual indication of its progress as early as possible. This can be accomplished by plugging a display board into the system bus, using existing LEDs on the board, or through a display to a screen. Each of these options should provide a progress indicator.

For example, assume that the design engineer included into the design an I/O port that displayed an 8-bit output to LEDs. This I/O port would be very helpful in the checkout process and can be used during bootstrapping. At each defined step in the boot-up process, an 8-bit value is displayed and defined as shown below:

Set up the I/O configuration port	(display 01)
Set up the memory configuration	(display 02)
Checksum the ROM BIOS	(display 04)
Keyboard Setup	(display 06)
Other steps...	

During boot-up, if the system fails to proceed, the value displayed indicates how far the system progressed before it failed.

3.1.2   Development tools

The old method of changing the program, then burning and replacing the EPROM, was very time consuming and frustrating. A variety of development tools have evolved to eliminate some of this frustration and, these are:

1. debug monitors
2. ROM emulators
3. logic analyzers
4. in-circuit emulators

A *debug monitor* provides the following (and many other) functions:

1. read and write I/O ports
2. read and write to memory
3. execute test programs
4. set software break points

Furthermore, the debug monitor requires only minimal hardware functionality. Many debug monitor programs can be purchased for almost any microprocessor.

An inexpensive *ROM emulator* can be used to replace the EPROM. The ROM emulator is superior to the EPROM during development because the program in the ROM emulator can be changed by downloading from a development system. This eliminates the need to burn a new EPROM for every change to the program.

A *logic analyzers* provides a visual indication of an electrical circuit, and it can retain a history of how a diagnostic program progressed. The logic analyzer can be set to trigger when a selected memory location or an I/O port is accessed. Many available logic analyzers provide more than 64 channels of visual display.

A more expensive *in-circuit emulator* can be purchased to replace the ROM emulator. The in-circuit emulator provides better control over the board under test. An in-circuit emulator provides the ability to:

1. download code
2. start and stop the microprocessor
3. set both hardware and software break points
4. examine and change the contents of memory and registers

3.2   ROM CRC Check

It is very difficult to test EPROMs or ROMs with anything other than a simple checksum. Most checksums consist of a 16-bit addition of all bytes in the block of ROM. The checksum is then placed in the last two bytes of the ROM.

There are many different checksum algorithms. One common algorithm adds each byte of the ROM to form a 16-bit sum. The ones complement of the sum is then placed in the last two bytes of ROM. If the checksum is recalculated and added to the last two bytes, the sum should be equal to zero.

The purpose of the checksum is to verify that the program in ROM remains unchanged. However, the algorithm we have described above is susceptible to error cancellation.

For example, the two groups of 4 bytes each shown below have the same checksum but have different data patterns.

				Checksum
A4	63	92	8B	224
84	23	B2	CB	224

3.3   RAM Testing

To test the microprocessor board thoroughly, you will need to write complex diagnostics involving subroutines. However, subroutines require the RAM area on the microprocessor board to store the program stack. The stack contains the context (e.g., registers and program counter) needed to return from a nested layer of subroutine calls.

The program cannot use the program stack to call and return from subroutines reliably until this memory is verified. Hence, the RAM on the microprocessor board must be tested early so that subroutines may be used for further diagnostic tests.

However, if the processor that you are using supports jumping via a register (register indirect jump), then a pseudo-subroutine may be used. This effect can be achieved by loading the return address in a register and then branching to the subroutine. The return address must be preserved for proper return to the calling routine via a register indirect jump.

Chapter 4 discusses many different methods of RAM testing. For now, we will simply note that this first test of RAM should (1) test the stack and data area only, and (2) be very fast test.

Once the on-board RAM has been verified, it then may be used for program stack and data storage. After the initial testing of RAM, more extensive testing should be undertaken.

3.4   Interrupts

This section deals with the important concept of interrupts. The term *interrupt* applies to an event that is either expected or unexpected and which causes a branch to a special routine called an *interrupt service routine (ISR)*. The interrupt provides a method for the processor to take action when exceptional events occur within the system (both internal and external to the CPU). The interrupt also provides an efficient method of performing I/O operations.

3.4.1   When do interrupts occur?

There are two conditions under which the instruction execution sequence should be altered from its normal program sequence (collectively called *exceptions*). The first is when an error condition occurs within the system, such as upon detection of an illegal op-code, memory parity, or power failure. The CPU interrupts its own normal execution and takes some special action.

The second condition arises when some device, such as a keyboard, device requires attention. When the device requires attention from the CPU, it issues an interrupt request to the CPU.

The interrupt is also an alternative method of I/O. When an interrupt occurs, it can be used to indicate that a device is requesting a transfer. The processor suspends its current activities and services the request. This method of asynchronous I/O is best suited for peripherals such as terminals, keyboards, and communication controllers.

3.4.2   The interrupt vector

When the CPU is interrupted, the normal execution must be suspended and program execution transferred to the ISR. Because there may be many different interrupt sources, each interrupt requires a unique ISR. In addition, each interrupt has an associated interrupt vector. A *vector* is a pre-defined location in memory that contains the address of the ISR routine.

When the CPU is interrupted, it identifies the type of interrupt and reads the address from the memory location specified at the appropriate vector address.

The interrupt vectors should be set up during initialization prior to allowing interrupts. If interrupts are enabled before the vectors are set, then unpredictable results may occur.

3.4.3   The interrupt sequence

Whenever an interrupt occurs, the following sequence of events takes place (refer to Fig. 3.2).

1. The CPU finishes the current instruction.
2. The current contents of the CPU flags are saved on the stack.
3. The current value of the program counter (PC) is saved on the stack.
4. The first location of the ISR is placed in the PC.
5. The interrupt is serviced.
6. The PC and flags are restored.

Steps 2 and 3 make it possible to return to the routine that was executing when the interrupt occurred. Step 4 allows the ISR to start exe-

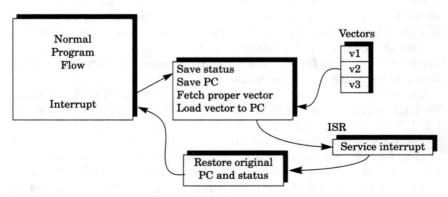

Figure 3.2 An interrupt sequence.

cuting. (In some microprocessors, steps 2 and 3 may not be performed automatically. In others, it needs to be written as part of the ISR.)

Because interrupts may occur at any time, the service routine must run transparently to any other program that is executing. Therefore, the service routing cannot change any register or CPU status flag. Still, it must accomplish its job and indicate that the interrupt occurred and was properly serviced.

3.4.4 Priorities

In most CPUs, interrupts have priorities. That is to say, some interrupts are more important than others. The more important interrupts have priority over those interrupts that are less important. For example, the clock interrupt has a higher priority than the UART (universal asynchronous receiver transmitter—an asynchronous I/O device) interrupt.

An interrupt with a higher priority may interrupt one with a lower priority. An interrupt of a lower priority device is not allowed to interrupt one of a higher or equal priority.

3.4.5 Polling

At times, it is not desirable to allow interrupts to occur. When this is the case, the program must read the controller periodically to determine if an interrupt condition has occurred. If an interrupt request has occurred, then a service routine must be called. This periodic checking of the controller is called *polling*.

3.4.6 Enable/disable

Interrupts may be enabled to allow the interrupts to occur, or they may be disabled so that the interrupts cannot occur. Interrupts may be individually disabled or globally disabled. Interrupts are disabled by the program itself when the program does not want to allow them. With many CPUs, immediately after an interrupt, further interrupts are disabled. It is normally the responsibility of the ISR to re-enable the interrupts.

Some interrupts cannot be disabled by the software. This type of interrupt is known as the *non-maskable interrupt (NMI)*. These generally occur under the following conditions:

1. power fail detected
 2. memory parity detected

3. single stepping program
4. watchdog timer timed out

3.5 Interrupt Test

Before the interrupt chip can be used, its registers must be tested. To do this, check all write/read bits and verify that the CPU has access to them. After verifying the data path to the interrupt chip, verify that the minimal operations can be accomplished. A generic register data path test is described at the end of this chapter.

Testing includes enabling interrupts and checking for any spurious interrupts in the system. *Spurious interrupts* are simply interrupts that should not occur.

Each possible interrupt must be generated as a test condition. When writing your tests, force each interrupt to occur while the interrupt controller has that interrupt disabled. Verify that the interrupt did not occur. Next, enable the interrupt and verify that the interrupt does occur. To generate some of the interrupts, you might need to wait until the component that issues the interrupt is tested.

If possible, check that an interrupt of a lower priority does not interrupt one of a higher or equal level. Also verify that all higher-priority interrupts can interrupt lower-priority ones.

3.6 Timers

All CPUs have some form of a clock, which might be part of the CPU chip or located in a separate controller circuit. The clock usually has a counter that is decremented each time an external signal triggers from a high to low condition. Once the counter becomes zero, the clock controller sets the interrupt, signaling that the timer has counted to zero and requires service.

Clocks have registers that must be tested. In addition, clocks are generally assigned to an interrupt. A check must be made to verify that the interrupt does occur when the clock times out.

To test the timers, load the clock registers and enable the timer. This should be preformed first with interrupts disabled, and again with interrupts enabled. Verify in both cases that when the counter goes to zero, the timer chip has requested action by setting the interrupt flag.

In some cases, the clock can be used as a counter rather than as a clock. When used as a counter, the clock is free running, and the register value is automatically reset when the clock counts down to zero. When in this mode, the clock applied to the chip can be divided to create a particular clock rate. This clock rate is often used with communications to synchronize the baud rate.

3.7   Time of Year

The *time of year* chip provides a means for the system to keep track of the date. Once the date and time are set, a rollover past midnight increments the day. If the day is the last day of the month, then the month advances to the next month. If the last month, the year is advanced. The system can set and read the date, and a battery allows the clock to keep time while power is removed from the system.

The test program should verify that the clock increments the second, minute, hour, day, month, and the year. This is achieved by setting the chip to a particular time and verifying the rollovers.

This may not be a test that someone would want in an operating system, given that it would tend to cause the system lose track of the time. But in a development or manufacturing system, this is a required test.

Many clock chips provide a small amount of memory. When power is removed from the system, the battery provides power to the low power consumption memory. Many systems store data in this battery-backed memory. A checksum algorithm should be used to verify that the data has not been corrupted.

3.8   Concept of DMA

The data transfer rate for I/O operations is a relatively slow. Some devices, such as disk drives, A/D converters, and magnetic tape drives, operate at high rates. In these cases, the CPU does not have the time to read each byte and place it into memory. For these higher data rates, *block transfers*, which use *direct memory access (DMA)*, take place under the direction of bus controllers.

Devices that use DMA transfer request the use of the bus from the CPU. When the CPU is not in need of the bus, the bus controller grants the bus to the device requesting DMA. This device now becomes the bus master and places a memory address onto the address bus and generates the necessary signals for either a read or write operation. Taking control of the bus from the CPU is called *cycle stealing* because it prevents the CPU from using the bus during its normal fetch-execute cycle. Cycle stealing does have a negative impact on system performance.

The DMA must be capable of storing the memory address and incrementing that address at the end of each DMA cycle. It must also know when to stop the DMA block transfer.

The following are the steps for a DMA write operation to memory:

1. The device sends a request for service to the DMA controller.
2. The device gains control of the bus.
3. The address is placed on the address bus.
4. The device acknowledges interface.
5. Interface places data onto the bus.
6. Data is transferred to memory.
7. The device relinquishes the bus.
8. The address register adjusted by 1.
9. The block count adjusted by 1.
10. If the block count is non-zero, we return to step 1; otherwise an interrupt occurs and DMA stops.

The CPU has the ability to perform other tasks while the DMA is transferring data. When all the data has been transferred to memory, the DMA controller issues an interrupt to the CPU. This interrupt is used by the CPU to recognize that all the data was read.

The process is reversed when the I/O controller requests a character to write via DMA. When DMA access is granted by the bus controller, the I/O controller places the proper address onto the memory bus and sets the proper control signal at the correct time. The I/O controller then fetches the data directly from memory. Once again, when all the characters are transferred to the I/O device, the DMA controller interrupts the CPU.

3.9   DMA Testing

The DMA controller, like other controllers, has read/write registers and control registers. The data path test described in this chapter should be performed on the DMA chip. In doing so, the address bus lines are indirectly tested.

After the data path tests are performed on the DMA controller, checks must be made to verify that it can transfer data from memory to the controller, and then from the controller to memory.

Once the preliminary test for the DMA is run, tests must be designed to check that the memory address in the DMA controller is incremented by 1 every time a character is transferred, and that the DMA controller has the ability to cause a CPU interrupt.

Some DMA controllers have limited memory access and require additional external registers to access the full range of memory. If this is the case, a test must be designed so that all areas of memory are accessed using DMA. Furthermore, tests must verify that the DMA functions correctly when errors occur. Such errors might include an attempt to access memory that is prohibited from DMA, or when a DMA memory wrap is detected.

A *DMA memory wrap* occurs when the last location of legal DMA memory has been accessed, but DMA controller must still attempt to access more memory. The address wraps to location 0 of the block.

3.10   Floating Point Coprocessor

Many existing microprocessors do not have the power to support floating point calculation internally. To provide hardware floating point calculations, many of these processors now use *coprocessors* that reside on the CPU bus.

Both the CPU and the coprocessor share the system address and data buses. The coprocessor reads all CPU instructions. When it detects a floating point instruction, it performs that instruction. The coprocessor, when required, takes control of the buses until it completes its processing function.

All connections to the coprocessor must be verified by exercising the device itself. For example, use the floating point *load* and *store* commands to verify these connections. The values can be loaded into memory via the CPU and then verified by the CPU.

Make sure that all bits of the data are read and written in both the low and high states. Verify that all the address lines are used in both high and low states.

For example, let us assume that our system has a 16-bit data bus and a 24-bit address bus.

Step 1   CPU loads integer value –1 (all bits set) into memory.
Step 2   CPU loads integer, converts it to floating-point value, and saves it.
Step 3   CPU verifies the expected result.

The above can be repeated with a number of values, such as all 0s, and alternating 1s and 0s. Special patterns that might stress the data bus may also be used. But always know what the expected result should be. These tests should be performed on several locations within the memory range. In doing so, we verify that the coprocessor is able to read and write to all of memory.

3.11   Generic Data Path Test

There are two generic data path register tests. These can be used to test any I/O port register. Many I/O register have bits that are read and write, other bits that are read only, and some that are write only.

The first test is used to verify registers that have all their bits as write and read. This test routine is found in Code Block 3.1.

The second test is used when some of the bits are read/write, while other are read-only or write-only. Code Block 3.2 is a listing for this partial data path test.

3.12 Summary

In this chapter, we found that the motherboard contains many components that require testing, in addition to the CPU. Generic register tests were introduced that can be used for many read/write hardware registers.

This chapter also introduced the concept of an interrupt, which is an event external to the program that can suspend the program and transfer control. We found that interrupts are used for two main purposes: to handle exceptions that occur, and as an alternative method of I/O operation.

We further discussed direct memory access, which can be used for asynchronous I/O. The idea here is that the CPU or other device can initiate a transfer of data to or from memory, while the CPU proceeds with other activities until the transfer completes. This can greatly enhance overall system performance.

3.13 Bibliography

1. Crooks, R. 1991. Debugging microprocessor-based boards. *Evaluation Engineering* (April), 28–31.
2. Stark, W. 1991. Combining strategies to test PC motherboards. *Evaluation Engineering* (October) 10–14.
3. Gelsinger, P. 1987. Design and test of the 80386. *IEEE Design & Test* (June) 42–50.
4. Sowell, E. 1984. *Programming in Assembly Language: Macro-11*. Boston: Addison Wesley.
5. Leventhal, L. 1987. *80386 Programming Guide*. New York: Bantam Books.

```
/*
    datapath_test()
    Description:
    This test routine accomplished a walking zero pattern
    test on the selected I/O register. The second part of
    the test accomplishes a walking 1 pattern test on the
    same I/O register.
*/
datapath_test(int reg, int width)
    {
    int value,data;
    int i;
    value = 0xfffe;                     // set initial value
    for (i=0;i<width,i++) {
        outreg(reg,value);             // write the value
        data = inport(reg);            // read the register
        if (data != value) return -1;  // report error
        value = (value << 1) + 1;      // shift zero
        }
    value = 1;
    for (i=0;i<width,i++) {
        outreg(reg,value);             // write the value
        data = inport(reg);            // read the register
        if (data != value) return -1;  // report error
        value = (value << 1);          // shift zero
        }
    return 0;
    }
```

Code Block 3.1 Register data path test.

```
/*
    partial_datapath_test()
    Description:
    This test routine accomplished a walking zero pattern
    test on the selected I/O register. The second part of
    the test accomplishes a walking 1 pattern test on the
    same I/O register.
*/
partial_datapath_test(int reg, int width,int bits)
    {
    int value,data;
    int i;
    k = 1;
    value = 0xfffe;                        // set initial value
    for (i=0;i<width,i++) {
     if (bits & k) {                       // Bit to test
       outreg(reg,value);                  // write the value
       data = inport(reg) | bits;          // read the register
       if (data != value) return -1;       // report error
       } // end of if bit to test
     value = (value << 1) + 1;       // shift zero
     k = ( k << 1);
     } // end of for loop
    k = 1;
    value = 1;
    for (i=0;i<width,i++) {
      if (bits & k) {
      outreg(reg,value);                   // write the value
      data = inport(reg);                  // read the register
      if (data != value) return -1;        // report error
      }
      value = (value << 1);           // shift zero
      k = k << 1;
      }
    return 0;
    }
```

Code Block 3.2 Partial data path test.

Memory Testing

4.0 Introduction

This chapter introduces the basic memory module and the testing of memories. It includes a description of the basic memory cell, memory array, and memory board. A brief introduction to static and dynamic memory is also provided. Next, several of the more popular memory test routines are described, and their algorithms are presented. Each step in the algorithm is defined, with the C source code provided. Finally, sample error reports are included, along with methods that can be used to isolate the fault to a chip or node.

4.1 Basic Memory Cell

The basic memory cell is the building block of all memory devices. Its purpose is to store one bit of binary information. To do this, it must be SET to store a one or RESET to store a zero.

Figure 4.1 displays the basic memory cell circuit called a *cross coupled NAND gate*. If the SET input is asserted and the RESET input is de-asserted, then the Q1 output is asserted. Q1 asserted along with RESET de-asserted forces Q2 to be de-asserted, which re-enforces the SET condition. Once this SET condition is established, the SET input can be removed and the circuit will remain stable.

When the RESET operation is asserted and the SET operation is de-asserted, Q1 becomes de-asserted, which drives Q2 to the set condition. Once the RESET condition occurs, the RESET input can be removed, and the circuit will remain stable.

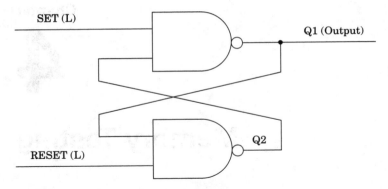

Figure 4.1 Basic memory cell, cross-coupled NAND gate.

4.2 Memory Array

A collection of memory cells form a *memory array*. Figure 4.2 shows a 1K by 1 memory array.

In this example, the memory cell is organized as 32 rows by 32 columns. Address lines 0–4 select one of the rows, and address lines 5–9 select one of the 32 columns. As a result, one of the 1024 memory cells is selected.

When the chip is selected in the read mode, the contents of the selected memory cell is placed onto the output. When the operation is a write, the data is saved into the memory cell.

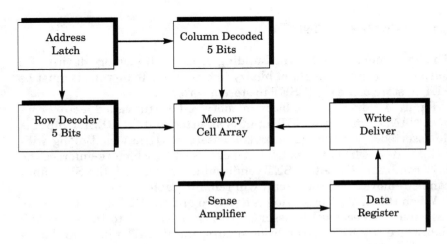

Figure 4.2 1k memory array.

Consider that the memory array in Fig. 4.2 can be directed to store input values and transfer them to its outputs at any given time. Once this command is completed, no input change can alter the outputs of the memory until the write operation is issued again.

Herein lies the fundamental concept of memory—it is a medium in which binary values can be stored and retained until a command is received to replace an old value with a new value. This stored binary value can be presented as output on request.

4.3 Types of Memory

Although many common memory arrays allow the system to both write data to and read from the memory cell, other memory cell arrays exist that allow the system only to read the data contained in the cell. When the memory cell can both be read from and written to, and if each location can be accessed in the same amount of time, the memory array is referred to as *random access memory* (RAM). The main memory of all computers is RAM. The other type is *read-only memory* (ROM).

RAM is designed to allow the CPU to both read and modify the memory. Most RAMs are classified as either *dynamic* or *static*. Dynamic RAMs require a periodic electrical refresh to maintain stored data, which makes them more complicated to use in a particular design. Static RAM requires no refresh and therefore can retain data even when powered down.

4.3.1 Static RAM devices

The static memory device contains several transistors for each memory cell, whereas the dynamic device contains fewer. Since the static cell requires more transistors, it generally requires more power. This disadvantage is offset in some applications, however, by the fact that it does not need to be refreshed.

4.3.2 Dynamic RAM devices

Like the static RAM, the dynamic RAM is organized in a matrix of rows and columns. As a result of the storage discharge or leakage of the capacitors used hold the data, the dynamic device must be repeatedly read and restored. This process is called *memory refresh*.

There are three main reasons why the dynamic RAM is attractive to designers. These are:

1. *High density.*   More cells of dynamic RAM can be placed onto a single chip than with static devices.
2. *Lower power consumption.*   A dynamic device generally requires less power.
3. *Economy.*   The dynamic devices costs less on a per-bit basis than static RAM.

4.3.3   Some RAM applications

In addition to employment as computer main memory, RAM has other applications within the computer system. These include cache memory and *sequential address memory* (SAM).

To avoid referencing the relatively slow memory devices on every memory cycle, high-performance microprocessors use *cache* memory, which consists of a small number of memory cells with a very fast access time.

Sequential address memories are very much like stacks. Two types of SAMs are the LIFO (last in/first out) and the FIFO (first in/first out) versions.

4.3.4   Read-only memory

As mentioned previously, if a memory can only transfer its data on request and cannot store new data into the memory array, the memory is referred to as ROM. The ROM chip was purposely designed so that its contents cannot be modified with a simple CPU memory write. Its purpose is to save data or instructions that do not generally change and therefore need only be read.

The actual process of "burning" values into the ROM is a process more formally called *masking.* The masking process burns fusible links within the ROM. Once burned, the ROM can never be restored.

Another type of ROM, *programmable read-only memory* (PROM), is similar to the ROM except that the device can be programmed by the user. Once programmed, however, the data cannot be changed.

A variation on the PROM concept, the *erasable programmable read-only memory* (EPROM), is very much like the standard PROM, but it has the ability to be erased and reprogrammed a number of times. One type of EPROM has a glass window, and when the device is placed under an ultraviolet light, the fusible links are reconnected. These EPROMS are called *UV PROMS.* Erasure and reprogramming of this type of PROM is rather involved and usually requires removal of the chip from the circuit board.

Electrically erasable PROM (EEPROM) or *flash PROM*, a more recent development, is a type of EPROM can be more easily erased and reprogrammed electrically. After the flash PROM is erased, it can be programmed in place by the on-board CPU. The use of flash PROM allows systems to be updated in the field without ever removing the PROMs.

4.4 Memory System Organization

Figure 4.3 is a block diagram of a 32k memory board. Notice that the system bus connects to three major parts of the board: the data bus, the address bus, and the control signals. The RAM is divided into four blocks of contiguous memory.

4.4.1 The data bus

The data bus provides a gate between the system bus and the internal data bus of the board. On control signal enables the data bus, and another control signal defines the direction of the data flow. If the CPU is in the read process, the data bus is enabled so that the direction is from the data bus to the system bus. If the CPU is in a write process, the bus is enabled from the system bus to the data bus.

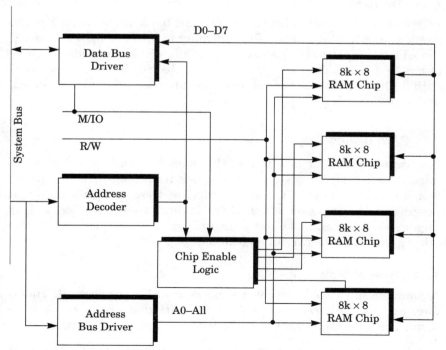

Figure 4.3 Block diagram of a memory board.

4.4.2 The address bus

The upper system address lines enter the board address decoder. The address decoder is used to determine if the address on the system bus is indeed addressing the memory on the board. The remaining bits of the address are latched in the address driver.

When addressing memory on the board, the data bus is enabled, and the proper select line is used to enable a bank of memory on the board. If we are not addressing memory on this board, then the data bus is not enabled, and none of the memory banks are selected.

4.4.3 The control lines

Several control lines enter the board. These control lines inform the board of the different stages of the CPU. If the CPU is in the read mode, then the read/write signal is high. The read/write signal in the low state indicates a write operation.

Another signal is the memory/IO. This signal is used to enable or disable the address decoder. If the signal indicates *memory,* then the decode is enabled.

4.4.4 The RAM

In Fig. 4.3, the memory board has four 8K banks of memory. For the moment, it does not matter if the memory is 8, 16, or 32 bits wide. If the address supplied on the system bus falls within the address range of the first bank, then the first bank is selected. If the address falls with in the range of the second bank, then the second bank is selected, and so on.

4.5 RAM Testing

Let use now consider how to test the memory board. Our diagnostic must isolate faults in a step-wise manner, beginning with circuity on which there is the greatest dependency (address and data line) and progressing to areas on which there is decreased dependency. This implies that the address and data line must be verified before any other areas of the board can be tested.

4.5.1 Types of faults

A complete functional test for a memory board is impractical. Therefore, we restrict ourself to a subset of faults that are more likely to occur. The faults that most likely to occur on a memory board are:

1. *Stuck bit.* One or more bits on the memory board cannot be changed.

2. *Coupling*. Two or more lines are said to be *coupled* if a transition in one line causes a transition in other lines. For example, assume that data line 1 is set high, and all other data lines are set low. If data line 2 becomes high as a result of data line 1 being set high, then data line 1 and 2 are coupled.

3. *Pattern sensitivity.* Certain patterns of zeros and ones cause the transition of other memory locations. As the density of the RAM increases, the cells become closer together and are more apt to affect surrounding cells.

4.5.2 Test Algorithms

There are many types of RAM tests designed to detect the above-described faults. The stuck bit test is usually are very simple and fast. The coupling tests are somewhat more complicated and take more time. The pattern sensitive tests are the most complicated and generally are restricted to a small number of patterns. The following sections describe these tests. Note that, in all the test algorithms discussed, the following symbols are used:

$v \rightarrow w[i]$	value written to memory location i
$r[i] = v$	read memory location i with expected value

4.5.2.1 Data bus test. The purpose of the data line test is to verify and isolate failures in the data lines between the system bus and the RAM. This type of test also detects faults in the memory data register.

This test writes a number of data patterns to one memory location in each RAM bank. The data pattern usually consists of a walking one (a one walked through a field of zeroes) followed by a walking zero (a zero walked through a field of ones) test. The result of each write is verified before the next write.

This test verifies that the data bits are not shorted, opened, or coupled with another signal. The algorithm for the data bus test is:

Step 1:	$0 \rightarrow w[0]$ $r[0] = 0$
Step 2:	$1 \rightarrow w[0]$ $r[0] = 1$
Step 3:	For k = width of memory, shift w[0] one bit left $r[0]$ = new pattern
Step 4:	Repeat step 1, interchanging 1s and 0s

The C code is provided in Code Block 4.1, at the end of this chapter.

This test executes very quickly. However, it only verifies that one memory location was accessed and that the data path between the CPU and the RAM is functioning properly.

4.5.2.2 Knaizuk memory test.   Knaizuk and Hartman developed a test algorithm, called the *algorithmic test sequence* (ATS), that detects multiple faults of any combination of cells stuck at 0 or 1.

Memory is grouped into three partitions—G0, G1, and G2—where

G0 memory location modulo 3 = 0

G1 memory location modulo 3 = 1

G2 memory location modulo 3 = 2

Starting at location 0, every third memory cell belongs to G0. Starting at location 1, every third memory cell belongs to G1, and starting at location 2, every third memory cell belongs to G2.

The algorithm is:

Step 1:	G0 is filled with all ones pattern.
Step 2:	G1 and G2 are filled with all zeros pattern.
Step 3.	G1 is read and verified to be all zeros pattern.
Step 4:	G1 is filled with all one's pattern.
Step 5:	G2 is read and verified to be all zero pattern.
Step 6.	G0 and G1 are read and verified to be all ones pattern.
Step 7:	G0 is filled with all zeroes pattern and then read and verified to be all zero pattern.
Step 8:	G2 is filled with all ones pattern then read and verified to be all ones pattern.

Sample C code given in Code Block 4.2, at the end of this chapter.

4.5.2.3 Marching test.   One of the more popular test algorithms is the *marching test*. Its popularity is largely a result of its simplicity.

One type of marching test is the *modified algorithmic test sequence* (MATS+) test. This test scans all memory in ascending then descending order. Each scan consists of reading the memory cell for a preloaded expected value, writing the complemented value, and then reading it a second time.

The idea is that, while scanning the memory in the ascending order, if there is a problem with coupling, the write operation may affect a higher memory location. This would be detected during the ascending portion of the test. While scanning in the descending order, any write that might affect a lower memory address would be detected.

The algorithm is:

Step 1:	Fill all memory with zeros.
Step 2:	From lower memory to high memory r[i] = 0 1→w[i] r[i] = 1
Step 3:	From high memory to lower memory r[i] = 1 0→w[i] r[i] = 0
Step 4:	Repeat above steps interchanging ones and zeros.

The C code is provided in Code Block 4.3, at the end of this chapter.

Note that in steps 2 and 3 above, the data is changed in each cell before the next cell is read and tested. This method guarantees that the memory block under test has n cells.

This test detects all stuck-at-faults and address decode faults. However it does not detect a coupling fault with the data lines.

4.5.2.4 Galloping test. The galloping ones and zeros test is quite often used in industry to test RAMs. This test verifies that all memory cells exist, that there are no stuck at bits in the data buffer, and that no coupling exists between memory cells.

The major disadvantage of this test is the long completion time. This make it very impractical for use with large memory modules.

The routine fills all memory under test with zeros and then writes to each memory cell. After writing to each memory cell, all other memory cells are read to verify that the single cell write did not affect any other cells in the module. After checking all cells, the cell under test is read, and it is verified that the data is correct. This process continues until all memory cells have been tested.

This test verifies that all cells are addressable and that there is no coupling between the cells. It also guarantees that there are no stuck-at-bits in the decoder, data buffer, or memory array. Remember, though, that this test is considered to be inefficient because of the time required to accomplish the test and the fault coverage.

The algorithm is:

Step 1:	Fill all memory with zeros.
Step 2:	From lower memory to higher memory $1 \rightarrow w[i]$ For all other cells (j) $r[j] = 0$ $r[i] = 1$ $0 \rightarrow w[i]$
Step 3:	Repeat above steps interchanging ones and zeros.

The C code is provided in Code Block 4.4, at the end of this chapter.

4.5.2.5 Marching B test. The purpose of this test is to detect any stuck or coupling faults in the RAMs or in the address and data lines between the bank controllers and the RAMs.

This test implements a cell-by-cell march test sequence, and it is an implementation of the Suk and Reddy Test B algorithm.

The algorithm is :

Step 1:	Fill all memory with Zeros
Step 2:	From lower to high memory $r[i] = 0$ $1 \rightarrow w[i]$ $r[i] = 1$ $0 \rightarrow w[i]$ $r[i] = 0$ $1 \rightarrow w[i]$
Step 3:	From low to high memory $r[i] = 1$ $0 \rightarrow w[i]$ $1 \rightarrow w[i]$ $0 \rightarrow w[i]$
Step 4:	From high to low memory $r[i] = 0$ $1 \rightarrow w[i]$ $0 \rightarrow w[i]$

The C code is provided in Code Block 4.5, at the end of this chapter.

This test is intended to be an all-inclusive data memory fault catcher, with the exception of the pattern sensitivity type of RAM faults. It verifies a RAM chip to be free of stuck-at or coupling faults, provided that the chip does not exhibit multiple access faults in its address decoder in conjunction with coupling faults in the cells.

4.5.2.6 Parity test.   Many systems with a large amount of memory have a built-in means of testing whether a memory byte is read correctly. This employs what is called the *parity bit*.

When data is written to the memory, the memory controller evaluates the bits written and counts the number of bit sets. The parity bit is appropriately set, depending on whether odd or even parity is selected. For example,

		Data bits						Odd
0	1	2	3	4	5	6	7	Parity
0	1	1	1	0	1	0	0	1
1	1	0	1	1	1	0	0	0

When reading the memory location, a check is made to verify that the parity bit is properly set. If incorrectly set, the CPU is interrupted, indicating the parity error.

Testing the parity logic simply requires that a memory location be initialized with a data pattern with parity enabled. Next, read the memory location and verify that no parity interrupt has occurred. Disable memory parity and change the value of one bit in the memory location. Re-enable parity and read the memory location. Now, a memory parity interrupt should occur. The steps are summarized as follows:

Step 1:	Set up for parity interrupt.
Step 2	Disable parity.
Step 3	Write byte with improper parity bit.
Step 4:	Enable parity interrupt.
Step 5:	Read memory location written with bad parity.
Step 6:	No interrupt should occur (parity detection disabled).
Step 7:	Enable parity.
Step 8:	Read memory location written with bad parity.
Step 9:	Interrupt should occur (parity detection enabled).

Memory parity detects whether an odd number of bits have changed. It cannot verify that an even number of bits changed.

4.5.2.7 Byte/word test.

If the memory has the ability to be accessed in more than one mode (such as byte, word, or long word), a test program must be designed to verify that writing in one mode allows the data to be read in another mode.

Let us assume that our system has the ability to read and write memory in both byte mode and word mode. If this is the case, then a test must be designed to write a block of code in byte mode and then read it in word mode. We must also write the memory in byte mode and read it in word mode.

4.5.2.8 Dual-access RAM testing.

In modern architectures, memory can be *dual ported* or *tri-ported*. This means that the memory can be accessed by more than a single host. For example, assume that you have a system as shown in Fig. 4.4. The DRAM in this system can be accessed by the host CPU, the DMA chip, and the external bus. In this case, a test must be designed that allows all three hosts to access the memory. Such a test requires some imagination. One test implementation follows.

First, the CPU can access a small portion of the memory block at the same time that the communications port is dumping data into the memory via the DMA. If this test succeeds, then proceed to the next part of the test wherein the CPU write to memories, and the external

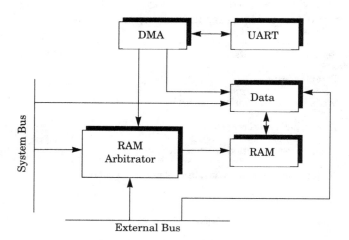

Figure 4.4 Tri-ported RAM.

bus dumps data into the memory. The next part of the test should consist of the DMA accessing the memory and the external port. This should be accomplished with both modules writing to memory at the same time, then reading and writing, and finally reading.

The last test must be accomplished with all three units accessing the memory.

4.5.2.9 Data retention test.   If the memory array is a dynamic, there is a potential that the memory may start losing its data after a few seconds. This would occur if the refresh circuity is not working properly. To test for this, fill the memory with data, allow a predetermined length of time to pass (for example, 10 ms), and the read the memory to verify that it has retained the data.

4.5.2.10 Bank testing.   When the memory is broken into banks, as it is in the board described in Fig. 4.3, a further test must be accomplished to ensure that each individual bank can be accessed without interfering with other banks.

This is a relatively easy test to perform. Fill all of memory with zeroes and verify it, then take a single location in each bank and write to it. Verify that all other locations are still zero.

4.5.2.11 Testing nonvolatile RAM.   *Nonvolatile RAM,* or NV_RAM, is a common type of RAM that is backed by a battery to retain data when the system is powered down. When power is applied, this data must be retained. The testing of NV_RAM is very risky.

If it is necessary to test the RAM during power up, then the test should be performed one byte or word at a time. Before testing a location, the contents of that location must be saved. After saving the location contents, then execute a test on that memory location only. After the test is complete, restore the original data to the memory location. This test is very limited and verifies only that each bit of a NV_RAM can be set both high and then low. The problem with testing NV_RAM is that, during the test, the power could be removed, with the result that the NV_RAM data would then contain the test data rather than the original data.

4.5.2.12 SAM testing.   Testing of SAMs involves filling them with a predefined pattern then making sure that all bits are set both high and low. After filling the SAM, verify that the SAM indicates that it is full.

Next, start reading each byte from the SAM. Verify that the byte read matches the data pattern that was written to the SAM.

After reading all the data from the SAM, verify that the empty indicator, if present, indicates that the SAM is empty. The steps of the test can be summarized as follows:

Step 1:	Fill the output buffer with data pattern.
Step 2:	Fill the SAM with the data pattern to location n-1.
Step 3:	Verify that *full* indicator is not set.
Step 4:	Fill last location of SAM.
Step 5:	Verify that SAM indicates full.
Step 6:	Read full SAM buffer until indicates empty.
Step 7:	Verify that *empty* is indicated when expected.
Step 8:	Verify SAM data.

4.6 Error Reporting

When an error is detected in a test, as much information as possible must be passed on to the tester. If a single error is detected, the address of the memory cell, the expected data, and the actual data should be reported. The error reporting routine can allow the test routine to continue and gather more information. For example, if the marching zeros test is executing and a single error is detected at cell 100H, and if the expected data was 0 but the actual data was 0xff, the error report would appear as:

cell address	100h	Actual	0xff	SB	0x00

If this test were allowed to continue, and if it could save all the errors and then interrogate them, you might see an error report similar to the following:

Cell	Actual	S.B.	Cell	Actual	S.B.
Testing ascending order			Testing descending order		
100h	0xff	0x00	300h	0x00	0xff
180h	0xff	0x00	180h	0x00	0xff
300h	0xff	0x00	100h	0x00	0xff
380h	0xff	0x00	080h	0x00	0xff

From the above information, the program could determine that there was a coupling error between address bits 7 and 8; that is, a high on address bit 7 or 8 forces a high on the adjacent address line.

4.7 Summary

In this chapter, we were introduced to the basic memory cell and the memory array. Many of the different memory devices were introduced, including

1. random access memory (RAM)
2. sequential address memory (SAM)
3. read-only memory (ROM)
4. programmable read-only memory (PROM)

A basic memory board and a description of its operation were also presented. Several of the better known RAM tests were described. "C" source code is provided hereing for several of the RAM memory tests.

4.8 Bibliography

1. Abadir, M.S., and H.K. Reghbati. 1993. Functional testing of semiconductor random access memories. *Computer Surveys* 15, no. 3:175–198.
2. Van de Goor, A.J., and C.A. Verruijt. 1990. An overview of deterministic functional RAM chip testing. *ACM Computing surveys* 22 (March):5–33.
3. Saluja, K.K., and S.H. Sng. 1987. Built in self testing RAM: A practical alternative. *IEEE Design & Test* (February):42–51.
4. Dekker, R., F. Beenker, and L. Thijssen. 1989. Realistic built-in self test for static RAMs. *IEEE Design & Test* (February):26–34.
5. Franklin, M., and K.K. Saluja. 1990. Built-in self testing of random access memories. *IEEE Computer* (October):45–56.

```
/*
    data_line_test()
    Description:
    This test routine verifiesthere are no shorts, opens,
    or coupled data bits in the memory block. A single
    memory location is tested. First a walking 1's
    pattern is executed, followed by a walking 0's pattern.
*/
data_line_test(int far *memory,int width)
  {
  int i;
  int data,data1,pass;
  data = 0;                         // initialize varaibles
  data1 = 1;
  pass =0;
  while(pass != 2) {                // loop for 2 passes
    *memory = data;                 // save data to memory
    if (*memory != data) {          // comapre data
      error_report(1,1);            // report error if failed
      memory_error(data,*memory);
      } // end of error report
    *memory = ~data;                // complment the data
    if (*memory != ~data) {         // comapre data
      error_report(1,2);            // report error if failed
      memory_error(data,*memory);
      } // end of error report
    for (i=0;i<width;i++) {         // test full width of data
      *memory = data1;              // save the data
      if (*memory!= data1)  {       // compare the data
        error_report(1,3);          // report the error
        memory_error(data1,*memory);
        }
      data1 = data1 << 1;           // walking 1 pattern
      if (pass == 1) data1++;
      } // end of for statement
    data = -1;                      // All ones
    data1 = -2;                     // bit zero = 0
    pass++;                         // bump the pass count
    } // end of while
  } // end of function
```

Code Block 4.1 Data line test.

```
/*
    ATS_Test()
    Description:
    This is the Knaizuk memory test. Memory is breaken into three
    blocks. The first location belongs to Group 0, the second to
    Group 1 and the third to Group 2. This is repeated for all of
    memory.
*/
ATS_Test(int far memory[], int size)
  {
  int i;
  unsigned int data = 0;
  for (i=0;i<size;i+=3)              // fill G0 with 1's pattern
        memory[i] = ~data;
  for (i=0;i<size;i+=3) {
    memory[i+1] = data;             // Fill G1 & G2 with
    memory[i+2] = data;   }         // 0's pattern
  for (i=0;i<size;i+=3)    {         // G1 is verified to be all 0's
    if (memory[i+1] != data) {      // if bad report the error
          error_report(2,1);
          memory_error(data,memory[i+1];  }
    }
  for (i=0;i<size;i+=3)              // Fill G1 with all 1's
        memory[i+1] = ~data;
  for(i=0;i<size;i+=3) {            // test G2 are all 0's
    if (memory[i+2] != data) {      // report error if not
          error_report(2,2);
          memory_error(data,memory[i+2];  }
    }
  for (i=0;i<size;i++)   {           // Test G0 & G1 are all 1's
    if (memory[i] != ~data) {
          error_report(2,3);        // report if G0 failed
          memory_error(~data,memory[i];  }
    if (memory[i+1] != ~data) {
          error_report(2,4);        // report if G1 failed
          memory_error(~data,memory[i+1];  }
    }
  for(i=0;i<size;i+=3)              // Fill G0 woth o's
      memory[i] = data;
  for(i=0;i<size;i+=3) {            // Test G0 to be all 0's
    if (memory[i] != data) {
            error_report(2,5);      // report error if failed
            memory_error(data,memory[i]);  }
    }
  for (i=0;i<size;i+=3)             // fill G2 with all 1's
      memory[i+2] = ~data;
  for (i=0;i<size;i+=3) {           // Test G2 to be all 1's
    if (memory[i+2] != ~data) {
            error_report(2,6);      // report if failed
            memory_error(~data,memory[i+2]) }
    }
  } // end of function
```

Code Block 4.2 ATS memory test.

```
/*
   marching_test()
   Description:
   This test scans memory first in the ascending and then in
   the descending order. Each scan consist of reading memory
   for a pre-set value, complementing the value, and then reading
   it a second time.
*/
marching_test(int far memory[], int size)
   {
   int i,j,done = 0;
   unsigned int data = 0;
   while (!done) {
   for (i=0;i<size+1,i++)              // fill memory with 0's pattern
           memory[i] = data;
   for (i=0;i<size+1;i++) {            // scan from low to high memory
       if (memory[i] != data) {            // compare location
               error_report(3,1);          // if failed report error
               memory_error(data,memory[i]); }
       memory[i] = ~data;                  // compelment the data
       if (memory[i] != ~data) {           // verify it's ok
               error_report(3,2);          // report error if failed
               memory_error(~data,memory[i]); }
       } //end of for loop
    for (i=size;i<0;i--) {              // scan from high to low memory
       if (memory[i] != ~data) {           // verify data
               error_report(3,3);          // report error if failed
               memory_error(~data,memory[i]); }
       memory[i] = data;                   // write original data
       if (memory[i] != data) {            // verify the data
               error_report(3,4);          // report error if failed
               memory_error(~data,memory[i]); }
       } // end of for loop
    data = ~data;                      // complement the data
    if (data == 0) done = 1;           // check if we are done
    } // end of while statement
   } // end of function
```

Code Block 4.3 Marching test.

```
/*
    galloping_test()
    Description:
    This test verifies that all memory cells exist, that there
    are no shorts, opens, or coupled bits. The test routine fills
    memory with the data pattern. It then write a single location
    at a time and verifies that no other location in that memory
   block was modified. This continues until all of memory is tested.
*/
galloping_test(int far memory[],int size)
 {
 int i,j,done = 0;
 unsigned int data = 0;
 while (!done) {                 // two pass test
    for (i=0;i<size;i++)         // fill memory with all 0's
          memory[i] = data;
    for (i=0;i<size;i++) {       // from low to high memory
    memory[i] = ~data;           // complement the data
    for(j=0;j<size;j++) {
      if (i == j) {              // verify all other location
        if (memory[i] !=~data){// this location all 1's
            error_report(4,1); // if yes report the error
            memory_error(~data,memory[i]); }
        }
      else
        if (memory[j] !=data){ // test other locations
            error_report(4,2); // report error
            memory_error(data,memory[j]); }
        } // end of if
      } // end of test loop
    memory[i] = data;            // save orginal data
    if (data == 0) done = 1;     // check if done
    } // end of while statement
 } // end of function
```

Code Block 4.4 Galloping test.

```
/*
   marching_b_test()
   Description:
   The routine start by filling all of memory with 0's.
   The from low to high memory each location is checked
   and then filled with all 1's.  A second pass checks
   from high to low memory, verifying all 1's writing 0's
   then 1's and again 0's. The third pass checks from
   high memory to low memory, verifying all 0's, then
   writing 1's followed by writing 0's
*/
marching_b_test(int far memory[],int size)
  {
  int i,j,done = 0;
  unsigned int data = 0;
  while (!done) {                 // loop tile done
   for (i=0;i<size,i++)          // fill memory with pattern
        memory[i] = data;
   for (i=0;i<size;i++) {        // from low to high memory
      if (memory[i] != data) {   // verify data
          error_report(5,1);      // if bad report error
          memory_error(data,memory[i]); }
      memory[i] = ~data;          // write complement data
      if (memory[i] != ~data) {  // check it
          error_report(5,2);      // if bad report error
          memory_error(~data,memory[i]); }
      memory[i] = data;           // write 0's again
      if (memory[i] != data) {   // and verify it
          error_report(5,3);
          memory_error(data,memory[i]); }
      memory[i] = ~data;          // finally write all 1's
      } // end of for loop
   for (i=size;i<0;i++) {        // now from high to low memory
      if (memory[i] != ~data) {  // check for all 1's
          error_report(5,4);      // report error if not
          memory_error(~data,memory[i]); }
      memory[i] = data;           // write all 0's
      memory[i] = ~data;          // all 1's
      memory[i] = data;           // all 0's
      } // end of for loop
   for (i=size; i<0; i--) {      //now from high to low
      if (memory[i] != data) {   // verify the data
          error_report(5,5);      // report if failed
          memory_error(data,memory[i]); }
      memory[i] = ~data;          // write all 1's
      memory[i] =data;            // and all 0's again
      } // of for loop
   data = ~data;                  // complment the data
   if (data == 0) done = 1;      // check if done
   } // end of while statement
  } // end of function
```

Code Block 4.5 Marching B test.

Chapter

5

Serial Communications

5.0 Introduction

Computers communicate using binary encoded information in the
form of logical ones and zeroes that are represented by discrete volt-
age levels. Data encoded in this form is transferred from one computer
to another computer or other device via communication lines. Moreover, computers can communicate with many other computers at the
same time or just listen as other computers communicate. Communications between two computers employ one of two basic methods. In
the first method, *serial communication,* one bit of information at a
time is sent over a single wire. In the second method, *parallel communication,* one bit at a time is sent over each of multiple wires.

At first, communications between computer systems were slow but,
as technologies improved, the rate became much faster. Recent advances allow data transfer rates greater than 10 million bytes per second. These higher speeds require new media technologies such as
coaxial cable and fiber optics. Collectively, these technologies—serial
communication, coaxial cable, and fiber optics—are used in many applications such as *local area networks* (LANs).

In this chapter, we will describe serial communication, the device
technology involved, and the testing of related hardware. Numerous
pseudo-code logic examples are given for performing these tests.

5.1 Serial Communication

Many I/O devices transfer data to and from the computer system serially; that is, one bit at a time over a single or paired communication

channel. A device called the *transmitter* transfers a byte of data one bit at a time over the communication channel using a shift register. The system at the other end reads each bit and forms those bits into the byte that was originally transmitted.

There are three accepted serial communication modes, which are:

1. simplex mode
2. half duplex mode
3. full duplex mode

The three modes are depicted in Fig. 5.1.

Simplex mode is defined as one-way data communication. That is, one system always acts as transmitter, and the other always acts as receiver. Conversely, *half duplex mode* is two-way communication, but only one system can transmit at a time. Communication is via a single channel. Finally, in *full duplex mode*, data communication is fully two-way, and both systems are able to transmit and receive at the same time. Full duplex communication requires two channels.

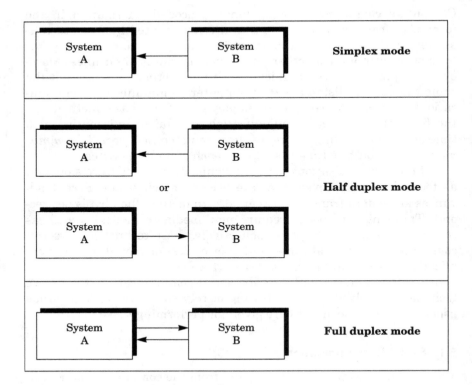

Figure 5.1 Serial communication modes.

For these three serial modes, there are two basic types of serial communication: *asynchronous* and *synchronous*. With asynchronous communication, each data character is transmitted independently and must carry its own start and stop information. With synchronous communication, characters are transmitted one after the other but must include special synchronization ("sync") characters as starting and ending designators.

5.1.1 Asynchronous communication

The format of a typical asynchronous character is shown in Fig. 5.2. Before the character starts to transmit, the transmitter marks the output line, otherwise known as the *idle state*. The start bit is always a zero and is followed by the data.

The data typically consists of five, six, seven, or eight bits per character. The *least significant bit* (LSB) of the data stream is always the first bit of the first byte to be transmitted. The parity bit, which is optional, follows the data bits. The last bits are the stop bits—generally 1, $1^{1/2}$ or 2 stop bits.

5.1.2 Synchronous communication

With asynchronous communication, each data byte must be surrounded by a start bit and a stop bit. In synchronous communication, the start and stop bits are not required. Because of the absence of these bits, another method of determining which groups of bits represent characters must be used. To accomplish this, synchronous communication requires that a clock be transmitted along with the data bits. This clock guarantees the synchronization of the transmitter and receiver.

Figure 5.3 shows the character format for synchronous transmission and the clock signal. Here, for example, bits 1–8 might represent a single byte, while bits 9–16 may be the second byte of data; or bits 1–3 may be part of a one character, bits 4–11 may be a second byte, and

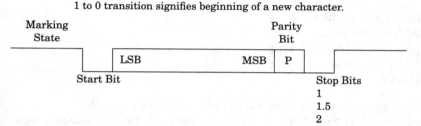

Figure 5.2 Asynchronous transmission.

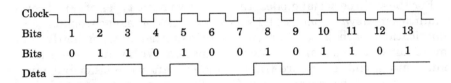

Figure 5.3 Synchronous transmission.

bits 12–16 could be part of a third character. To determine proper framing, the transmitter must send a unique byte pattern that signals the start of data transmission. This byte is referred to as the *sync byte*. At the receiver, the communication chip searches the data stream until it finds the sync byte. When the sync byte is found, the receiver starts shifting in data characters.

Synchronous communication is most appropriate where blocks of data are to be transmitted, whereas asynchronous data communication is best suited where single characters are to be transmitted.

5.2   Standards

Transmission rates are measured in *bits per second* (bps), more commonly referred to as *baud* rate. Currently, standard baud rates are 110, 300, 600, 1200, 1800, 2400, 4800, 9600, 19,200, and 28,800. Most system are capable of handling 9600 baud. At 9600 baud, the maximum number of characters that can be transmitted in one second would be 9600/10 = 960. This maximum rate can be attained only if there is no time lost between transmitting characters. The value 10 in the formula assumes that each character requires by one start bit, eight data bits and one stop bit.

5.3   Description of a Serial Communication Board

Figure 5.4 is a block diagram of a typical serial communication board. There are five major components on this board:

1. internal data bus
2. address decoder
3. programmable clock chip
4. DMA controller
5. UART

These components are described in subsequent paragraphs.

One way of testing this board is to divide the logic into smaller, testable segments. Once the board's logic has been divided, we can see

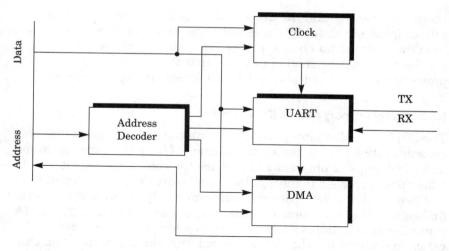

Figure 5.4 Serial controller block diagram.

that all data entering or leaving the board must pass through the internal data bus and the data bus driver. For this reason, the data bus and data bus driver should be the first logic blocks tested. Once this logic is tested, you may start using the tested logic to test other parts of the board, starting with the address decoder.

5.3.1 The data bus

The data bus driver is a gateway between the system data bus and the internal data bus of the board. Signals on the system bus determine whether the driver becomes enabled and set the direction of data flow.

During a CPU read operation, the CPU places the I/O address onto the address bus and sets IO/M low. While IO/M is low, the address decoder selects the proper chip. The selected chip is enabled and places data onto the board's internal data bus. The data bus driver is enabled and allows that data to flow from the board's data bus to the system bus.

During a write operation, the CPU places data onto the system data bus, along with the address, and sets IO/M low. The on-board logic allows the data on the system bus to be passed onto the internal data bus of the board. Once the data is on the internal data bus, the selected chip reads the data into one of its internal registers.

5.3.2 Address bus and decoder

The address bus and address decoder are used to decode the I/O address presented by the CPU to the system address bus. When an I/O operation is active and the decoder detects the board address, a chip select signal is raised. The selected chip then either reads the data from the internal data bus or places data onto the internal data bus. A test routine must be created to verify that the address decoder works properly for a legal address, and that it filters all illegal addresses.

5.3.3   Direct memory access (DMA) chip

The DMA controller chip provides the interface for the programmable communication chip to the system memory. Using the communication and DMA chips, a program can prepare the communication device to transmit or receive a number of bytes and start the transfer operation.

When receiving data, the communication chip receives a character and signals the DMA controller that it needs to be serviced. The DMA controller chip initiates a memory write cycle to the proper memory location and places the character received from the communication chip into that memory location. After the character is placed into memory, the address in the DMA controller is incremented, and the counter is decremented. When the DMA count equals the required number of bytes, the DMA controller issues a *receive complete* signal. This signal is used to interrupt the CPU, signifying that a full message was received.

When transmitting, the communication chip informs the DMA controller that it needs a character to transmit. In response, the DMA controller places the memory address on the system bus and causes a memory read to occur. The read operation places the next byte to transmit onto the internal data bus. At this time, the communication chip reads the data and transmits it. The DMA controller increments the address and decrements the byte count. Once the entire message is transmitted, the DMA controller issues the DMA complete signal.

5.3.4   The clock chip

The clock chip is used to provide the communication chip with an internal, synchronizing signal that is used to transmit characters in serial form. The rate of that clock signal determines the baud rate. Generally there is one clock input for each port, which allows for different baud rates. Each clock can be initialized at the start of the system and need not be changed, assuming the baud rates remains fixed during program operation.

5.3.5   The UART

The *universal asynchronous transmitter/receiver* (UART) is a programmable chip that converts bytes of data into a serial stream of bits, plus the start and stop bits. This conversion takes place while bytes of data are transmitted from the UART. The UART also has the ability to convert an incoming serial data stream to bytes and present these bytes to the CPU as incoming data. Figure 5.5 displays a block diagram of the typical UART. From this diagram, note that there is more to the UART than simply receiving and transmitting data.

The receive logic consist of:

1. the receiver timing and control block
2. the receiver shift register
3. the receiver holding register

The transmit logic consist of:

1. the transmitting holding register
2. the transmitting shift register
3. the transmitting timing and control logic

Also included on the chip are:

1. the modem control logic
2. the status register logic
3. the interrupt control logic

Many of the newer chips also have BIST logic to support self-testing of the chip.

5.4   Test Routines

The test routines that are described in this section start with verifying that the lowest level of logic common to all blocks is tested first. After testing these blocks, the diagnostic can start checking the programmable chips and their interfaces.

The code in each code block is generic code that can be used to test most communication boards. The actual hardware I/O drivers must be developed for each particular communication device. At the end of this section is a brief specification for the diagnostic communication driver.

5.4.1   Address decoder test

The address decoder examines the address that is presented to the communication board. If the address decoder decodes the proper address, the board's data bus is enabled. The output of the address decoder selects one of the programmable chips or registers on the board.

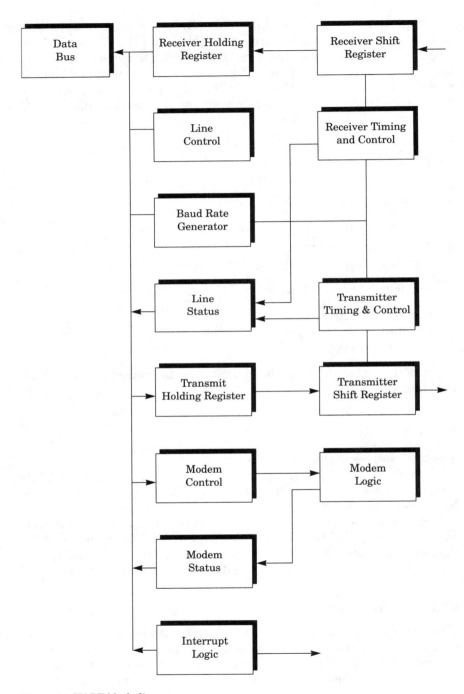

Figure 5.5 UART block diagram.

The address decoder test must verify that the proper chip is selected when the chip's address is presented to the board. However, this might be harder to achieve than you might expect. For example, if no programmable chip has a unique ID stored in one of its registers, then special testing must be performed to verify that the proper chip was selected. In many cases, this diagnostic test is combined with the data bus test described in Chap. 3.

5.4.2 Data bus test

From block diagram in Fig. 5.4, we can see that the internal data bus is connected to each of the programmable chips and the data bus drivers. The purpose of the data bus test is to verify that internal data bus is capable of transferring data between the system bus and the selected programmable chip. The test also verifies there are no stuck data bits and no coupled data bits.

The data bus test should select a register within each programmable chip that has full write/read ability (see Code Block 3.1, Chap. 3). If no register has this ability, then a register that gives the maximum number of write/read bits should be used. In this case mask the bits that are not write/read (see Code Block 3.2).

5.4.3 Internal loopback test (polling)

This test routine verifies that the communication port is able to transmit and receive characters using the I/O polling method. This test should be accomplished using the internal loopback mode. *Internal loopback mode* loops the transmitted data stream back into the receiver, internal to the chip. No data stream is applied to the output of the chip.

After transmitting each character, the program should verify that the character was transmitted and then wait for that character to be received. Make sure that there is a time-out—otherwise, the program could hang waiting for a character to be received.

The program should attempt to transfer and receive several bytes. A check should be made after transferring each byte to ensure that the chip is ready to transfer another character.

The process is summarized as follows:

Step 1:	Initialize the transmitter for internal loopback.
Step 2:	Set up to transmit X characters.
Step 3:	Transmit the first character.
Step 4:	Wait for received character.

Step 5:	If error, report it and break.
Step 6:	Verify that character is the same as transmitted.
Step 7:	Loop until all characters are transmitted.

Sample C code for this test is provided in Code Block 5.1, at the end of the chapter. Refer to the sample communication driver specification (Exhibit 5.1) defined at the end of this section.

5.4.4 Interrupt test

The internal loopback test, using interrupts, verifies that the UART is able to cause a CPU interrupt when the transmitter buffer is empty and when the receiver buffer is full. The test routine needs to set up the ISR vector and the number of data characters to transmit. In many cases, the test routine must "kick start" the UART by sending the first character to the UART. Thereafter, as each transmit buffer empty interrupt is received, another character is transmitted. This continues until the last character is transmitted. As each receive buffer full interrupt is received, the character is read from the UART and placed into the receive buffer.

The process is summarized as:

Step 1:	Set up the interrupt vectors.
Step 2:	Initialize the UART for transmit and receive (interrupts enabled).
Step 3:	Set up to transmit X characters.
Step 4:	Transmit the first character.
Step 5:	Wait for error condition or transmit complete.
Step 6:	Reset the vector and the UART.
Step 7:	Compare the transmit buffer with received buffer.

Sample C code for this test is provided in Code Block 5.2, at the end of this chapter.

5.4.5 DMA loopback test

This DMA loopback test routine is designed to check the interface between the DMA controller, the communication chip, and the system memory. The program sets up the DMA controller to transfer and receive a number of characters. Once the first transfer byte is loaded to the communication chip, the DMA controller then transfers all the remaining character to the communication chip. As each character is received (internal loopback), the UART requests the DMA controller to transfer the character into memory. Once the proper number of characters have been transferred, then the DMA controller terminates the transfer and issues and interrupt to the CPU.

The DMA test is summarized as:

Step 1:	Set up the DMA interrupt vectors.
Step 2:	Initialize the UART for transmit and receive (DMA).
Step 3:	Initialize the DMA controller.
Step 4:	Set up to transmit X characters.
Step 5:	Transmit the first character.
Step 6:	Wait for error condition or DMA receive complete.
Step 7:	Reset interrupt vector, DMA controller, and UART.
Step 8:	Compare the transmit buffer with receive buffer.

Sample C code for this test is provided in Code Block 5.3.

5.4.6   Baud rate test

The UART transmits a character from its holding register to the serial output line. Each bit is transmitted during a clock pulse that is supplied by the on-board clock. The clock chip sends these clock pulses at a particular rate that depends on the clock crystal. Proper synchronization of the clock pulses is crucial to the transmission and reception of characters in asynchronous mode—if the transmitting and receive units are at different clock frequencies, then the receiving station will never be able to read a character from the transmitting station.

The baud rate tests verifies that the crystal, the clock connected to the UART, and the internal clock divider are working properly. This test must transmit data for a number of seconds, and for as fast as the transmitter allows. At the completion of that time, the transmitter should be turned off. Afterwards count the number of characters transmitted and multiply by 10 (for 10 bits per character), and then divide by the time expired. This gives the baud rate.

Example Let the transmitter transmit at 9600 baud for four seconds. At the end of four seconds, the program is allowed to transmit 3839 characters. The baud rate is then

$$(3839 \times 10)\,/4 \;=\; 9598 \text{ baud}$$

When comparing the actual transmission rate to the desired one, a small tolerance must be allowed, due to variation and granularity of the clock. To determine the tolerance, check with the system engineer.

Sample C code for the baud rate test is provided in Code Block 5.4 at the end of this chapter.

5.4.7 All baud rate test

The test described in Sec. 5.4.6 will verify that a crystal is working at the correct frequency and that the clock is providing the proper pulses. The test described in this section verifies that the UART's internal clock division circuitry is working properly. For each baud rate, repeat the baud rate test described in Sec. 5.4.6. A one-second transmit time is more than adequate for this test.

5.4.8 External loopback test

The UART supports both internal and external loopback. In the case of external loopback, the data is actually transmitted off the board and then returned back onto the board. To complete this testing, you must have an external loopback connector.

To perform the test, connect the external loopback connector. Next, initialize the UART so that it executes in external loopback mode. Finally, proceed in the same manner as the internal loopback test described in Sec. 5.4.3.

5.4.9 Operational test

An operational test is designed to test the system under simulated operating conditions. The test requires two systems. One system acts as the master, and the other is the slave station. The test routine verifies that the communication option, the disk, and the video display can operate at the same time.

The test program starts by sending a command to the slave and waits for the slave station to respond. After the slave station responds, the program opens a file on the disk and reads the first sector of the disk file.

Next, a buffer of data is transmitted to the slave station. As each character is transmitted to the slave station, it is displayed on the screen of the master. When there are less than 32 characters in the buffer, the program issues a command to the disk drive to read the next sector. That sector is placed in a second buffer. This continues until the entire file has been transferred.

The slave station echoes each received character onto its screen. After it receives a complete sector, that sector is written to its local disk.

When the entire file has been transmitted, the slave station transmits the file back to the master station.

The operational test starts at baud rate 50 and is repeated until all 16 baud rates have been tested. Exhibit 5.1 provides a description of the diagnostic serial communication driver.

Exhibit 5.1 Serial Driver Specification

There are several routines that the diagnostic will use. These are:

reset_uart()   This routine is used to reset the UART, disable any pending interrupts, reset any flags.

init_uart()   This routine initialize the UART, The following arguments must be set before calling this routine.

1. bits   The number of bits per data byte.
2. Loopback   0 = non-loopback 1 = loopback
3. INT   0 = non interrupt mode
    1 = interrupt mode
4. DMA   0 = non DMA mode
    1 = DMA mode
5. BAUD   The BAUD Rate

send_serial()   This routine places the character passed to it in the UART transmit buffer.

get_serial()   This routine waits for a character to be received. The character is returned in the lower 8 bits. The upper 8 bits represent status.

enable()   Enables the UART interrupt.

disable()   Disables the UARt interrupt.

delay()   Delay 1 millisecond per count.

setup_DMA   Sets up the DMA with arguments that are passed. The DMA channel, the count, and the pointer to the buffer.

serial_ISR()   This is the communications interrupt service routine. It is entered every time the UART or the DMA requires an interrupt service.

Pseudo Code:
```
Save all registers
read reason for interrupt
if DMA complete (Transmit Channel)
        indicate DMA transmit complete
if DMA complete (Receive Channel)
        indicate DMA receive complete
if (Transmit buffer empty)
        if (xmit_cnt != 0)
                send next data byte
                decrement xmit_cnt
if (Receive buffer full)
        read the data byte
        place into buffer
        increment rec_cnt
        reset interrupt chip
        restore all registers
        return to interrupted routine
```

5.5 Local Area Networks

Local area network (LAN) technology provides for transmission of data at a much faster rate than the serial communication techniques we have already visited. LAN technology also provides suitable communications for other types of devices, such as document scanners and video monitors.

The task of the network communication chip can be categorized into two basic functions:

1. transmission of packets
2. reception of packets

Data is transmitted in the form of *packets* whose typical format is shown in Fig. 5.6. The leading eight bits form a synchronization byte, followed by a six-byte destination address, then the source address. The data field has a minimum as well as a maximum length, followed by a 32-bit *cyclic redundancy check* (CRC). These fields, along with the ring buffer data structure used to hold the packets and tests to exercise the LAN, are described in the following paragraphs.

5.5.1 Destination address

The destination address indicates the destination of the data packet and is used to filter unwanted data packets from reaching the system. There are three type of destination addresses supported:

1. *Physical address*—an address that identifies a unique system in the network.
2. *Multicast address*—an address that identifies a subset of system in the network.
3. *Broadcast address*—an address that is used to address all systems in the network.

5.5.2 Source address

The source address is the physical address of the system that sent the data packet. The source address is not allowed to be a multicast or broadcast address. The network chip simply passes the source address with the packet information to a memory buffer.

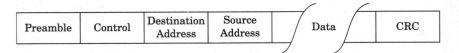

Figure 5.6 Typical network packet.

5.5.3 Ring buffers

Received packets are stored in a ring buffer data structure composed of a series of contiguous buffers that form a first in/last out (FILO) (see Fig. 5.7). The location of the receive buffer ring is programmed during the initialization of the chip. The first byte of each buffer has a flag to indicate whether the host owns the buffer or it belongs to the LAN chip. If the host owns the buffer, the LAN chip cannot place data into the buffer.

The transmission ring buffer has the same format as the receive buffer ring. If the host owns the buffer, the host may place data into the buffer. When the packet is ready to transmit, the host sets ownership of the packet to the LAN. The LAN chip detects that it owns the packet and then transmits that packet. At the completion of the transmission, ownership is returned to the host.

There is a possibility that packets may be transmitted out of sequence. For example, assume that packets 4, 5, 6 are built and ownership given to the LAN chip. The next buffer that the LAN chip checks is packet number 6. That packet is transmitted before packets 4 and 5.

Most LAN chips have built-in DMA logic. The DMA logic provides support so that the LAN can access memory locations by either placing data into a buffer (receiving a packet), or taking data out of the buffer (transmitting a packet).

5.5.4 Node ID test

The Node ID PROM contains the system's network physical address. The node ID is a unique ID number for each machine. Because this ID is used in the transmission and reception of message packets, it is

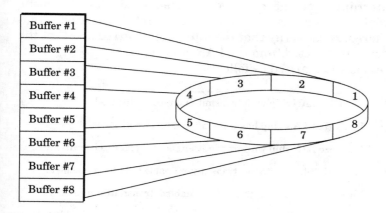

Figure 5.7 Ring buffer.

essential that the PROM contains the proper ID—an incorrect address could result in improper communication on the network.

During the test, the six-byte address and the two-byte check-sum are read from the ID ROM. A check-sum, CS, is calculated from the six-byte address using the equation:

$$CS = (A \ll 8 + B) + (C \ll 8 + D) + (E \ll 8 + F)$$

$$CS = MOD(2**16-1)(CS)$$

The term $\ll 8$ represents a left shift by eight bits, and A through F represent bytes 0 through 5. CS is compared to the actual check-sum, which is derived from bytes 7 and 8 of the ID ROM (represented by G and H) in the following way:

$$Check\text{-}sum = (G \ll 8 + H)$$

If CS does not equal check-sum, then the test fails.

5.5.5 Network chip test

This test verifies that the network chip can cause an interrupt. First, the interrupt is masked at the interrupt controller, and a packet is transmitted in loopback mode. The LAN chip is checked to verify that the controller did indeed set its interrupt bit. Also, a check must be made to verify that the system did not get interrupted. Exhibit 5.2 contains a description of the diagnostic LAN driver needed for this and other tests.

The second part of this test is to re-initialize the LAN chip and enable the interrupt. A second message is transmitted. The diagnostic interrupt routine sets a flag to indicate that an interrupt service routine was entered. Next, verify that the interrupt occurred and that the proper status was detected from the LAN chip.

The process is summarized as follows:

Step 1:	Initialize LAN chip with transmit and receive disabled.
Step 2:	Verify that LAN chip has transmit and receive disabled.
Step 3:	Initialize LAN chip with transmitter enabled and receiver disabled.
Step 4:	Verify that LAN chip has transmitter enabled, receiver disabled.
Step 5:	Initialize LAN chip with receiver enabled, transmitter disabled.
Step 6:	Verify that LAN chip has receiver enabled, transmitter disabled.

Step 7:   Initialize LAN chip with both transmitter and receiver enabled.

Step 8:   Verify that both transmitter and receiver are enabled.

Exhibit 5.2   LAN Driver Specification

Init_port	This routine is called to initialize the hardware, setup the buffers and the interrupt vector.
Start_Lance	Called to active the Lance.
Stop_Lance	Called to stop the Lance.
Reset_port	Called to reset the Lance, and the transmit and receive buffers.
Set_addr	Logical hardware address.
Read_addr	Read logical hardware address.
Mode	This routine allows the calling routine to enable and disable promiscuous mode, and enable and disable multi-cast mode.
Xmit_frame	This routine searches the transmit buffer ring, find a free transmit buffer, copy the transmit frame to the transmit buffer and then give ownership of the buffer to the Lance.

5.5.6   Internal loopback and DMA test

The network chip provides an internal loopback. The internal loopback mode is used for a majority of the diagnostic testing. Using the internal loopback mode allows the system to undergo testing and not disrupt traffic on the network.

During the following test all packet destinations are to the system that is transmitting the message. That is the destination address is the same as the source address.

The first loopback test should be a simple data packet and accomplished in the poll mode. This verifies the proper operation of chip initialization, packet transmission, and reception. These tests should include a time-out waiting for initialization, transmission, and the reception to complete. An error should be reported if a time-out occurs or if the receive packet is not the same as the transmitted packet. This test also sends multiple packets having varying length and alignment in memory in order to exercise the DMA addressing bits. The process is summed up as follows:

Step 1:   Initialize the test setup.

Step 2:   Initialize the network chip.

Step 3:	Set up pointer for packet length and memory alignment.
Step 4:	Create the next packet.
Step 5:	Transmit the packet and check for errors.
Step 6:	Verify that a packet was received and check for errors.
Step 7:	Compare the transmit and receive packets.
Step 8:	Advance to the next packet.
Step 9:	Loop until done.

5.5.7   CRC test

The network chip uses a cyclic redundancy check (CRC) on both the transmission and reception of packets. When a packet is being transmitted, the CRC is calculated and sent as the last characters of the transmitted packet. When the chip receives a packet, it calculates the CRC for the incoming packet. When the chip receives the CRC, a comparison with the calculated CRC and the transmitted CRC is made. If they do not match, then a CRC error flag is set.

Hence, the CRC test verifies the LAN's ability to receive a good CRC without flagging a CRC error, to correctly generate a CRC on transmission, and to flag a bad CRC on a received packet.

The ability to correctly receive a good CRC is verified by placing the LAN chip in a mode that enables transmission and disables the receiver CRC. A packet is then transmitted and received. Since the CRC calculation is disabled at the receiver, this routine should return with an error.

The correct generation of a CRC upon transmission is verified by transmitting a packet with the LAN generating and appending a CRC. The packet is received with no LAN CRC checking. A CRC is calculated and compared on the receive buffer. If the CRC is not equal, then an error is reported.

The ability to flag a bad CRC is verified by transmitting a packet with a manually appended faulty CRC. This is done by disabling transmit CRC logic and enabling the receive CRC logic. When the packet is received, the LAN is expected to flag the fault CRC.

These tests are summarized as follows:

Step 1:	Initialize test setup.
Step 2:	Initialize the chip to transmit and receive CRCs.
Step 3:	Create packet for CRC test.

Step 4:	Transmit packet and check for errors.
Step 5:	Verify that packet was received with no errors.
Step 6:	Initialize chip for non-transmission of CRC.
Step 7:	Insert bad CRC at end of packet.
Step 8:	Transmit packet with bad CRC.
Step 9:	Verify that packet was received with CRC error.
Step 10:	Initialize network chip not to check for CRC on receive packets.
Step 11:	Send packet and check for errors.
Step 12:	Verify that packet was received without errors.

5.5.8 Address filtering test

One of the functions of a network chip is to check each incoming packet to determine if it is addressed to the station. This check is done internal to the network chip. The address filtering test verifies that the network chip correctly filters the destination address of an incoming packet and determines whether to accept or reject the packet. Specifically, the chip must reject a physical address, accept a multicast address packet, and receive logical address while in *promiscuous mode.*

The ability to reject the physical address is verified by placing the network chip in a mode that is non-promiscuous and non-multicast mode. A packet with the destination address not equal to the system's physical address is transmitted. The packet should be rejected.

The reception of a multicast address is verified by setting a bit in the logical address filter. A multicast packet is expected whose address corresponds to that transmitted set bit.

The next test verifies that the chip can receive a non-broadcast packet which is not physically addressed to it while in promiscuous mode.

All packets that are received should be error free, and the data in the packet should be verified.

To summarize these tests:

Step 1:	Initialize test setup.
Step 2:	Initialize chip.
Step 3:	Transmit broadcast packet.
Step 4:	Verify that packet was received.

Step 5:	Compare packets.
Step 6:	Transmit packet with multicast address.
Step 7:	Verify that packet was not received.
Step 8:	Transmit packet with different physical address.
Step 9:	Verify that packet was not received.
Step 10:	Initialize chip for multicast bit set.
Step 11:	Transmit multicast packet.
Step 12:	Verify that packet was received.
Step 13:	Transmit packet with different multicast address.
Step 14:	Verify that packet was not received.
Step 15:	Initialize chip in promiscuous mode.
Step 16:	Transmit packet with different address.
Step 17:	Verify that packet was received.

5.5.9 Missed packets

The network chip should detect occasions when a packet is addressed to it and there are no buffers to place the packet. If this occurs, it is refereed to as a *missed packet,* and a MISS error is reported. The following test verifies that the network chip has the ability to detect when a MISS error occurs and that the proper status bit is set to indicate the error.

To start this test, the chip is initialized so that there are no receive buffers belonging to the chip. A packet is transmitted to the chip in loopback mode. The test routine must then verify that the chip did detect the MISS error and that the appropriate bit was set.

The second part of the test verifies that the chip is able to recover from the MISS error and receive packets when the ownership bit is set properly. This is accomplished by setting the ownership bit in a packet and transmitting a second packet. The test then verifies that the packet was received without errors and compares the two packets.

To summarize these tests:

Step 1:	Initialize test setup.
Step 2:	Initialize chip with no receive buffers allocated.
Step 3:	Send a packet to itself.

Step 4:	Verify that a MISS error was reported.
Step 5:	Set ownership bit in a buffer.
Step 6:	R-send the packet.
Step 7:	Verify that the packet was received without errors.
Step 8:	Compare the packets.

5.5.10 Collision detection

In a network environment, the likelihood of more than two stations attempting to transmit packets at the same time is very high. When two or more stations transmit at the same time, it is refereed to as a *collision of packets*. Collisions will corrupt the data contained in both packets. The network chip can detect collisions so that it can re-transmit the packet again. The network chip can also falsify this signal in internal loopback mode for test purposes. Hence, the collision detection test verifies that the chip can detect when a collision occurs and re-transmit the message by faking a collision.

To summarize the test:

Step 1:	Initialize test setup.
Step 2:	Initialize network chip with force collision.
Step 3:	Transmit test packet and check for collision.
Step 4:	Verify that the retry error occurred.
Step 5:	Verify that the transmitter is still enabled.
Step 6:	Initialize chip.

5.5.11 Certification test

The certification test, although not a diagnostic, is used to certify that the designed board is fully functional and operational. The certification test program for a network chip requires that the system be an active component on the network.

The certification test program allows the node to continuously transmit sequentially numbered packets. While in the process of transmitting continuous data, the node must also be able to receive packets from other stations. In this case, there are two types of packets.

The first packet would be a reply packet to the node. The reply packet is simply an acknowledge packet and consists of the sequence counter, the original data, and the station that replied. When a reply packet is received, a check of the data and the sequence number should be implemented. The sequence number may be received out of sequence. If a packet sequence is not acknowledged within a specified time period, count that packet as missing or lost.

The second type of packet that may be received is a command packet from another node. When this packet is received, the packet is echoed back to the sending station.

The certification test program must keep track of the number of packets transmitted, the number of packets received, errors detected, and possibly the rate of transmission and reception.

5.6 Summary

This chapter addressed two different types of serial communications: synchronous and asynchronous. Although both transfer data serially, they differ in the speed of transmission. The faster synchronous communication is better for block transfer, while the slower asynchronous is better suited for transferring single characters. Although most of the testing was defined for asynchronous mode, many of the tests can be modified for synchronous communications.

We also discussed other, newer technologies used in local area networks, which transfer data at a much faster rate using data packets. We noted that the testing of the LAN circuit is completely different from that of testing serial communications. We also saw that testing must cover transmitting and receiving packets, the filtering of packets that are not for the station, and checking for collisions and missed packets.

5.7 Bibliography

1. McNamara, J.E., 1982. *Technical Aspects of Data Communications*. Burlington, Mass.: Digital Press, Digital Equipment Corp.
2. McNamara, J.E., 1985. *Local Area Networks*. Burlington, Massachusetts: Digital Press, Digital Equipment Corp.
3. 1988. *Data Communications, Local Area Networks, UART*. Santa Clara, California: National Semiconductor.

```
/*
   internal_loopback_test()

   Description:
   This test routine setup the UART for asynchronous mode
   with internal loopback enabled. After the UART is
   initialized, 256 characters are transmitted and received.
   If at any time a character is not transmitted, or one
   is received, when expected, an error is reported.

   As each character is received, it is compared with the
   character that was transmitted.
*/
internal_loopback_test()
   {
   bits = 8; loopback = 1        // set for internal loopback
      inter = 0; dma = 0; BAUD = 9600
      reset_uart();             // reset the UART
      initialize_uart();        // initialize the UART
      for (i=0;i<256;i++) {
         send_serial(i);        // transmit a character
         if (error_code) break; // break if failed
         char_in = get_serial();// get the next character
         if (error_code) break; // break if error
         if (char_in != i) {
            error_code = 5;     // se t error code
            break;
            } // end of if
      } // end of for loop
   } // end of function
```

Code Block 5.1 Forward/backward seek test.

```
/*
    interrupt_test()

    Description:
    This routine enables the UART in asynchronous mode with
    interrupts enabled. The transmit butter is filled with
    the data pattern. Next the first character is transmitted.
    The routine then waits for 1 second. The UART is disabled,
    the interrupt is restored. The routine then checks if
    all 256 characters were transmitted and received. Then it
    compares the transmit buffer with the receive buffer.
*/
interrupt_test()
    {
    old_vector = read_vector(INTR);
    bits = 8; loopback = 1          // set for internal loopback
    inter = 1; dma = 0; BAUD = 9600;
    set_vector(INTR,serial_isr);
    reset_uart();                   // reset the UART
    init_uart();                    // initialize the UART
    for (i=0;i<256;i++) {
      t_buffer[i] = i;              // fill the buffer
      r_buffer[i] = 0;   }          // clear receive buffer
    enable();                       // enable interrupts
    send_serial(i);                 // transmit first character
    if (error_code) break;          // break if failed
    delay(1000);                    // 1 second delay
    disable();                      // disable interrupts
    reset_uart();                   // reset UART
    set_vector(INTR,old_vector);// reset to old vector
    if (x_cnt != 255)  {
            error_code = 10;        // set error code
            break;          }
    if (r_cnt != 255); {            // check receive count
            error_code = 12;        // set error code
            break;          }
    // verify receive buffer
    for (i=0;i<256;i++) {
      if (r_buffer[i] != t_buffer[i]) {
          error_code = 12;          // set error code
          break;  } // end of if compare
      } // end of for loop
    } // end of function
```

Code Block 5.2 Interrupt test.

```
/*
    DMA_test()

    Description
    This routine enables the DMA to transfer and
    receive 256 characters. At the completion of
    the timeout, a check is made to see if all 256
    characters were transmitted and received, if not
    an error is reported. Otherwise, the two buffers
    are compared.
*/
DMA_test()
    {
    bits = 8; loopback = 1;        // set internal loopback
    inter = dma = 1; BAUD = 9600;
    reset_uart();                  // reset the UART
    init_uart();                   // initialize the UART
    setup_DMA(CHN1,256,t_buffer);
    setup_DMA(CHN2,256,r_buffer);
    for (i=0;i<256;i++) {
      t_buffer[i] = i;             // fill the buffer
      r_buffer[i] = 0;  }          // clear receive buffer
    send_serial(i);                // transmit first character
    if (error_code) break;         // break if failed
    delay(1000);                   // 1 second delay
    if (!x_done) {
         error_code = 20;          // set error code
         break;  }
    if (!r_done); {                // check receive count
         error_code = 22;          // set error code
         break;  }
    // verify receive buffer
    for (i=0;i<256;i++) {
      if (r_buffer[i] != t_buffer[i]) {
         error_code = 22;          // set error code
         break;
         } // end of if compare
      } // end of for loop
    } // end of function
```

Code Block 5.3 DMA test.

```
/*
    BAUD_test()

    Description:
    This test routine enables the UART in asynchronous mode
    and at 9600 BAUD. Interrupts are enabled for the transmitter
    only. After sending the first character, the interrupt
    Service routine continues to send characters. After 4
    seconds, the transmitter is turn off. A check is made
    to verify that the number of characters transmitted were
    within tolerance
*/
BAUD_test()
    {
    error_code = 0;
    bits = 8; loopback = 1;      // set loopback mode
    inter = 1; dma = 0; BAUD = 9600;
    old_vector = read_vector(INTR);
    set_vector(INTR,serial_isr);
    reset_uart();                    // reset the UART
    init_uart(1);                    // initialize the UART
    enable();                        // enable interrupts
    send_serial(i);                  // transmit first character
    if (error_code) return(error_code; // break if failed
    delay(5000);                     // 5 second delay
    disable();                       // disable interrupts
    set_vector(INTR,old_vector);  // restore old vector
    reset_uart();                    // reset the UART
    if (x_cnt < 4790 | x_cnt > 4810)
        error_code = 30;             // set error code
    return(error_code);
    } // end of function
```

Code Block 5.4 Baud rate test.

6

Secondary Storage Devices

6.0 Introduction

Secondary storage devices provide the computer with long-term bulk data storage. This chapter deals with two particular types of secondary storage devices: the magnetic tape and the magnetic disk.

The *magnetic tape drive* is very similar to cassette tape drives used for music, given that both use *serial* access. The tape machine is serial because it must pass over the first and second songs to get to the third song. Similarly, if the magnetic tape device needs to get to the third file on the tape, it must pass over the first and second files on its way.

The *magnetic disk* is a circular magnetic platter. It is divided into *tracks,* and each track is divided into *sectors*. The CPU can write data to, and read data from, each sector. To access a particular sector, the *read/write heads* are positioned above the proper track. As the selected sector passes under the heads, the heads perform the read or write operation. This type of access is referred to as *direct random access*.

6.1 Generic Test Routines

Review the block diagram of Fig. 6.1, which depicts a storage device controller. There are generic hardware functions that must be provided by all types of device controllers. For example, inside the controller resides the following:

1. data bus
2. address bus

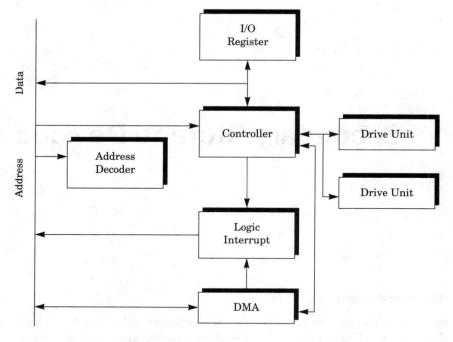

Figure 6.1 Device controller block diagram.

3. I/O registers
4. interrupt control logic
5. DMA
6. programmable chips

Although individual tests used to diagnose subsystems vary according to the controllers and devices used, a core set of tests for these generic functions can be used for most storage device controllers.

This section describes generic test routines that can be used with almost any type of controller. These generic tests should be performed before any advanced testing of the device. If the generic tests fail, then it is most likely that the advanced testing would also fail.

6.1.1   Register test

To verify the data path and the address decoder of the controller, the tester should first execute a data path test to each of the I/O registers. After completing the data path test for the I/O registers, a data path test should be performed on each of the programmable chips.

To test the I/O registers, use the generic register test routines provided in Chap. 3. If each bit of the register is readable and writable, use the full data path test; otherwise, use the partial data path test. These routines require the I/O address and the testable bits as arguments.

If any errors are detected, they should be reported by the test routine. An integer value is returned from the data path test routine. A zero indicates no error, and a non-zero indicates that the test failed.

6.1.2   Interrupt test

After checking the data path to each of the programmable chips and any I/O registers that exist on the controller board, a basic interrupt test must be performed. There are several parts to the interrupt test. The first interrupt test should be the *spurious interrupt* check. A spurious interrupt is an unwanted interrupt from the controller.

Figure 6.2 indicates that an interrupt to the CPU can be caused by several events. As discussed in the previous chapter, when the DMA completes transferring all the required bytes, it has the ability to cause an interrupt. Similarly, when the control completes certain functions (such as seeking, recalibration, and completing initialization events), it also can cause an interrupt. Some devices return signals to the controller board that can also cause interrupts.

To perform the spurious interrupt test, set the system interrupt vector to point to an interrupt service routine that services an interrupt from the controller under test. Enable the interrupt level for the controller and verify that no interrupt occurred. If an interrupt occurred, and there was no cause for the interrupt, then the system received a spurious interrupt.

After testing for spurious interrupts from the controller, test to verify that the controller board can indeed issue an interrupt to the CPU. This test should be performed by the simplest means possible. The *interrupt service routine* (ISR) should be very simple and fast. It should only signal the test routine that an interrupt occurred, service the interrupt, and clear the interrupt condition.

The test routine should verify that the interrupt that occurred was the expected one. The test routine should also have a time-out while waiting for an interrupt. If the test routine does not have a time-out, the system could hang waiting for an interrupt to occur.

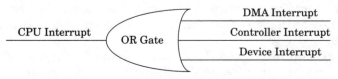

Figure 6.2 Controller interrupts.

6.1.3 DMA test

The DMA test checks that the DMA controller is able to interface with the device controller as well as with the system bus. The test routine must verify that the DMA controller is able to transfer data to or from any legal block of memory within the system.

For example, if the system under test has 128k of RAM on the mother board, 256k on an extended memory board, and another 256k board, and the DMA controller has the ability to transfer data into all those memory blocks, then the test should transfer data between each of those blocks.

The test should also verify that the DMA cannot transfer data to or from illegal memory locations. Assume that your system does not allow DMA to access the video RAM. A test should be designed that transfers data between the DMA controller and the video RAM. Know the expected results of this test.

To test the transfer of data, the DMA controller must be able to read and write data using the device controller. This test should be done and, in most cases, must be accomplished with the read and write test.

6.1.4 Illegal command test

The CPU issues commands to the device controller chip. These commands inform the controller of the operation that the CPU wishes it to perform. It is the responsibility of the diagnostic tests to verify that the controller is able to accept and perform all of the legal functions.

It is also the responsibility of the diagnostic to issue illegal commands to the controller and verify that the controller responds as expected. What could be a legal command in one case may be an illegal command in another. To properly design this test, be sure you have a full understanding of the legal and illegal commands and what happens in response to an illegal command.

6.2 Generic Disk Test

Many common functions exist both in *hard disk drive* and *floppy disk drive* subsystems. There are also features that one type of drive provides and the other does not.

Many storage devices that reside in an operational environment have programs and data on these drives. When using diagnostics test programs, care must be taken so that the data is not corrupted during diagnostic testing.

In many systems, multiple tracks of data are reserved for diagnostic use. These tracks can be formatted by the diagnostic, used to write or read data, and used to force sector data errors. Before writing data to

any hard disk drive, be sure that the drive or track can be used for diagnostics. It is not wise to develop a hard disk drive diagnostic using a
drive that is used with an operating system. When possible, always
use a diagnostic test drive.

6.2.1 Overview of disk structure

This section provides an overview of the structure of a formatted magnetic disk platter. As displayed in Fig. 6.3, the circular platter known
as a disk contains data. The data is recorded as magnetic pattern in
circles around the platter. Each of these circles is a *track* of data. The
inner track, contains as much information as the outer tracks even
though the diameter gets smaller as the tracks get closer to the center
of the circular platter.

Each track of data is divided into equal segments called *sectors*.
Each of the sectors contains information in a *header*. The information
in the header identifies the head, track, sector, and bytes per sector.
Following the header is the data, whose size in bytes is generally a
power of 2, from 128 to 2048 bytes per sector. The data is followed by a
sector CRC.

Different read/write heads are associated with each side of the platter (see Fig. 6.4). These heads are moved in or out until they are positioned above the track that needs to be read. Once the heads are in
position, the selected head waits for the correct sector to pass under it,
at which time the head is enabled to read or write the sector of data.

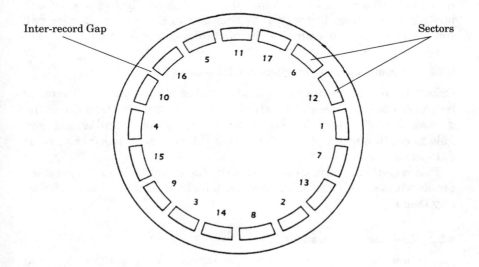

Figure 6.3 Format of a magnetic disk platter.

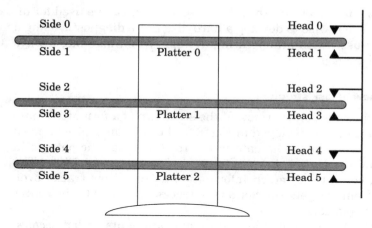

Figure 6.4 Multi-platter disk drive.

Between each sector of the disk is a gap called the *inter-record gap*. This gap is used to provide the heads and logic with time to complete the action of accessing one sector before the following sector is accessed.

In most cases, by the time the disk controller has prepared the read/write head to access the next sector, the edge of the next sector has already passed under the heads. This causes access to the next physical sector to be delayed one full revolution of the disk. To enhance the performance of the access time of the disk data, sectors are not numbered in a sequential order but are *interleaved*. Figure 6.3 displays a track having an interleaf factor of 3:1. This allows the disk controller two full sector times to prepare for the next disk access operation.

6.2.2 Differences between floppy and hard disks

Other than the obvious physical attributes, the main difference between a floppy disk and a hard disk is the density of the data on the disk surface. The hard disk has a much higher density and is therefore able to contain much more information. The hard disk also can access data much faster.

To increase capacity, most hard disks have more than a single platter, and it is not uncommon to find hard disks with more than ten platters (see Fig. 6.4).

6.2.3 Summary of operations

The following is a list of generic operations that both the floppy and hard disk controllers and drives can perform:

- *Seek*. This command causes the selected disk drive to seek to a particular track.
- *Recalibrate*. This command causes the selected disk to recalibrate and set the heads to track zero. This is used so that the drive can regain a reference.
- *Format track*. This command allows the drive to write new data with a specific format onto the currently selected disk drive.
- *Read data*. This command allows the system to read a number of sectors from the currently selected track.
- *Write data*. This command allows the system to write a number of sectors to the currently selected track.

6.2.4   Recalibrate test

As mentioned previously, the heads of a disk move from track zero to the innermost track. On a floppy drive, the innermost track is track 79. On a hard disk drive, there may be over several hundred tracks. Seek commands cause the heads to move relative to their current positions. If for some reason the drive does not know what track the heads are on, then it is lost. A recalibrate function is provided so that the drive is able to position its heads from any position to the home or outermost track.

The recalibrate test verifies the drive's ability to reposition the heads to track zero. To accomplish this, the test issues a recalibrate command, followed by a seek to the maximum cylinder, then another recalibrate command. After this is done, a check should be made to verify that the disk is at track zero. Some drives do provide a status flag to indicate that the heads are at track zero.

6.2.5   Forward/backward seek test

When a seek command is issued to the controller, the controller issues stepping pulses, in or out, relative to where the heads are currently positioned. A single step pulse is issued for each track that the heads must move. The forward seek test verifies the drive's ability to seek forward to all tracks. The test starts with recalibrating the drive. It then issues a seek command to seek to each track in an incremental fashion. At the completion of the seek, the header data of each track is read to verify that seek reached the correct track.

When the innermost track is reached, the test starts seeking backward. It performs this in the same manner except the track number is decremented after each seek.

To summarize this test:

Step 1:	Recalibrate drive.
Step 2:	For track = 0 to maximum perform Step 3.
Step 3:	Seek track and verify.
Step 4:	Recalibrate drive.
Step 5:	For track = maximum to 0, perform Step 6.
Step 6:	Seek track and verify.

Sample C code for this test is provided in Code Block 6.1, at the end of this chapter.

6.2.6 Hourglass seek test

While the forward and backward seek test verifies that the drive is able to step in and out of a single track, the hourglass seek test verifies the drive's ability to seek with different lengths of head travel. This test instructs the controller to move the head to every possible length between the minimum and maximum movements, in both directions.

The test starts by recalibrating the drive. The inner track is set to the maximum, and the outer track set to zero. The test routine then seeks the inner track and then the outer track. The inner track counter is decremented by one, and the outer track counter is incremented. Then the process is repeated until the inner track count reaches zero.

To summarize the test:

Step 1:	Recalibrate.
Step 2:	Inner_track = maximum.
Step 3:	For outer_track = 0 to maximum, perform Steps 4 through 7.
Step 4:	Seek to inner_track.
Step 5:	Seek to outer_track.
Step 6:	Increment inner_track.
Step 7:	Decrement outer_track.

Sample C code for the hourglass test is provided in Code Block 6.2, at the end of this chapter.

6.2.7   Read data test

The read data test is the first test routine that tests the ability of the controller to transfer data between main memory and the drive. It checks that the disk controller is able to read data from the disk. It also verifies that the DMA controller is able to interface properly with the disk controller, can place data into the system memory, and can cause an interrupt at the completion of the read operation. The test assumes that the disk is already formatted and has data that can be transferred to main memory.

To summarize the test:

Step 1:	Recalibrate drive.
Step 2:	Set up DMA size and transfer address.
Step 3:	Fill read buffer with predetermine data pattern.
Step 4:	Issue read command to controller.
Step 5:	Verify that no errors were detected.
Step 6:	Verify that data was transferred.

Sample C code for the read data test is provided in Code Block 6.3, at the end of this chapter.

6.2.8   Write data test

In addition to the read data test, a test is needed to verify that the disk storage device can transfer data from the CPU to the storage media. The write data test verifies this. This test must be used in conjunction with a read test because, once the data is written to the storage device, the only way to verify that the data was properly stored onto the drive is to read the data. It is assumed that the storage device has already been formatted.

To summarize the test:

Step 1:	Recalibrate drive.
Step 2:	Fill buffer with data pattern.
Step 3:	Issue write command to controller.
Step 4:	Verify that no errors exist.
Step 5:	Recalibrate drive.
Step 6:	Issue read command to controller.

Step 7:	Verify that no errors exist.
Step 8:	Compare input buffer with output buffer.
Step 9:	Report any data errors.

Sample C code for the write data test is provided in Code Block 6.4, at the end of this chapter.

6.2.9 Format test

Before the controller can transfer data to or from a disk, the disk must be formatted. The controller issues a format command to the controller, which specifies the track, head, number of sectors, format data pattern, and interleaving, and guarantees that each sector has a header, data block, CRC, and correct inter-record gap.

The test program must be able to format a single track or the entire disk. In addition, care must be taken when the diagnostic is executing on a drive that has real data and programs, because formatting a track destroys all the data that might be on that track.

To summarize this test:

Step 1:	Recalibrate drive.
Step 2:	Set up format information.
Step 3:	Seek to proper track.
Step 4:	Issue format command.
Step 5:	Check for any errors.
Step 6:	Read and verify data for each sector of track.

Sample C code for the format test provided in Code Block 6.5, at the end of this chapter.

6.2.10 Random seek and read test

When loading data or a program from disk, the disk drive is requested to seek to a track, load several sectors from that track, seek to another track, loads sectors from that track, and so on until the entire program or data has been loaded. The random seek and read tests verify the ability of the controller and drive to randomly seek cylinders and read the data from that track.

There are three different ways to perform the random read test:

1. Provide a continuous random read until the operator interrupts the test.
2. Perform a specified number of random reads.
3. Permit the operator to enter the number of random read operations.

Overall, the test should fill the read buffer with all zeroes and, after the read, verify that data was placed into the buffer. We cannot assume that the data pattern is known; therefore, this test does not attempt to verify the data. If the data on the disk is all zeroes, a second attempt to read should be made after the buffer is filled with another pattern.

This test routine is a nondestructive test, so the data on the disk is not modified or altered. The procedure for this test is:

Step 1:	Recalibrate drive.
Step 2:	(Top of loop.)
Step 3:	Select random track and number of sectors.
Step 4:	Select random start sector.
Step 5:	Clear input buffer.
Step 6:	Set up DMA count and address.
Step 7:	Issue seek command.
Step 8:	Check for any errors.
Step 9:	Issue read command.
Step 10:	Check for any errors.
Step 11:	Verify that data pattern is different.
Step 12:	Go to top of loop (Step 2), repeat until done.

Sample C code for this test is provided in Code Block 6.6, at the end of this chapter.

6.2.11   Write-read-verify test

The purpose of this routine is to test the data integrity of the device. This is a destructive test and should be performed only on areas of the drive that do not contain useful data.

As with the random read test, there are three different ways to perform the write-read-verify test:

1. Provide a continuous test until the operator interrupts the test.
2. Perform a specified number of test.
3. Permit the operator to enter the number of random test.

To summarize:

Step 1:	Recalibrate drive.
Step 2:	Initialize controller and setup.
Step 3:	Loop to for count.
Step 4:	Set up write buffer.
Step 5:	Clear read buffer.
Step 6:	Write to selected sector.
Step 7:	Read the selected sector.
Step 8:	Issue verify command to legal sector.
Step 9:	Compare write and read buffer.
Step 10:	Go to step 3, repeat until done.

6.2.12   Forced error tests

All the tests that we have seen so far exercise the drive by performing legal activities. Now we will examine the need to force certain errors to ensure that the drive behaves properly under illegal conditions. For example, one forced error test would check the ability of the drive and controller to detect that the drive attempted to seek to an illegal track or to read from an illegal head or sector.

Another forced error verifies that a bad sector CRC is detected. Some controllers have the ability to write bad CRCs to a disk sector. If this option is available, then you should write a sector with a bad CRC, and then read that sector. During the read operation, the controller should indicate a CRC error.

Each controller has different kinds of error detection. If there are other errors that can be forced, these should be tested as well.

The following pseudo-code summarizes a few forced error tests:

Step 1:	Recalibrate drive.
Step 2:	Initialize controller.
Step 3:	Seek to illegal track.
Step 4:	If no error detected.

Report error and exit.

Step 5:   Recalibrate drive.

Step 6:   Initialize controller.

Step 7:   Attempt to read from illegal head.

Step 8:   If no error detected.

Report error and exit.

Step 9:   Recalibrate drive.

Step 10:   Initialize controller.

Step 11:   Attempt to read an illegal sector.

Step 12:   If no error detected.

Report error and exit.

Step 13:   Recalibrate drive.

Step 14:   Initialize controller.

Step 15:   Write legal sector with bad CRC.

Step 16:   Read sector with bad CRC.

Step 17:   If no error detected.

Report error and exit.

6.2.13   Motor test

A disk motor is used to rotate the platter at 360 rpm or 166 milliseconds for each revolution of the disk. The rotation speed of a disk becomes very important when comparing the performance of one drive with another.

To verify that the motor speed is as expected, set a test to read the first sector of a track 60 times. This should take 10 seconds since:

$$360 \text{ rpm} = 166 \text{ ms/rotation}$$

$$60 \times 166 \text{ ms} = 10 \text{ s}$$

Start the test by seeking to the selected track and issuing the first read command. At the completion of that read, start two clocks—one to keep track of total time and the second to provide the time between the completion of each read operation. Do not keep track of the first read operation, because the first operation provides an inaccurate time. When the read command is issued, the sector could just be starting to move under the heads, or it could be just completed.

When all 60 read operations are completed, display the minimum and the maximum time along with the average time. The total time should indicate 10 seconds. It might be necessary to compare the interval time of each operation and report if out of tolerance. The tolerance should be defined in the disk specification.

To summarize the motor test:

Step 1:	Recalibrate drive.
Step 2:	Initialize setup.
Step 3:	Clear clock count array.
Step 4:	Issue first read operation.
Step 5:	Set for 60 operation.
Step 6:	Wait for completion.
Step 7:	Start both clock counters.
Step 8:	Issue next read operation.
Step 9:	When completed, save clock count.
Step 10:	Display minimum and maximum values.
Step 11:	Check for tolerances.
Step 12:	If out of tolerance, report error.

6.2.14 Seek performance

Seek performance is used as a method of determining overall performance for disk subsystems. A test should be designed to seek to individual tracks and keep time for seeks on a one-track increment, a ten-track increment, and the maximum track increments.

This performance test should perform each seek at least 10 times, and the high time, low time, and average time should be reported.

6.3 Floppy-Only Tests

The floppy disk drive is different from the hard disk drive. Some operations required by the floppy drive would not conform to the hard disk environment. Two of these operations are:

1. door open
2. write protect

Additional tests are then needed to fully exercise the floppy drive.

6.3.1 Door-open test

When the disk drive door is opened, it is generally for the purpose of removing the current diskette and replacing it with another. When the door is open, the system is unable to access the floppy diskette, and the door open status is returned to the controller.

The door open test requires the door to be opened while verifying that the controller does detect the door open status. While the door is open and the disk is in place attempt to access the diskette. The controller should return an error during this attempt.

Next, the tester must close the drive door, with the diskette still in place. Verify that the drive indicates that the drive door was opened and then access the diskette without errors. The CPU must reset the door open status appropriately. You should notice that the door open status remains until it is reset by the CPU action. This is because if a diskette is removed, the door opened, and a new diskette is inserted into the drive and the door shut, then the CPU must know that the door was open and that possibly a new diskette was inserted.

To summarize this test:

Step 1:	Recalibrate drive.
Step 2:	Initialize controller.
Step 3:	Open drive door.
Step 4:	If no drive door open, status detected.
Step 5:	Report error and exit.
Step 6:	Close drive door.
Step 7:	Door open status remains, otherwise.
Step 8:	Report error and exit.
Step 9:	Execute required function to reset door open status.
Step 10:	If drive door open status still set,
Step 11:	Report error and exit.

6.3.2 Write-protect test

Most floppy diskettes have a write protect tab or a notch that the disk can sense. If the notch is open, the drive allows data to be written to the diskette. If the notch is closed, the drive should prevent data from being written to the disk and issue an error back to the controller if a write is attempted.

The test of these features requires the tester to take an active role; that is, to insert a write-protected disk into the drive and then remove the disk. After beginning the test, the program asks the tester to insert a write-protected diskette (notch is covered or tab is slid to write-protect position) into the system. After the disk is in place, the test program attempts to write data to the disk. An error should occur indicating the operation could not be accomplished because the disk is write protected.

To summarize this test:

Step 1:	Recalibrate drive.
Step 2:	Initialize setup.
Step 3:	Wait for write-protected disk to be inserted.
Step 4:	Issue write to drive.
Step 5:	Verify that write-protect error occurred.
Step 6:	Report error if incorrect result.
Step 7:	Request tester to replace diskette.

6.4   Hard-Disk-Only Tests

The following tests are specific to the hard drive controller and drive mechanism. Because the data on the hard drive is much denser than on a floppy disk, there is a greater risk of data corruption. Moreover, possible bad blocks must be identified and logged on the bad block track.

6.4.1   Find bad spots (read only)

This test is used on a live disk system where the data on the disk cannot be overwritten. If the disk does not have data that has to be preserved, then one should use the "find bad spot" test in conjunction with the write/read/verify test.

The find bad spot test reads each track, starting at track zero. It reads each sector on the disk, one sector at a time, ten times. The purpose is to find which sectors of the disk report consistent errors.

6.4.2   Find bad spots (write/read/verify)

This test writes and then reads each sector of the disk starting at track zero. It writes and then reads to that sector ten times. Any anomalies are reported.

6.4.3   ECC correction

Many controllers have the capability of correcting certain types of data errors using CRCs or other types of *error correcting code* (ECC). The data read from the disk passes through the controller, and the controller performs a CRC or other type of check (such as Hamming or Golay codes) on the data. Depending upon the severity of the error, the controller may be able to correct it.

To perform the test, a disk sector should be written that results in a correctable ECC error. The controller should attempt to read that sector with ECC enabled. The test should ensure that the error was corrected and that the controller reported correctly. Also, issue the same read without ECC enabled and verify that the error was detected. Finally, force a sector to have a non-correctable CRC error and verify that the controller reports it as such. A sample disk diagnostic driver is provided below.

Exhibit 6.1 Disk Diagnostic Driver

The diagnostic driver has several functions that are generic to all disk drivers. Each function is expected to text for errors, and if errors are detected, set the flag "error." The number placed into this error flag identifies the type of error.

An interrupt service routine must also be provided that acknowledges the disk interrupt, saves the status, resets the interrupt, and returns. Each function that must wait for the interrupt must also have a time-out in case the interrupt does not occur.

Init_Cont   Initializes controller, interrupt vector, reset buffers, and flags.

seek_track   Seek to the specified track that is passed to the functions.

read_track   Read the track over which the heads are currently positioned.

recalibrate   Recalibrate the drive, verify that the heads are positioned over track zero.

format   Format the specified track using the table of information supplied by the calling routine.

read_sector   Read from the drive the specified number of sectors starting at the specified track, head, and sector. Place the data into the specified buffer.

write_sector   Write to the drive the specified number of sectors starting at the specified track, head, and sector. Take the data from the specified buffer.

6.5 Tape Diagnostics

Before a discussion of diagnostics for a tape drive, we need a brief review of the tape drive, the format of the tape, and the type of instructions it requires.

The tape drive is a sequential device, and Fig. 6.5 shows the layout of a small portion of tape. At the start of the tape is the *beginning of tape* (BOT) mark. After the BOT mark, there is a file that contains three records, followed by a *file mark*. After the file mark, there is a second file with four records, followed by another file mark. Any number of records may be in a file, and there can be many files on a single tape. Although in some systems standardized length records are required, in others variable length records are allowed. Between each record, there is a uniform inter-record gap. This gap is used by the controller to detect the end of each record.

Tape drives normally have either seven, eight, or nine tracks and a data density of 800 or 1600 *bits per inch* (BPI)—or more, depending on the tape technology. This is not to say that all units have this speed or number of tracks.

6.5.1 Summary of tape operations

The following is a list of generic operations that the tape controller and drive can perform.

- *Select.* The controller may control multiple tape drives. The controller must be able to select the unit to access.
- *Rewind.* The tape drive rewinds the tape until it reaches the beginning of tape (BOT).
- *Write record.* The tape controller writes the next sequential record on the tape.
- *Read record.* The tape controller reads the next sequential record on the tape.
- *Write file mark.* The controller writes a special record on the tape that specifies the end of the current file.
- *Skip records.* The tape controller can detect inter-record gaps and therefore can skip a single or multiple record.
- *Skip file mark.* The tape controller skips over a single or multiple file mark.

BOT	R1	R2	R3	FM	R1	R2	R3	R4	FM

Figure 6.5 Sequential tape format.

6.5.2 Select unit test

The purpose of this test is to verify that the controller can select the proper tape drive. This is accomplished by issuing the select command to the drive and checking for the correct reply from the drive. The test does not verify that we are communicating with the proper unit in a multiple drive controller; it simply verifies that a unit responded properly. A later test verifies that the proper unit replied.

6.5.3 Drive reset test

This test verifies the drives ability to be reset, to issue the drive reset command, and to check for the correct status. The drive reset may cause the tape drive to rewind to BOT. It might also send the tape drive through an internal self-test. Be sure of the expected results before issuing the drive reset command.

To summarize this test:

Step 1:	Reset drive and controller.
Step 2:	Wait for reset to complete.
Step 3:	Read the results and compare with expected results.
Step 4:	If results differ, report as error.

6.5.4 Rewind test

Because the tape drive is a serial device, there must a means of returning to the beginning of the tape. The rewind command, when issued, starts the rewind process. The rewind continues until the BOT is detected. When the BOT is detected, the rewind is complete and the drive stops rewinding.

The rewind test checks the rewind ability of the drive and is a multiple-part test. The test should be started by setting the controller and drive to a reset condition.

The test process is:

Step 1:	Reset controller and drive.
Step 2:	Disable Interrupt.
Step 3:	Issue rewind command to the controller, poll for complete.
Step 4:	Operation complete and the verify status.
Step 5:	Enable interrupts.
Step 6:	Issue rewind command, check that interrupt occurred, and check for proper status.

Notice that the tape has not been moved from the BOT marker. The purpose of this test is to verify that the controller is able to detect the BOT from the drive and issue an interrupt. Later, a second rewind test can be performed after we can move the tape from the BOT.

6.5.5   Write and read file mark

The write and read file mark is the first test that accesses data on the tape drive. The purpose of this test is to verify the controller's ability to issue the commands, and the drive's ability to react properly to the commands.

To summarize the test:

Step 1:   Reset controller and drive.

Step 2:   Interrupt disabled.

Step 3:   Write one file mark from the BOT position.

Step 4:   Check for valid status return.

Step 5:   Interrupt enabled.

Step 6:   Rewind the tape and check for BOT and correct interrupt.

Step 7:   Write five file marks on the tape and check for expected interrupt and the response.

Step 8:   Issue instruction to controller to skip over one file mark.

Step 9:   Verify interrupt occurred and proper status.

Step 10:   Issue to controller to skip over 3 file marks verify.

Step 11:   Interrupt occurred and proper status.

Step 12:   Rewind and reset drive and controller.

Sample C code for this test is provided in Code Block 6.7, at the end of this chapter.

6.5.6   Write/read/verify single record

This test verifies the ability of the controller and drive to write data to the tape and then read the data. This test is performed with interrupts enabled, and after every operation the program checks for the proper interrupt and the status from the controller.

To summarize this test:

Step 1:	Reset controller and drive.
Step 2:	Enable interrupts.
Step 3:	Write a single data record.
Step 4:	Write a file mark.
Step 5:	Rewind and read the single record.
Step 6:	Check for data errors.
Step 7:	Compare the write buffer with the read buffer.

Sample C code for this test provided in Code Block 6.8, at the end of this chapter.

6.5.7 Write/read/verify multiple records

This test verifies the ability of the controller and drive to write multiple record to the tape and then read multiple reads from the tape. This test also verifies that the drive lays the records sequentially on the tape with no overlap of the records.

The test summary is:

Step 1:	Reset controller and drive.
Step 2:	Enable interrupts.
Step 3:	Write 10 records followed by a file mark.
Step 4:	Rewind the tape drive.
Step 5:	Read 11 records.
Step 6:	Check that controller read only 10 records and that a file mark was detected.
Step 7:	Check for data errors.
Step 8:	Compare the buffers.

6.5.8 Write/read/verify full length

This test routine writes records until the end of tape is detected or the maximum number of records is written. The program then randomly selects a record to read, reads that record, and verifies the data. This routine can be set up to execute indefinitely or for a certain number of passes.

Each write buffer for each record starts with a seed equaling the record number, and the remaining data is built from the seed. This allows the program to rebuild each buffer to compare data.

To summarize the test:

Step 1:	Reset controller and drive.
Step 2:	Enable interrupts.
Step 3:	Rewind tape.
Step 4:	Write full length of tape or maximum records.
Step 5:	Loop until done.
Step 6:	Select random record.
Step 7:	If current record < next record.
Step 8:	Skip to next record and read.
Step 9:	Rewind the skip to record and read.
Step 10:	Verify controller status.
Step 11:	Compare buffers.
Step 12:	Reset controller.

6.5.9   Write protection

This test verifies the controller's ability to handle write-protected errors and the ability of the drive to recognize file-protect status.

In summary:

Step 1:	Reset controller and drive.
Step 2:	Rewind the drive.
Step 3:	Write a record onto the tape.
Step 4:	Rewind the drive.
Step 5:	Prompt user to set write protect.
Step 6:	Attempt to write to tape.
Step 7:	Check controller for proper error code.
Step 8:	Rewind to BOT.
Step 9:	Read record and verify original data.

Step 10:	Prompt user to disable write protect.
Step 11:	Reset controller.

6.5.10 Erase entire tape

This test checks the ability of the controller and drive to erase the entire tape.
In summary:

Step 1:	Reset the controller and drive.
Step 2:	Enable interrupts.
Step 3:	Rewind drive.
Step 4:	Issue erase command.
Step 5:	Check controller status.
Step 6:	Rewind and check for BOT.
Step 7:	Attempt to read one record.
Step 8:	Check for expected "blank tape" error code.

6.5.11 Skip forward files

This test checks the ability of the controller to stop correctly after skipping to a file mark and then to read the data.
The steps are:

Step 1:	Reset the controller and drive.
Step 2:	Enable interrupts.
Step 3:	Rewind the drive.
Step 4:	Write 10 records, followed by a file mark.
Step 5:	Write 20 records, followed by a file mark.
Step 6:	Write 30 records, followed by a file mark.
Step 7:	Write 40 records, followed by a file mark.
Step 8:	Write 50 records, followed by a file mark.
Step 9:	Write 60 records, followed by a file mark.

Step 10:	Write 70 records, followed by a file mark.
Step 11:	Rewind drive, skip to first file mark, read and compare data for second record.
Step 12:	Skip two file marks, read data, and verify proper file.
Step 13:	Skip three file marks, read data, and verify proper file.
Step 14:	Rewind drive and skip four file marks, read data, and verify proper file.
Step 15:	Rewind drive, reset drive and controller.

6.5.12   Space forward/reverse file marks

This routine tests the ability of the drive to space by file mark and stop and start again correctly. It also tests the ability of the controller to execute the "skip file mark" command.

The steps are:

Step 1:	Reset the controller and drive.
Step 2:	Enable interrupts.
Step 3:	Rewind the drive.
Step 4:	Write 20 file marks.
Step 5:	Repeat 20 times or until an error occurs.
Step 6:	Space forward one file mark.
Step 7:	Report error if < 20 file marks were read.
Step 8:	Repeat 20 times or until BOT or error occurs.
Step 9:	Space backward one file mark.
Step 10:	Report error if < 20 file marks were read.
Step 11:	Report error if at BOT (early BOT).
Step 12:	Space backward one more file mark.
Step 13:	Report error if BOT not found.

6.5.13   Space forward /reverse records

This routine tests the ability of the drive to space by records and to stop and start again correctly. It also tests the ability of the controller to execute the "skip record" command.

The steps are:

Step 1:	Reset the controller and drive.
Step 2:	Enable interrupts.
Step 3:	Rewind the drive.
Step 4:	Write 20 records.
Step 5:	Repeat 20 times or until an error occurs.
Step 6:	Space forward one record.
Step 7:	Report error if < 20 records were read.
Step 8:	Repeat 20 times or until BOT or error occurs.
Step 9:	Space backward one record.
Step 10:	Report error if < 20 records were read.
Step 11:	Report error if at BOT (early BOT).
Step 12:	Space backward one more record.
Step 13:	Report error if BOT not found.

6.6 Summary

This chapter introduced two mass storage devices: the serial magnetic tape unit and direct-access disk devices. The structure of the disk platter was also introduced. We saw that a disk platter is broken into tracks, that each track has sectors, and that the sectors contain the data.

There are many similarities between the floppy disk drive and the hard disk drive. Although the drivers are different, the basic functions are similar, and this allowed us to define tests that can be used for both devices. Conversely, the magnetic tape is different from the disk unit in its structure and method of data access, so it requires a separate set of tests.

A sample diagnostic drive specification was provided for each type of device. Please note that these specifications only define generic functions for the devices. The test specifications for your particular device most likely will have significant differences.

6.7 Bibliography

1. Norton, P., and R. Jourdain. 1988. *The Hard Disk Companion.* New York: Brady Books.
2. Liu, Y-C., and G. Gibson. 1986. *Micro Computer Systems.* Englewood Cliffs, NJ: Prentice-Hall.

```
/*
    FB_seek_test()
    Description
    This test verifies that the disk drive is able to step one
    track at a time from the outer tracks to the inner tracks.
    The second part of the test verifies that the drive is able
    to step one track at a time from the inner to outer tracks.
*/
FB_seek_test()
   {
   int i;
   init_cont();                          // initialize controller
   if (!error) {                         // if no error continue test
     recalibrate();                      // recal drive
     if (error) break;                   // exit if error
     for(i=0;i<MAX_TRACK+1;i++) {        // seek from outer to inner
       seek_track(i);                    // seek to track
       if (read_track() != i)            // verify correct track
           error_report();               // report error if not
       } // end of for loop
     recalibrate();
     for(i=MAX_TRACK;i>=0;i--) {         // seek from inner to outer
       seek_track(i);                    // seek to track
       if (read_track() != i)            // verify correct track
           error_report();               // report error if not
       } // end of for
     } // end of if
   } // end of test
```

Code Block 6.1 Forward/backward seek test.

```
/*
   Hourglass_test()
   Description:
   This test causes the drive to seek the maximum number of
   tracks, to the minimum of tracks. The test routine starts
   with two track value, inner and outer tracks.
*/
Hourglass_test()
  {
  int   inner,outer;
  init_cont();                      // initialize controller
  recalibrate();                    // recal drive
  if (!error) {                     // if no error continue
  inner =MAX_TRACK;                 // set inner track number
  for (outer=0;outer < MAX_TRACK+1;outer++) {
    seek_track(inner);              // seek inner track
    if (read_track() != inner)      // verify position
        error_report();             // report error
    seek_track(outer);              // seek outer track
    if (read_track() !~= outer)     // verify position
        error_report();             // report the error
    inner--;  }                     // decrement track
    } // end of if
  return(error);
  } // end of function
```

Code Block 6.2 Hourglass seek test.

```
/*
   read_test()
   Description
   This test routine verifies that a disk section can be read,
   and its contents placed into memory via DMA.
*/
read_test()
  {
  init_cont();            // initialize controller
  if (!error) {
    recalibrate();        // recal drive
    if (error) break;     // break if error
    fill_buffer(record)   // fill the buffer
    read_sector();        // read the specified sector
    if (error) break;
    compare_buffer(buff1,buff2);
    } // end of if
  return(error);
  } // end of function
```

Code Block 6.3 Read sector test.

```
/*
   write_sector()
   Description
   This test accomplishes a single write command to the drive.
   After the write is complete, the read of the same sectors is
   accomplished. If no error is detected, then the two data
   buffers are compared.
*/
write_sector()
   {
   init_cont();              // initialize controller
   if (!error) {
   recalibrate();           // recal drive
   if (!error)
      fill_buffer(buff1);    // load data pattern
   if (!error)
      write_sector(buff1);   // write sector
   if (!error)
       recalibrate();        // recal drive
   if (!error)
       read_sector(buff2);   // read sector
   if (!error)
       comp_buffer(buff1,buff2);
     } // end of if
   return(error);
   } // end of test
```

Code Block 6.4 Write disk sector.

```
/*
   format_test()
   Description:
   This routine verifies that the disk controller is able to
   issue a format command to the disk drive, and the disk drive
   is able to actually format the track.
*/
format_test()
  {
  int i;
  init_cont();              // initialize controller
  if (!error) {
    recalibrate();          // recal drive
    for(i=FIRST,i<=LAST;i++) {
      set_format_table(i);  // set up format tables
      format_track(i);      // format the track
      if (error) break;     // break if error
    } // end of for statement
  } // end of if
  return(error);
  } // end of function
```

Code Block 6.5 Format disk cylinder.

```
/*
   random_seek()
   Description:
   This test routine select rand sector, heads, and track. Then
   the drive must seek and read the selected sectors.
   The test does not verify the data other than checking that
   the buffer have some other values other than all nulls.
*/
random_seek()
   {
   int i;
   init_cont();               // initialize controller
   if (!error) {
     recalibrate();           // recal drive
     track = rnd(MAX_TRACK);  // get random track #
     sector = rnd(MAX_SECTOR); // get random sector number
     head = rnd(MAX_HEAD);    // get random head number
     clear_buffer(buff1);     // clear input buffer
     if (!error_code)
     read_sector(buff1);      // read the buffer
     if (!error_code)
     NON_zero(buff1);          // verify buffer non-zero
     } //end of if
   return(error);
   } // end of test
```

Code Block 6.6 Random seek test.

```
/*
    filemark_test()
    Description:
    This test verifies that the controller is able to write
    a file marks, and skip over file marks. The test starts
    by writing a single file mark and verifying proper status.
    This is followed by writing 5 file marks and verifying
    proper status return. The tape is rewound and the controller
    is issued command to skip a single and multiple file marks.
*/
filemark_test(unit)
    {
    int i;
    init_tape();              // initialize tape subsystem
    disable();                // disable interrupts
    rewind(unit);             // rewind tape unit;
    if (!BOT) return 1;       // return if not at BOT
    w_filemark(unit);         // write filemark to unit
    if (!FM) return 1;        // return if no file mark written
    rewind(unit);             // rewind unit
    if (!BOT) return 1;       // return if not at BOT
    for(i=0;i<5;i++) {
        w_filemark(unit);     // write another filemark
        if (!FM) return 1;    // return if no filemark
        }
    rewind(unit);             // rewind unit
    if (!BOT) return 1;       // return if not at BOT
    skip_filemark(unit,1);    // skip 1 filemark
    if (!SKIP) return 1;      // return if SKIP not performed
    skip_filemark(unit,3);    // skip 3 filemarks
    if (!SKIP) return 1;      // return if Skip not performed
    expect_error = 1;         // expect error code
    skip_filemark(unit,3);    // try again should get error
    if (SKIP) return 1;       // return with error
    rewind(unit);
    if (!BOT) return 1;       // return if not at BOT
    init_tape();              // initialize tape subsystem
    return 0;                 // return test passed
    }
```

Code Block 6.7 Filemark test.

```
/*
   w_test1()
   Description:
   This test routine is used to write a single record to
   the tape device, rewind the device, and the read the
   record. After reading the record, the data is compared.
*/
w_test1(int unit)
   {
   int i,ok,byte_cnt;
   init_tape();                            // initialize tape subsystem
   enable();                               // enable interrupts
   rewind(unit);                           // rewind unit
   if (!BOT) return 1;                     // return if not at BOT
   for (i=0;i<10;i++) {                    // now write 10 records
     fill_buffer(i);                       // fill buffer with record data
     w_data(unit,w_buffer,SIZE);           // write record
     if  (!WR) return 1;                   // return if we got an error
     }
   w_filemark(unit);                       // write file mark
   if (!FM) return;                        // return if failed
   rewind(unit);                           // rewind unit
   for (i=0;i<10;i++)  {                   // now read the records
     clear_buffer(r_buffer);               // clear the read buffer
     fill_buffer(i);                       // set up expected buffer
     byte_cnt = r_data(unit,r_buffer);     // read next record
     if (!RR) return 1;                    // return if failed read
     ok = comp_buffer();                   // compare the buffers
     if (ok)  return 1;                    // return if failed
     }
   rewind(unit);                           // rewind to BOT
   init_tape();                            // initialize tape subsystem
   return 0;
   } // end of test
```

Code Block 6.8 Write test.

Video Graphic Devices

7.0 Introduction

The video terminal has become a vital component of the computer system. Because of graphic controllers, previously unimagined tasks are now being done by the computer. Computer graphics has brought us computer video games, computer aided design, and an added new dimension to computer presentations. We now can find the graphics terminals in thousands of offices and homes. Computer graphics can present data in the form of graphs, charts and text. With scanners, the computer is now able to read a picture into its memory bank and display that picture on its graphical display.

This chapter provides an overview of the functionality of the graphical terminal and provides diagnostic tests that are used to verify that the graphics controller and terminal are properly functioning.

Most graphic controllers provide very little feedback. Therefore, many of the tests described in this chapter require that the tester evaluate the output.

7.1 Theory of Operation

To develop good video diagnostics, you must first have a firm understanding of the design and operation of the video circuit to be tested.

7.1.1 The CRT

In the *cathode ray tube* (CRT), an *electron beam* is swept across the face of the screen, from left to right, as shown in Fig. 7.1. As the beam

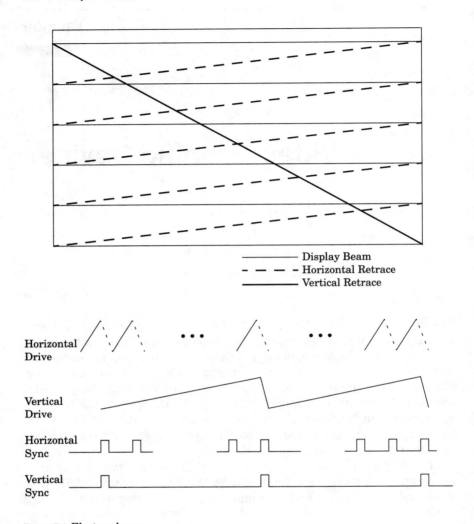

Figure 7.1 Electron beam.

is swept across the screen, the beam intensity changes, as determined by the CRT controller, to display a pattern.

The beam begins in the upper left corner. As the beam reaches the right of the screen the beam must return to the left side of the screen, but to a position slightly below where it started. While the beam is returning to the left side, the beam is turned off so that there is no display. The turning off of the beam is called *horizontal blanking* and as the beam moves from right to left is called the *horizontal retrace*.

After the horizontal retrace, the electron beam starts to move across the screen again. This process continues until the last horizontal beam is displayed and the beam is at the bottom right corner of the screen.

At this time, the beam must return to the top left corner of the screen. This is called the *vertical retrace*. During the vertical retrace, the beam is again shut off.

The display controller must be capable of controlling the motion of the beam so that it moves across the display in synchronization with the data in the beam. To accomplish this, the CRT controller issues horizontal and vertical sync pulses. By pulsing these sync signals, the display performs horizontal and vertical *blanking*.

The horizontal beams moving from left to right are called *scan lines*. As these scan lines are presented to the screen, the data causes the electron guns to adjust the intensity of the electron beam. The intensity cause bright and dark spots to appear on the screen.

An electron gun inside the CRT projects the electron beam to a spot on the screen. The purpose of the gun is to produce a beam that has the following properties:

1. It must be highly focused to produce sharp image.
2. It must have high velocity because brightness depends on the velocity.
3. It must provide proper beam intensity control.

In a black-and-white CRT, there is a single gun that controls the electron beam. In a typical color system, there are three guns that control the three primary colors: red, green, and blue.

The inside of the CRT is coated with phosphor, which glows when an electron beam strikes it. The phosphor used with CRTs is selected for color and persistence qualities.

The beams are aimed at *electroluminescent phosphor* dots. In a color CRT, the dots are grouped into a triad of three dots. Each dot displays one of the three colors mentioned above.

7.1.2 Resolution

The computer divides the scan lines into a series of data bits. High-resolution graphics may have 640 bits per scan line, while the low-resolution graphics may have only 320 bits. Each data bit on the screen is referred to as a picture element or *pixel*.

The number of pixels per line determines the resolution of the display. The higher the resolution, the sharper the picture.

7.1.3 CRT controller

The CRT controller has several basic functions:

1. It communicates graphics data from the host system to the CRT.
2. It keeps track of the color that is being displayed.
3. It stores each pixel in video memory.
4. It sends the signal that represents the stored picture.

The CRT controller reads the data from main memory and places the data in pixel format into the video display buffer. In some cases, the computer may write this video data directly into main memory. Two operations are always occurring in the video memory:

1. The CRT controller is making changes that will project new video images to the screen.
2. The screen signal is being generated from the video memory.

7.1.4 Color representation

In a black-and-white display, each pixel can have one of two states: black or white. It requires only one data bit to represent these two states. In a standard color system, each pixel is represented by four bits, so each pixel can have one of 16 colors. (High-end color graphics terminals provide even greater bit depth to display a much wider range of colors.)

Two methods are used to store color information,

1. the packed pixel
2. the color plane

When using the packed pixel, all the color information is packed into one byte. Using the plane approach, however, the display memory is separated into independent planes of memory. Each plane is dedicated to controlling one color component. Each pixel of the display occupies one bit position in each plane. Refer to Fig. 7.2 for a graphical representation of the packed pixel versus the color plane.

7.2 The Video Controller

Figure 7.3 provides a high-level block diagram of a graphics controller. The block indicating that the controller is the data path between the processor and the display.

The RAM is a large bank of dynamic memory that can be divided into four color planes. This RAM holds the screen display. The serializer takes the display information from the display memory and converts it into a serial data stream. The attribute controller controls the colors that are being displayed.

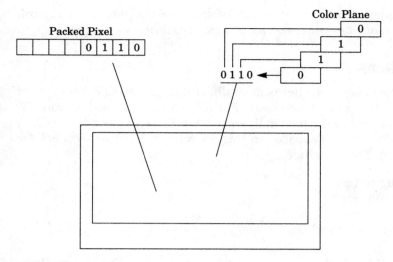

Figure 7.2 Packed pixel vs. plane pixel.

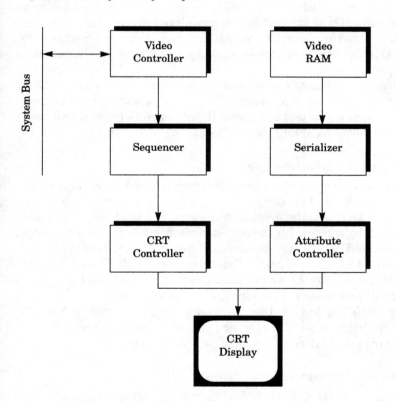

Figure 7.3 Scan pattern block diagram.

The sequence controls the overall timing of all functions on the board. The CRT controller generates the timing signals for sync signals.

7.3   Video Tests

Testing the video controller is more difficult than testing other types of controllers that provide feedback. For the most part, the video controller outputs data to the terminal, and very little is fed back to the CPU.

Some of the tests described in this section require user feedback for verification. These include:

1.   the cursor test
2.   the scroll test
3.   the attribute test
4.   graphics color test

7.3.1   Board self-test

Many video boards now have the ability to enter a self-test mode when power is applied. Once the self-test is completed successfully, the system is able to use the controller board. In many cases, the host is able to issue a self-test command to the controller and wait for the controller to complete its test.

The controller self-test is able to exercise and test many points that the host system is unable to detect. The first test that should be performed is to issue a self-test command to the controller board and wait for the controller to complete the self-test.

7.3.2   Text mode vs. graphics mode

There are two basic operating modes for graphic controllers: text mode and graphics mode. In text mode, a byte in video memory represents a text character that is to be displayed. In graphics mode a single pixel is represented by a single bit in the video memory. Text mode requires less memory and places less burden on the processor. However, text mode is limited in that only text characters can be displayed. In any one system there may be several text modes and several graphics mode. Each different mode provides different features.

The diagnostic must verify that controller is able to enter each mode and cause the right type of character generation on the screen. There is no standard test that checks all the different mode.

7.3.3   Text character display

Most graphics adapters have a *font* character ROM. The character ROM contains the pixel representation of the characters that are displayed on the screen. Each character may be 8 pixels wide and 16 pixels high, as shown in the sample characters of Fig. 7.4. Each zero in the font character represents a dark pixel, and each 1 represents a light pixel.

Two bytes of video memory are generally used to define the character set. The first byte is the character itself, and the second byte is the attribute for that character.

A test must be written to display all characters. The developer or tester must check each character and determine whether that character font is correct.

7.3.4 Text and font test

Three test screens are used in testing of the text characters. The first test screen displays all the characters on the screen. Use the full screen to display these characters. Separate each character so that you are able to evaluate each one individually. Determine whether each character appears properly.

The second test screen display lines of text. Each line uses a different character color. The character color should be defined in the message. While this screen is displayed, the tester should be able to press a key to change the background color.

The third screen contains a full screen of text. The purpose of this test screen is to check for readability and clarity over the entire dis-

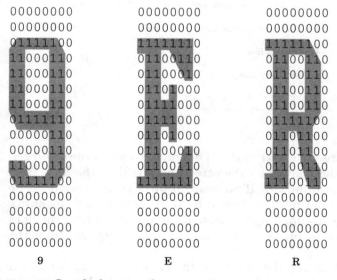

Figure 7.4 Sample characters from screen font.

play. The tester should have two keys to allow the changing of the character and background colors.

7.3.5 Cursor test

Logic internal to the CRT controller handles the placement, size, and shape of the cursor. The cursor test verifies the functionality of the cursor control logic. The test places a full block cursor at several specific locations on the screen and then queries the tester as to whether the cursor is at the correct position.

After the cursor placement test, the cursor is placed at the center of the screen, and it shape and size is changed. Once again, the tester is queried if the size and shape is correct. Test code is in Code Block 7.1, at the end of this chapter.

To summarize:

Step 1:	Initialize CRT controller.
Step 2:	Setup to display five or ten cursor locations.
Step 3:	Display next cursor location.
Step 4:	Query tester if ok.
Step 5:	If failed, log answer.
Step 6:	Set cursor to middle of screen.
Step 7:	Set up to display different cursor size and shapes.
Step 8:	Display next cursor size and shape.
Step 9:	Query test if ok.
Step 10:	If failed, log answer.
Step 11:	If test failed, display results.

7.3.6 Scroll test

An area of the screen, in text mode, is define in terms of rows and columns. To scroll the display on the screen up one line, the data from row x must move to row x–1. If all rows on the screen are scrolled up one line, then the top row is removed from the screen, and the entire screen display moves up. Conversely, to scroll down one line, the data on row x is move to row x+1. The bottom line is remove from the screen.

The scroll test checks the ability of the controller to perform text scrolling functions. Lines of text are scrolled from the bottom of the screen to the top, and the test is queried if the function is executing properly. If the system provides an ability to read the data at the present cursor position, then write a routine that read the screen after the screen and verify that the text on the screen is correct. Test source code is in Code Block 7.2, at the end of this chapter.

To summarize:

Step 1:	Initialize test set.
Step 2:	Fill the screen with text.
Step 3:	Start the screen scroll for maximum lines.
Step 4:	Scroll up one line.
Step 5:	Delay one second for tester to visually see scroll.
Step 6:	After all scrolls, query tester.
Step 7:	Fill screen with text.
Step 8:	Start the screen scroll for maximum line.
Step 9:	Scroll down one line.
Step 10:	Delay one second.
Step 11:	After all scrolls, query tester.

7.3.7 Attribute test

The CRT controller has the ability to add special functions to a character, these are:

1. blinking and non-blinking
2. high and low intensity
3. underline and non-underline

The test program determines if the attribute controller is functioning correctly. This is accomplished by displaying a text string with each attribute function. The string should indicate the attribute under test. For example,

```
This string is high intensity.
```

The tester is queried for each attribute display. If correct, the program passes on to the next attribute. Another possible scenario is to display these messages all together on a single screen, then query the tester.

To summarize:

Step 1:	Initialize test setup.
Step 2:	Pointer to attribute table.
Step 3:	Display string with attribute character.
Step 4:	Next attribute string.
Step 5:	Wait for the tester reply.
Step 6:	Log any error reported.

7.3.8 Color paint test

Each system provides a different set of colors. To verify that the color is properly displayed, the entire screen should be painted one color. The program should perform two operations:

1. Request that the tester acknowledge the color is correct.
2. Paint the screen and leave it for a few seconds before passing on to the next color.

Some systems allow for the adjustment of the color guns via program control. If your system allows for the adjustment, paint the screen with the selected color and adjust the intensity from the lowest to the highest.

To summarize:

Step 1:	Perform for all colors.
Step 2:	Perform for each scan line.
Step 3:	Write each pixel selected color.
Step 4:	Adjust intensity at slow rate.

7.3.9 Graphics test

This test verifies the graphic system's ability to output text and color graphics in several different graphics modes. This is one of the more important tests for the graphic system because of the range of modes that must be exercised.

The test starts by placing the system into monochrome text mode. A pattern is placed on the screen of horizontal lines, vertical lines, dots, solid white blocks, and text. The tester is queried as to whether the display looks correct. The above test should be performed for all monochrome modes.

Next, the low-resolution graphic mode is entered. A pattern of small boxes is displayed in different colors. In each graphic mode, each color palette is displayed. Once again, the tester is queried at each screen.

7.3.10   Animation test

Graphic displays are generally used for drawing pictures or animation. Although your program does not need to draw a picture to verify that the graphics system is working properly, remember the old saying, "a picture is worth a thousand words."

If you are able to display an animated picture on the screen, this is a somewhat pleasing task for the tester, and it also provides information about whether the system is functioning correctly. Several animations have been used as diagnostic routines, including

1. water flowing by trees
2. a spiral continuously moving outward
3. animated figures moving around on the screen

7.3.11   Sync pulse testing

In many of the newer video controllers, design engineers have begun to insert test feedback circuitry to aid the test diagnostic engineer in verifying the logic. Two signals that help in testing the board are the horizontal and vertical sync pulses. These signals are feed back through an IO port.

The width of these pulses and the time between each pulse can be measured by a test program. Measure these pulses and verify that the time durations are correct.

7.4   Monitor Alignment

The tests defined in this section are more of the nature of utilities than tests. Their purpose is to provide the technician with tools for monitor adjustment. This provides several screens for use in aligning the guns and setting the focus, vertical and horizontal position, and linearity.

There are several test patterns that can be used to test linearity of your video system. Linearity is defined as a line on the screen having equal width, length, and straightness over the entire screen area.

The first test pattern (see Fig. 7.5) is used to set up the size and position controls. Adjust the controls to position the outer rectangle until centered on the screen. The inner square should appear as a square, and the circle should appear uniform, smooth, and round.

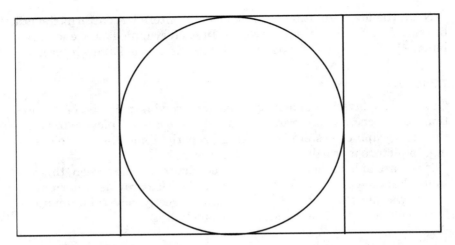

Figure 7.5 Linearity test pattern.

A second test is used to check for curvatures in both horizontal and vertical lines. This test requires two patterns. The first is a set of vertical lines from the top of the screen to the bottom. The second screen consist of horizontal lines from the left to right of the screen.

A third test consists of creating screens with grids. The grids help detect geometric linearity. There should be three or four grids, including at least a large grid, a medium-size grid, and a very small grid. Collectively, these test patterns will allow the tester adjust the terminal controls for the best possible picture.

7.5   Color Testing

The tests described in this section verify that the colors' registration, alignment, and convergence are proper. The first test pattern checks for proper color timing, the second test checks for proper color, and the third checks for purity of color.

The color timing test verifies that the color gun signals are arriving at the CRT display at the same time. The bands display a complementary color pair. Notice that the upper part of the screen is high-intensity, and the lower part of the screen is low intensity. A timing problem appears as a black gap at one border and a bright spot at another. Keyboard input allows the user to change the color pairs. The color pairs are:

Yellow—Purple
Blue—Red
Red—Cyan

The color bar test is used to verify the quality and purity of the colors the system is able to produce. The first test should display a screen with colors bars running from left to right on the screen. Once the color bars are displayed, the user should have the option of changing the color palette, which will also change the color.

The second part of the test checks for purity of the color over the entire screen area. The screen should be painted one color. The test describing the color should be placed on the screen.

7.6 Video Driver Specification

The video diagnostic requires a video driver. The video driver defined in Exhibit 7.1 has a very limited number of functions. In most cases, the specification defined here must be expanded to support other features that may exist in whatever system that you are testing. Identify the additional features and expand the diagnostic driver to include the use of those features.

7.7 Summary

This chapter introduced a method used to display data on the CRT. It provided a basic understanding of how the computer converts charac-

Exhibit 7.1 Video Driver

```
The following is a description of the diagnostic video driver.

init_crt()        This routine is called to initialize the hardware
                  and to set up the buffers and interrupt vectors.

set_cursor()      This is called to set the hardware cursor to a
                  specific location (column-row) combination.

new_cursor()      This routine is used to set the hardware cursor
                  so that it has a new appearance on the screen.

scroll_up()       This is used to scroll the screen up one line.

scroll_wn()       This is used to scroll the screen down one line.

co_out()          This routine writes a single character to the
                  display at the current cursor position using the
                  current define attribute.

read_pos()        This routine reads the character at the current
                  cursor position on the screen.

clear_screen()    This routine clears the scree to the currently
                  defined background color.

set_colors()      This sets the foreground and background colors.

set_attr()        This sets the character attribute.
```

ters to a display on the screen. We also have a understanding of how the colors are represented internally in the memory map and how they are displayed.

We found that many of the video tests require manual intervention, which is to say, the user must verify the result displayed on the screen. The reason is that video systems generally provide very little feedback.

Again, several sample C code programs are provided, with some of the test, and a sample diagnostic video driver specification was included.

7.8 Bibliography

1. Newman, W., and R. Spraull. 1973. *Principles of Interactive Computer Graphics.* New York: McGraw-Hill.
2. Sutty, G., and S. Blair. 1988. *Programmers Guide to the EGA/VGA.* New York: Brady.

```
/*
   cursor_test()

   Description:
   This test routine places the cursor at the four connors of
   the screen and then in th emiddle of the screen. At each
   position, an Asteric is displayed, followed by a message.
   The user must press a 'Y' if correct, otherwise an error
   is reported.
   The second part of the test will position the cursor at
   the middle of the screen, and display the eight sizes of
   the cursor. Between each size display, a delay occurs.
*/
int t[5][2] = { 1,1,24,1,1,79,24,79,12,40 };
char mess[5][20] = {"Cursor at 1,1", "Cursor at 24,1",
                    "Cursor at 1,79","Cursor at 24,79",
                    "Cursor at 12,40" };
cursor_test()
  {
  int i;
  char reply;
  init_crt();                  // initialize crt
  clear_screen();              // clear the screen
  for(i=0;i<5;i++) {
      set_cursor(t[i][0],t[i][1]);
      printf("*");
      set_cursor(5,30);
      printf(mess[i]);
      reply = getche();
      if (reply != 'y' & reply != 'Y')
   return(1);   }
  // now display all sizes of cursor
  clear_screen();                    // clear the screen
  for(i=0;i<8;i++) {
    set_cursor(12,40);               // position to center of screen
    new_cursor(i);                   // set new cursor type
    delay(1000);                     // 1 second delay
    } // end of loop
  return(0);
  }
```

Code Block 7.1 Cursor test.

```
/*
    scroll_test

    Description
    This routine fills the screen with lines of text, then
    will start to scrool the screen down one line at a time,
    with a delay between each scroll. Again the screen is
    filled with test and the test is repeated with scrolling
    up the screen.
*/
scroll_test()
 {
 int i,j;
 init_crt();                    // initialize crt
 set_cursor(0,0);               // home the cursor
 for(i=0;i<26;i++) {            // do all 26 lines
    for(j=0;j<80;j++)           // 80 character per line
      co_out(i+0x41);}          // issue character
 scroll_up();                   // scroll up 1 line
 set_cursor(0,0);
 for(i=0;i<25;i++)  {           // now check for successful
    for (j=0;j<80;j++) {
     if (read_pos() != i+0x42)
        return(5); }            // report the error
      }
 for (j=0;j<80;j++) {
    if (read_pos() != 0)
      return(6);   }
 scroll_dwn();                  // now scroll down
 set_cursor(0,0);
 for (j=0;j<80;j++) {
    if (read_pos() != 0)
      return(7);   }
  for(i=1;i<26;i++) {
    for(j=0;j<80;j++) {
      if (read_pos() != i+0x41 )
    return(8);   }
   }
  return(0);                    // return good
 } // end of function
```

Code Block 7.2 Scroll test.

8

Diagnostic Executive

8.0 Introduction

There are two parts to every diagnostic program: the *executive* and the test routines. The test routines provide the primary functions of the diagnostic in that they find and isolate faults. By themselves, however, these routines are of little value. The executive is needed to make the test routines coherent.

The diagnostic executive is a series of routines that provide all the support needed for the diagnostic test procedures. The executive controls what test executes and how it executes. It provides all the routines to interface with the keyboard and the video. Routines are provided for error reporting and for disk access. The test engineer may spend many weeks defining and developing the test executive. This chapter is provided to help the engineer in the development of the test executive.

This chapter includes several diagnostic executives with different functionalities that have been developed by the author. These executives are provided to assist in the development of your specific diagnostics. Since they were developed on an IBM AT system, you may have to modify some of the code for the executive to run on other systems.

8.1 Pick and Link Menu

The *Pick & Link* is very powerful diagnostic executive that can be used by design engineer when verifying the functionality of a board under test. It is also very helpful to the test technician when attempting to debug a board.

Figure 8.1 is a display of the *Pick & Link* executive main screen. The top window of the screen contains a menu displaying the tests. There may be several menus, and each menu can display up to eight tests. To display the different menus, use the Page Up and Page Down keys. These menus are only displayed as an aid and can be removed if the developer does not wish to use them. The lower window in Fig. 8.1 displays the options. This window is also used as a work area during the execution of test.

The next subsections describe the features of the *Pick & Link* executive in more detail. For each subsection, refer back to Fig. 8.1.

8.1.1 Entering test suite

The tester may choose from the available tests and initiate the execution of those tests in the sequence that the tester specifies. The program is designed to accept a maximum of 20 tests into each test suite.

To enter a test suite, enter a two-character representation (the two characters preceding the test name) of the test that you wish to execute, then depress the space bar. A check is made to verify that the two-character name is a legal test name. If an illegal test name is entered, an error is reported, and the test name is removed from the

```
┌──────────── Pick & Link Diagnostic Executive ────────────┐
│                                                           │
│   A1   -   Data Line Test                                 │
│   A2   -   ATS Memory Test                                │
│   A3   -   Marching 1s and 0s Test                        │
│   B1   -   Galloping 1s Test                              │
│   B2   -   Marching B Test                                │
│   C1   -   Data Path Test                                 │
│   C2   -   Partial Data Path Test                         │
│                                                           │
│   Select ==>   A1   A2   A3   B1   A2   D1   A3           │
│                                                           │
└───────────────────────────────────────────────────────────┘

┌──────────────────────── Options ─────────────────────────┐
│                                                           │
│   ESC  -   Exit program          PgDn -  Next Page        │
│   F1   -   Execute Indefinite    PgUp -  Previous Page    │
│   F2   -   Execute Passes                                 │
│   F3   -   Logging                                        │
│   F4   -   Action on Error                                │
│   F5   -   Save Script                                    │
│   F6   -   Load Script                                    │
│                                                           │
│                                                           │
└───────────────────────────────────────────────────────────┘
```

Figure 8.1 Pick & Link executive.

string. After entering the twentieth test, the program automatically executes the test suite once. For example,

$$\text{Suite} ==> \text{A1 A2 A3 (CR)}$$

The test suite may be executed at any time by pressing the ENTER key. To execute the suite indefinitely, press the F1 function key. To have the test execute a defined number of passes, press the F2 functions key, followed by the number of passes. To terminate testing, press the ESC key.

The program allows the tester to enter a suite and change the help menus without affecting the suite that is currently entered. The tester may also use several of the function key operations without affecting the test suite.

As each test suite is executed, the test suite is saved in a buffer. The tester may recall the last five test suites by pressing the up arrow key.

8.1.2   Saved test suite

Certain test suites are executed many times during hardware development. This executive allows the user to save particular test suites. After the tester has entered a test suite, the suite may be saved to a file.

To save the test suite press F5. The tester is then prompted to verify the save instruction. Next, press the Y key to indicate "yes." Upon entering the Y key, the tester is requested to enter the name of the file. Do not enter the file extension—this is automatically attached. The suite is then save to the specified file. If the file has already been created, the test suite is appended to the end of the file. For example,

Enter the file name: SUITE1

8.1.3   Load and execute test suites

To execute a test suite that has already been saved, the user must select the option to load test suite (F6). Upon selecting this option, the user is requested to enter the test suite name. Again, do not enter the file extension.

All test suites of the file are executed. If any test in the currently selected suite is illegal, or the format of the suite is incorrect, that suite terminates and the next suite starts to execute.

The following is a sample saved test suite. Notice that comments may be place in the suite file (preceded by a semicolon). The first two lines of the file are legal scripts, the third line results in the script being ignored. The forth script has an illegal test in the middle of the script (Z1), which results in that script being terminated.

C1	C2	A1							
A1	A2	A3	A4						
; Comment line									
A1	A2	D3	D1	C1	B4	B1	Z1	A5	D2

As each script is loaded, it is displayed on the select log output device. Any illegal test routine is flagged as an error on the output logging device.

8.1.4 Error reporting

The diagnostic provides the user with option for reporting errors. A standard error format is provided, and can be easily changed to a format that best fits the developers requirements. Error reports are displayed as follows:

```
May 6, 1992 Time 12:45
Error Code 0C.0430
```

The tester may select options such as printing the error to the print port, sending the error to a log file, or ignoring the error reports. Many times during hardware debugging, it is desirable to disable error reporting. This option is provided. The tester also has the option to sound an alarm when an error occurs.

Options are available for the user to select stop on error, continue on error, or loop on error. To select the error action code, press the F4 key while in the main menu.

8.1.5 Log report

The user has the option of logging all the test reports and error reports to the monitor, printer, and/or disk files. The user can define the log output by selecting the log option F3. Table 8.1 is a sample log file.

If logging to a disk file, the user is able to review the log file at some later time. All log files are ASCII text files. All text, including error reports, are sent to the selected log device. The options are:

1. Set Log File
2. Display Log file
3. Set Error File
4. Display Error File

TABLE 8.1 Sample Log File

A1   A2   A3
Sample Data Path Test
Test Routine A2
Test Routine A3
; comment line
A1   A2   A3   A1   A2
Sample Data Path Test
Test Routine A2
Test Routine A3
Sample Data Path Test
Test Routine A2
End of pass #1

8.1.6 Adding and deleting menus and test routines

The sample program has two menus. To add another menu, create a routine that will display the options available on a page similar to the routines page0 and page1. Increment the argument MAX_PAGE by one and add a call to the new page menu in the routine display_page() (see source code in Appendix A).

To add another test routine to the *Pick & Link* executive, simply create the test code. Then in the routine *create_test_table* select the proper place element of *test_tab[x]*. Assume that you wish to add another test to menu B and call the test B4. Element 7 is assigned the address for B4. All test routines from the seventh element on are incremented by one.

In the *test_table[ ]* array, *B4* must be inserted between *B3* and *C1*.

8.2 The Menu Executive

The second sample executive to be discussed is the Menu executive. This executive is used when a single diagnostic suite must be created to support manufacturing, field service, and the customer. This executive provides an easy-to-use interface for the user.

The tester generally executes the diagnostic and reports that the diagnostic has passed or failed. When starting the diagnostic from the command line, the tester can set the pass count and the logging file along with other switches. Once the program is entered, all default conditions are selected and the diagnostic executes a predefined set of tests. After the predefined tests are executed, the diagnostic exits the program. For example,

```
fl_test /p=5 /l
```

The menu mode can be selected from the command line. Use the sample executive provided to evaluate its features. To enter the menu mode, use the example below:

```
fl_test /m
```

The executive provided has several menus. Each of these menus allow the tester to select certain diagnostic test or options. The last option on each menu allows the tester to exit the program. To move between the screens, simply use the PgDn and PgUp keys.

The following subsections describe the command line arguments in more detail.

8.2.1 Command line arguments

The menu executive accepts command line arguments. The arguments are:

- The /m switch allows the user to enter the menu mode. The default is to start executing the diagnostic suite.
- The /p=xx switch allows the tester to set the number of passes for the diagnostic.
- The /lc switch informs the diagnostic that the logging device is the disk file *log.txt*. A new file is created if it does not exist.
- The /la switch informs the diagnostic that the logging device is to the disk file *log.txt*. The file must exist; if it does not, an error is reported. The file is opened in the append mode.
- The /pr switch informs the diagnostic that the logging device is the printer.
- The /es indicates stop-on-error mode.
- The /ec indicates continue-on-error mode.
- The /el indicates loop-on-error mode.
- The /a informs the diagnostic to use the alternate address of the I/O device that is under test.
- The /u switch is a user-defined switch. The test program may use this switch for any purpose.

8.2.2 Automatic test suite

When the diagnostic program is started without entering the menu mode, the diagnostic screen is displayed, and the diagnostic will execute a predefined test suite. The tester has some control over how errors are reported, the logging options, and the pass count. This mode of operation exists for the nontechnical tester who only wants to know if the tested device failed or passed.

8.2.3   Menu mode

When the Menu Mode has been selected, the program is loaded, and the screen appears as shown in Fig. 8.2. This mode allows the user to select a test from the display. Once the test is executed, control is returned to the user via the menu executive.

There are several options to select from the menu. To select an option, use the up and down arrow keys to position the arrow so that it is pointing at the option desired, then press the *enter* key.

8.2.4   Diagnostic configuration window

The configuration window at the top of the screen displays information concerning the hardware configuration, diagnostic configuration, and error status information. This window is easy to modify. You might want to display the error report in this window rather than elsewhere on the screen, or display the accumulation of the errors as the are obtained.

8.2.5   Menu window

The menu window (bottom window of Fig. 8.2) is used to display the current menus and is the active window during the execution of the diagnostic.

8.2.6   Diagnostic configuration option

This option provides the user with the ability to:

```
┌──────────────── Diagnostic Configuration ────────────────┐
│                                                           │
│  Drive Under Test    A:       Drive Type          360k    │
│  Last Access Sector  1:5:12   Total Read Access    40     │
│  Action on Error     Stop     Total Write Access   40     │
│  Pass Count          0        Total Errors Detected 40    │
│  Required Passes     10                                   │
│                                                           │
└───────────────────────────────────────────────────────────┘

┌───────────────── Main Diagnostic Menu ──────────────────┐
│                                                          │
│  ──────> Automatic Test Mode                             │
│          Diagnostic Configuration                        │
│          Individual Test                                 │
│          Exit to DOS                                     │
│                                                          │
│       Use up/down arrows to select your option           │
└──────────────────────────────────────────────────────────┘
```

Figure 8.2 Menu executive.

1. set the pass count
2. set up the hardware
3. logging options
4. setting action on error

To select an option from this menu, use the up and down arrow keys. The last option on this menu is to return to the main menu.

The tester can set the number of passes that are required. If the pass count is set to zero, it indicates that the selected option is to be executed indefinitely until the *ESC* key is pressed.

The diagnostic also allows the tester to set up a particular hardware configuration. The user may set the hardware address of the board, the interrupt vector, and the amount of memory—the diagnostic must be flexible to allow the user to make changes. In many cases, the diagnostic might be "smart" enough to recognize the hardware configuration.

The logging of the test report and errors can be selected in the same manner that was used in the *Pick & Link* executive. The output options are to the screen, the line printer, a disk file, or no output. This executive also provides an option to the user to set the action to take when an error is detected.

8.2.7   Adding menus and text routines

To add a new page of menus, the argument *PAGE* must be incremented. Also, a new routine to display the menu must be created, and the routine *create_page_table* must be updated to reflect the function name of the menu. For each page, there are two arguments that are used with the menu, *Menux_Min* and *Menux_Max*. These value represent the menus option addresses in the *test_table* array.

To add new an option to a menu, increase the *test_table[]* array and update the routine *create_test_table* to assign the new routines. If, for example, you would like to add a new routine for the first page and make it the third option for that page, all other options after the third must be moved down one element of the *test_table*. Modify the routine *page1* and *page1*'s max value, add a new *write_position* line to the appropriate place. Also modify the line placements below the insert line of text.

Next you must update the array *test_table*, placing the new option at the proper place in the array.

8.3   Stand Alone Diagnostic Executive (SADE)

The third, and last, sample diagnostic executive to be discussed is the Stand Alone Executive or (SADE). SADE provides a very powerful interface, which can load any *.exe* file in the current directory, and any diagnostic program designed to execute with the executive.*

When the executive is loaded, it displays two main areas on the screen as shown in Fig. 8.3. The upper is the control window and the lower window is the work window. We will discuss the operation of SADE in more detail in the next subsections.

8.3.1 Control window

The control window provides several options for the tester, which are:

1. Run   Run the set of selected test routines
2. Select   Select the test routines
3. Config   Configure the diagnostic system
4. Option   Select option for testing
5. Log   Set log file reporting

Use the left and right arrows keys to select the option. At any time, pressing the ESC key returns you to the previous window or, if at the Control Window, exits the program. These options are described in the following text.

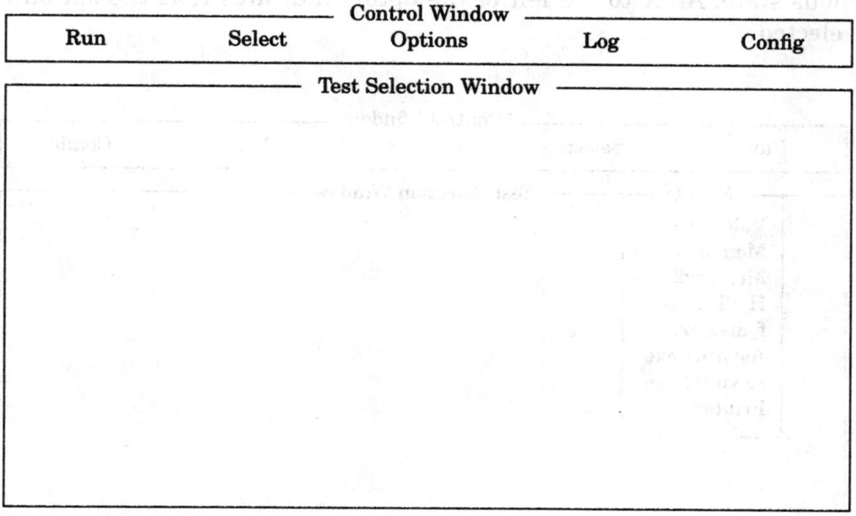

		Control Window		
Run	Select	Options	Log	Config

Test Selection Window

Figure 8.3 Sade windows.

---

*This file, SADE.EXE, is included on a supplemental floppy disk that may be obtained from the author. See the notice following the index for information.

- *Run.*   If any diagnostics are selected, control is transferred to the RUN routine. The run routine loads and executes each diagnostic selected.
- *Select.*   This option allows the user to enter the test selection menu.
- *Config.*   This option allows the user to load and save the current diagnostic configuration and set the default directory.
- *Option.*   This option allows the user to set the diagnostic mode, the action to take on an error report, flag to remove a test from the suite if multiple errors have been reported, and set the pass count.
- *Log.*   This option allows the user to select the logging device for the standard log and for the error log. The log files may also be displayed, if they exist.

8.3.2 Select option

The *Select* option allows the user to select test programs. When the select option is highlighted and the *ENTER* key is pressed, a pull-down menu appears below the option as shown in Fig. 8.4. This menu displays the test programs that are available to the tester.

To select a test programs, use the up and down arrows to highlight the test option, then press the *ENTER* key. After pressing the *ENTER* key, that option is either selected or de-selected, depending on its previous state. An *X* to the left of the option indicates that the option is selected.

```
┌──────────────────────── Control Window ────────────────────────┐
│   Run          Select       Options        Log          Config │
├────────────────────────────────────────────────────────────────┤
│┌───── Select ─────┬──── Test Selection Window ─────────────────┐│
││ Video.exe        │                                            ││
││ Memory1.exe      │                                            ││
││ Memory2.exe      │                                            ││
││ H_disk.exe       │                                            ││
││ f_disk.exe       │                                            ││
││ Async01.exe      │                                            ││
││ Async02.exe      │                                            ││
││ Printer.exe      │                                            ││
│└──────────────────┘                                            ││
│                                                                ││
│                                                                ││
│                                                                ││
└────────────────────────────────────────────────────────────────┘
```

Figure 8.4 Select option.

To add test programs to the list, the user must update the file *prog.lst*. This file contains an ASCII list of the test options available. The file can contain a maximum of 20 file names. The programs in this list can be any form of *.exe* files. The test option could be a stand-alone program or a program that requires the SADE executive to be executing.

The user may select any number of test programs to execute. Once the test suite has been selected, exit the selection process and select the *RUN* option.

8.3.3 Configuration option

Setting up the diagnostic configuration and selecting the test routines is sometimes a very cumbersome job. Once the entire configuration has been set up, the tester may save that configuration to a disk file. Figure 8.5 is a display of the configuration pull-down menu, which allows you to do this.

To save a configuration or load a configuration enter the *Config* option. The functions available from the Config option are:

1. save the configuration
2. load the configuration
3. change disk directory
4. directory

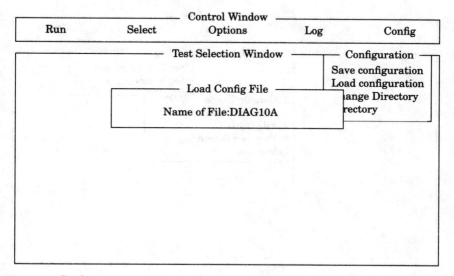

Figure 8.5 Configuration.

The following items are saved in the configuration file:

1. selected test options and test names
2. pass count
3. all error options
4. all logging options

To load a configuration file, enter the load option. Use the up and down arrows to select the proper configuration file to load. When the proper file is highlighted press the *ENTER* key.

8.3.4 Options

This option allows the tester to set up the hardware configuration, the pass count, and action on error, and to remove a test from the selected loop if that test is failing. Figure 8.6 is a display of the pull-down menu for the options option.

The first three options are very similar to the previous executives. The last option, *remove a test*, is new. This option can be used to inform the executive that if a particular test is constantly failing, remove that test from the test suite.

The tester can also specify which test routines can be removed and the number of errors that has to be exceeded before the test is removed. When the test is removed, a report of the removal is sent to the output logging device.

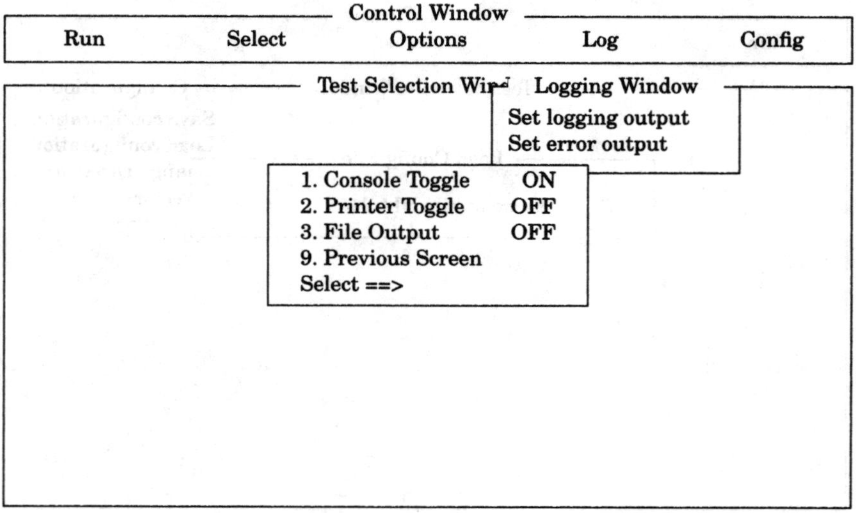

```
──────────────────────── Control Window ────────────────────────
    Run              Select          Options          Log              Config

┌──────────────────────── Test Selection Wir┌─ Logging Window ────────────┐
                                             │ Set logging output          │
                                             │ Set error output            │
                        ┌────────────────────┴───┐                         │
                        │ 1. Console Toggle    ON │─────────────────────────┘
                        │ 2. Printer Toggle    OFF│
                        │ 3. File Output       OFF│
                        │ 9. Previous Screen      │
                        │ Select ==>              │
                        └─────────────────────────┘
```

Figure 8.6 Logging window.

8.3.5 Logging options

As in the previous executives, logging of a test report and error reports can be to the console, the line printer, and a disk file. To set up the logging options, select the *log* option. A pull-down menu appears (see Fig. 8.7). Use the up and down arrow keys to select the desired option. The options are: select a log file, an error file, or view an ASCII file. Generally, this ASCII file is either a log file or an error file.

When viewing a file, the user must enter the name of the file and then press the *ENTER* key. After pressing *ENTER*, the file is displayed in the work area. As each page is displayed, the user may select to print the current page, stop the display, or continue to the next page.

8.4 Summary

When developing a diagnostic, many hours are spent on the executive that provides the user interface, and all utilities needed. In this chapter, we discussed three sample diagnostic executives, each containing many important features. Many of these features may be used as models in the development of your own diagnostic executive.

Pick.c Source Code

```
/************************************************************************
 *                                                                      *
 *    Name    Pick.c                                                    *
 *                                                                      *
 *    This test executive program is a demonstration executive         *
 *    program that allows the user to pick and choose the test          *
 *    suite that they wish to executive.                                *
 *                                                                      *
 *    The maximum number of test that may be linked together           *
 *    is 20 test routines.                                              *
 *                                                                      *
 ************************************************************************/
#define TW1    1                           // Top window values
#define TW2    1
#define TW3    80
#define TW4    13

#define BW1    1                           // Bottom window values
#define BW2    14
#define BW3    80
#define BW4    23


#include    <conio.h>
#include    <stdio.h>
#include    <string.h>
#include    "diag.h"
#include    "data.h"
#include    "proto.inc"


FILE    *handle;
/*
    If a new page of test is added this argument must be incremented
*/
#define MAX_PAGE     2                      // current page count
#define SEL_ROW      10                     // Row for select message
#define MAX_TEST     20                     // Max test count

/************************************************************************
 *    This character array represents the legal test names.            *
 *    To add a test name, this array must be updated.                  *
 *                                                                      *
 *    Example - If you wish to add the name B4 and it will             *
```

```
*    chronologically be after B3, then insert "B4"              *
*    between "B3" and "C1"                                      *
***************************************************************/
char test_table[20][3] = { "A1","A2","A3","A4","B1","B2",
                           "B3","C1","C2","C3","C4","C5","D1"
                         };

/***************************************************************
*  Name    main()                                              *
*                                                              *
*  Description:                                                *
*                                                              *
*  This routine is the main entry routine for the Pick & Link  *
*  execute. Once entering this routine, the system attributes are *
*  set, the screen is cleared, the windows is set up and the first *
*  page is displayed.                                          *
*                                                              *
*                                                              *
*  Input Arguments:     None                                   *
*                                                              *
*  Output Arguments:    None                                   *
*                                                              *
*  Local Arguments:     int i                                  *
*                                                              *
*  Functions called:    create_test_table()                   *
*                        clrscr()                              *
*                        open_window()                         *
*                        display_page()                        *
*                        execute_script()                      *
*                        get_decimal()                         *
*                        clear_buffer()                        *
*                        write_position()                      *
*                        log_menu()                            *
*                        error_menu()                          *
*                        save_script()                         *
*                        load_script()                         *
*                        get_key()                             *
*                        delete_key()                          *
*                                                              *
***************************************************************/
void  main()
    {
    int i,good;
    suite_num = 0;                      // default value
    create_test_table();                // set up test table
    textattr(0x17);                     // set background & foreground
    clrscr();                           // clear the screen
    open_window(TW1,TW2,TW3,TW4,23,1,"Pick & Link Diagnostic Executive");
    display_page();                     // display the current page
    pnt = str1;                         // initialize string pointer
    position = count = 0;               // and counters
    test_count = 0;                     // set test count to zero
    /*
    This while loop is used to allow the user to enter character
    on the keyboard. It will control all functions. This loop
    exits when an ESC key is pressed.
    */
    while ( (ch & 0xff) != 0x1b) {      // loop till ESC pressed
        ch = get_key();                 // get a key
        if (ch ==  PGDN) {              // Page down key
    if (page < MAX_PAGE-1)              // if not a maximum page
        page++;                         // bump to next page
    display_page();                     // display the new page
    cprintf( str1); }

        if (ch == PGUP) {               // display previous page
    if (page > 0)                       // if not at top of page
        page--;                         // back up
    display_page();                     // display new page
    cprintf( str1); }

    if (ch == F1) {
        pass_cnt = 0;                   // set pass count to zero
        execute_script();               // execute script
        clear_buffer(str1,80);          // Clear the string
```

```
        pnt = str1;                          // save the address
        count = 0;                           // reset the count
        display_page();                      // re-display the page
        position = 0;
        test_count = 0; }                    // set test count to zero

if (ch == F2) {
        gotoxy(3,SEL_ROW + 1);
        cprintf("Number of passes: ");
        get_decimal(&pass_cnt);              // enter number of passes
        execute_script();                    // execute the script
        clear_buffer(str1,80);               // clear the buffer
        pnt = str1;                          // save the address
        count = 0;                           // reset the count
        display_page();                      // re-display the page
        position = 0;
        test_count = 0; }                    // set test count to zero

if (ch == UP_ARR) {                          // recall previous suites
        if (suite_num < 5)  suite_num++;
        clear_buffer(str1,80);               // clear the string
        for (i=0;i<60;i++)  str1[i] = suites[suite_num-1][i];
        gotoxy(14,SEL_ROW);
        cprintf("                                              ");
        write_position(14,SEL_ROW, str1); }

if (ch == F3)  log_menu();       // Select the log menu
if (ch == F4)  error_menu();     // error menu
if (ch == F5)  save_script();    // save the current script
if (ch == F6) {
        load_script();                       // load new script file
        clear_buffer(str1,80);               // Clear the string
        pnt = str1;                          // save the address
        count = 0;                           // reset the count
        display_page();                      // re-display the page
        position = 0;
        test_count = 0; }                    // set test count to zero
if (ch == CR || test_count == 20 || ch == F10)
        {                                    // single pass selected
        pass_cnt = 1;                        // set pass count to 1
        execute_script();                    // execute suite
        clear_buffer(str1,80);               // clear the buffer
        pnt = str1;                          // set address
        count = 0;                           // reset count
        display_page();                      // redisplay page
        position = 0;
        test_count = 0;                      // set test count to zero
        }
if (ch ==  DEL) {                            // delete a character
        if (pnt != str1)                     // not at the start of
           delete_char();                    // string del a character
        }
if ((ch & 0xff) == 0x20) {       // insert a space
        *pnt++ = ch;                         // place it in the string
        putch(ch);                           // display the space
        position++;                          // bump pointer
        count = 0;                           // reset count
        }
// convert lower case to upper case ALPHA
if ((ch & 0xff) >= 'a' && (ch & 0xff)<= 'z') ch -= 0x20;
// if alpha or number place in string
if ((ch & 0xff) >= 'A' && (ch & 0xff) <= 'Z' ||
    (ch & 0xff) >= '0' && (ch & 0xff) <= '9' ) {
        if (count == 0 || count == 1) {  // if count < 2
        *pnt++ = ch;                         // place character in string
        putch(ch);                           // display the character
        position++;                          // bump the position
        count++;                             // keep count
        if (count == 2) {                    // if count equal 2
           good = 0;                         // check if legal test
           for (i = 0; i < 20; i++) {  // all possible test
              if (!strcmp(&str1[position - 2],test_table[i]))
              {
              good = 1;                       // indicate good test name
              test_count++;                   // count the test
```

```
                break;                    // cause break
                } /* end of the if statement */
            } /* end of for statement  */
        if (good == 0) {          // if illegal report
            beep();               // sound bell first
            write_position(3,SEL_ROW+1,"Illegal test name.");
            get_key();                // wait for keystroke
            write_position(3,SEL_ROW+1,"                    ");
            gotoxy(14+position,SEL_ROW);// reposition cursor
            delete_char();        // delete the previous 2 char
            delete_char();
            count = 0;            // reset the count
            } // if (good = 0)
        } // end if (count == 2)
    }
    else {                       // if 3 character in a row
    beep();                      // sound bell
    write_position(3, SEL_ROW+1, "Illegal test name format. ");
    get_key();                   // wait for keystroke
    write_position(3,SEL_ROW+1, "                          ");
    gotoxy(14+position,SEL_ROW);// reposition cursor
    } // end of the else statement
} // end of the if statement
    } // end of the while statement
 window(0,0,79,25);                         // reset full page window
 clrscr();                                  // clear the entire screen
 }  // end of function


/*******************************************************************
 *      Name execute_script()                                      *
 *                                                                 *
 *      This routine will cause each of the test routine specified *
 *      in the input string to be executed in the order that they are *
 *      found in the string. A check has already been made to verify *
 *      that the format and the test names are legal. Therefore no *
 *      checking is required.                                      *
 *                                                                 *
 *      Input Arguments:    None                                   *
 *                                                                 *
 *      Output Arguments:   None                                   *
 *                                                                 *
 *      Local Arguments:    None                                   *
 *                                                                 *
 *      Functions Called:   save_suite()                           *
 *                          open_window()                          *
 *                          execute_test()                         *
 *                          display_options()                      *
 *                                                                 *
 *******************************************************************/
void execute_script()
  {
  save_suite();                            // save the current suite
  open_window(BW1,BW2,BW3,BW4,30,1, "Diagnostic Work Screen");
  clrscr();                                // clear the window
  execute_test();                          // execute script
  display_options();                       // restore window
  window(TW1+1,TW2+1,TW3-1,TW4-1);         // Set proper window
  } // end of function

/*******************************************************************
 * Name   error_menu                                               *
 *                                                                 *
 * Description:                                                    *
 * This routine allows the user to select the options for the error *
 * reporting. The routine will set up the proper window, then display*
 * the proper selections on the screen, and then allow the user to *
 * select the option. Pressing a '9' will cause the routine to     *
 * re-establish the previously selected window and exit the screen. *
 *                                                                 *
 *      Input Arguments:    None                                   *
 *                                                                 *
 *      Output Arguments:   None                                   *
 *                                                                 *
 *      Local Arguments:    int i                                  *
```

```
*                                                                  *
*         Functions Called:  get_cursor()                          *
*                            open_window()                         *
*                            write_position()                      *
*                                                                  *
********************************************************************/
void error_menu()
  {
  int i;
  cursor = get_cursor();
  open_window(BW1,BW2,BW3,BW4,30,1,"Error Menu");
  ch = 0;
/*
  Loop in while statement until a '9' is pressed on the keyboard
*/
  while (ch != 0x39)
    {
    clrscr();                               // clear the screen
    // display status of stop[ on error
    write_position(2,2, "1. Stop on Error      ");
    if (error_mode == 0) cprintf("[Y]");
    else                 cprintf("[N]");
    // display status of continue on error
    write_position(2,3, "2. Continue on Error");
    if (error_mode == 1) cprintf( "[Y]");
    else                 cprintf( "[N]");
    // display status of loop on error
    write_position(2,4, "3. loop on Error      ");
    if (error_mode  == 2) cprintf( "[Y]");
    else                 cprintf("[N]");
    // display status of bell on error
    write_position(2,5, "4. Bell on Error      ");
    if (error_bell)       cprintf( "[Y]");
    else                 cprintf("[N]");
    gotoxy(2,6);
    cprintf("9. Return to Main Menu");
    ch = (get_key() & 0xff);
    switch(ch)
      {
      case '1': error_mode = 0;
        break;
      case '2': error_mode = 1;
        break;
      case '3': error_mode = 2;
        break;
      case '4': error_bell = !error_bell;
      case '9': break;
      default:  beep();                     //sound warning
        break;
      }
    } // end of while statement
  window(BW1+1,BW2+1,BW3-1,BW4-1);      // set bigger window
  clrscr();                             // clear it
  ch = 0;                               // reset character
  display_options();                    // display the options
  window(TW1+1,TW2+1,TW3-1,TW4-1);      // set proper window
  gotoxy(cursor >> 8,cursor);           // restore cursor
} // end of function

/********************************************************************
*    Name log_menu()                                               *
*                                                                  *
*    Description:                                                  *
*    This routine will allow the user to set the type of logging   *
*    and display the log files.                                    *
*                                                                  *
*                                                                  *
*        Input Arguments:    None                                  *
*                                                                  *
*        Output Arguments:   None                                  *
*                                                                  *
*        Local Arguments:    None                                  *
*                                                                  *
*        Functions Called:  get_cursor()                           *
*                           disp_log_menu()                        *
```

```
*                          get_key()                                      *
*                          display_options()                              *
*                                                                         *
*************************************************************************/

void log_menu()
  {
  cursor = get_cursor();                  //save the cursor position
  open_window(BW1,BW2,BW3,BW4,30,1, "Log Menu");
  disp_log_menu();                        // display the log menu
/*
  Loop on the while statement until a '9' is pressed
*/
  while ((ch = (get_key() & 0xff)) != 0x39) {
      switch (ch)
{
case '1':   set_log();               //set the log file
            break;
case '3':   set_error_log();         // select the error log file
            break;
case '2':   display_log(&log_file);
            window(BW1+1,BW2+1,BW3-1,BW4-1);
            break;

case '4':   display_log(&error_log_file);       // display the file
            window(BW1+1,BW2+1,BW3-1,BW4-1);
            break;
case '9':   break;                   // return to previous menu
default:    beep();
            break;
} // end of switch statement
    disp_log_menu();
    } // end of while statement
  ch = 0;                                 // reset character
  display_options();                      // display the options
  window(TW1+1,TW2+1,TW3-1,TW4-1);        // set up proper window
  gotoxy(cursor >> 8,cursor);             // restore cursor
  } // end of function

/*************************************************************************
*   Name:   disp_log_menu                                                 *
*                                                                         *
*   Description:                                                          *
*   This routine will display the log menu                                *
*                                                                         *
*       Input Arguments:    None                                          *
*                                                                         *
*       Output Arguments:   None                                          *
*                                                                         *
*       Local Arguments:    None                                          *
*                                                                         *
*       Functions Called:   write_position()                             *
*                                                                         *
*************************************************************************/
void disp_log_menu()
  {
  clrscr();
  write_position(3,1, "1. Set Log File");
  write_position(3,2, "2. Display Log File");
  write_position(3,3, "3. Set Error Log File");
  write_position(3,4, "4. Display Error Log File");
  write_position(3,5, "9. Previous Menu");
  write_position(3,6, "Select ==> ");
  } // end of function

/*************************************************************************
*   Name    display_page                                                  *
*                                                                         *
*   Description:                                                          *
*   This routine clears the working area, display the title in work       *
*   area, then display the selected page options, and finally the         *
*   footer of the page.                                                   *
*                                                                         *
*   If a new page is added, then this routine must be updated to          *
```

```
*    display the new page.                                            *
*                                                                     *
*                                                                     *
*         Input Arguments:    None                                    *
*                                                                     *
*         Output Arguments:   None                                    *
*                                                                     *
*         Local Arguments:    None                                    *
*                                                                     *
*         Functions Called:   page0()                                 *
*                             page1()                                 *
*                             display_options()                       *
*                             write_position()                        *
*                                                                     *
***********************************************************************/
void display_page()
   {
   clrscr();                             // clear current window
   if (page == 0) page0();               // if page 1 then display it
   if (page == 1) page1();               // else display page 2
   if (ch != PGDN & ch != PGUP)          // if only not page up/down
      display_options();                 // display options
   window(TW1+1,TW2+1,TW3-3,TW4-1);      // set proper window
   write_position(3,SEL_ROW, "Select ==> ");
   } // end of function
/***********************************************************************
*    Name    display_options                                          *
*                                                                     *
*    Description:                                                     *
*    This routine is used to display the special key options into the *
*    option window.                                                   *
*                                                                     *
*         Input Arguments:    None                                    *
*                                                                     *
*         Output Arguments:   None                                    *
*                                                                     *
*         Local Arguments:    None                                    *
*                                                                     *
*         Functions Called:   None                                    *
*                                                                     *
***********************************************************************/

void display_options()
   {
   open_window(BW1,BW2,BW3,BW4,30,1,"Options");
   clrscr();
   write_position(3,1, "ESC  - Exit Program  ");
   write_position(3,2, "F1   - Execute Indefinite ");
   write_position(3,3, "F2   - Execute Passes ");
   write_position(3,4, "F3   - Logging ");
   write_position(3,5, "F4   - Action on Error");
   write_position(3,6, "F5   - Save the Script");
   write_position(3,7, "F6   - Load Script");
   write_position(43,1,"PgDn - Next Page ");
   write_position(43,2,"PgUp - Previous Page");
   write_position(43,4,"F10  - Execute Script");
   write_position(43,3,"UpAR - Recall Script");
   } // end of function
/***********************************************************************
*    page0                                                            *
*                                                                     *
*    Description:                                                     *
*    This routine displays the option for the first page.             *
*                                                                     *
*         Input Arguments:    None                                    *
*                                                                     *
*         Output Arguments:   None                                    *
*                                                                     *
*         Local Arguments:    None                                    *
*                                                                     *
*         Functions Called:   None                                    *
*                                                                     *
***********************************************************************/
void page0()
   {
```

```
   write_position(2,1, "A1 - Data Line test");
   write_position(2,2, "A2 - ATS Test");
   write_position(2,3, "A3 - Marching Test");
   write_position(2,4, "B1 - Galloping Test");
   write_position(2,5, "B2 - Marching B Test");
   write_position(2,6, "B3 - Data Path test");
   write_position(2,7, "C1 - Partial Data Path Test");
   write_position(2,8, "C2 - Dummy Routine");
   } // end of function

void page1()
    {
   write_position(2,1, "C3 - Dummy Routine");
   write_position(2,2, "C4 - Dummy Routine");
   write_position(2,3, "C5 - Dummy Routine");
   write_position(2,4, "D1 - Dummy Routine");
   write_position(2,5, "");
   write_position(2,6, "");
   write_position(2,7, "");
   write_position(2,8, "");
   } // end of function


/***********************************************************************
*                                                                      *
*    Name save_script                                                  *
*                                                                      *
*    Description:                                                      *
*    This routine saves the current script to a file. If the          *
*    file already exist, the script will be appended to the end       *
*    of the file.                                                      *
*                                                                      *
*       Input Arguments:    None                                      *
*                                                                      *
*       Output Arguments:   None                                      *
*                                                                      *
*       Local Arguments:    None                                      *
*                                                                      *
*       Functions Called:   None                                      *
*                                                                      *
***********************************************************************/
void save_script()
    {
    int i,j,x,y,t_cursor;
    char  ans;
    char file_name[20],temp[80];
    t_cursor = get_cursor();                 // Save cursor location
    open_window(BW1,BW2,BW3,BW4,30,1,"Save Script File");
    clrscr();                                // clear the new window
    write_position(2,2,
     "Do you really want to save the script.(Y/N)");
    ans = get_key();                         // get answer
    if (ans == 'Y' || ans == 'y')            // if Yes
      {
      write_position(2,3,"Enter the file name: ");
      gets(file_name);                       // get the file name
      strcat(file_name,ext);                 // add extension
      // open the file
      handle = fopen(file_name,"a");
      // if unable to open file report an error
      if (handle == NULL)  {
    write_position(4,4,"Unable to open file");
    get_key();                               // wait for key
    return;                                  // return to caller
     }
      strcpy(temp,str1);                     // copy test suite to temp
      i = strlen(temp);                      // insert a CRLF
      temp[i] = 0xa;
      temp[i+1] = 0xd;
      temp[i+2] = 0;                         // and a null
      // write string to the file
      fwrite(temp,strlen(temp),sizeof(char),handle);
      fclose(handle);                        // close the file
      }
    clrscr();                                // clear the window
    display_options();                       // restore screen
```

```
        window(TW1+1,TW2+1,TW3-1,TW4-1);    // Set proper window
        gotoxy(t_cursor >> 8,t_cursor);     // restore cursor
    } // end of function

/*************************************************************************
 *    Name    load_script                                                *
 *                                                                       *
 *    This routine loads the script and execute the script file.         *
 *    if the script file has more than one script, then each and         *
 *    every script is loaded and executed.                               *
 *    The routine returns a value of zero if the file was opened,         *
 *    otherwise an error code will be returned.                          *
 *                                                                       *
 *    Error Code                                                         *
 *       1                                                               *
 *                                                                       *
 *      Input Arguments:    None                                         *
 *                                                                       *
 *      Output Arguments:   None                                         *
 *                                                                       *
 *      Local Arguments:    None                                         *
 *                                                                       *
 *      Functions Called:   None                                         *
 *                                                                       *
 *************************************************************************/
int  load_script()
    {
    int i,j,t_cursor;
    char file_name[20];
    t_cursor = get_cursor();                // get cursor location
    open_window(BW1,BW2,BW3,BW4,30,1,"Load Script File");
    clrscr();                               // clear the screen
    write_position(3,2,
    "Enter name of script file to load:");
    gets(file_name);                        // get file name
    strcat(file_name,ext);                  // add extension
    // open the file
    handle = fopen(file_name,"r");
    // report any error during opening
    if (handle == NULL) {
cprintf("Unable to open file");  // report unable to open file
get_key();                              // wait for key
return(1);                               // return to caller
}
    str1[0] = 'a';
    pass_cnt = 1;                           // set pass count
    open_window(BW1,BW2,BW3,BW4,30,1,"Diagnostic Work Screen");
    clrscr();
    // loop here until all scripts are loaded and executed
    while (str1[0] != 0) {
//if (p_log)  printer = 1;
//if (f_log)  file_act2 = 1;
str1[0] = 0;                            // null the string
//fread(handle,80,sizeof(char), str1);
fgets(str1,80,handle);
//if (str1[0] == 0) break;
cprintf("\n\r%s\n\r", str1);    // display string
if (str1[0] != ';')
run_test();                             // the execute test
printer = 0;
file_act2 = 0;
}
    fclose(handle);
    wait_press();
    clrscr();                               // clear the window
    display_options();                      // restore screen
    window(TW1+1,TW2+1,TW3-1,TW4-1);        // Set proper window
    gotoxy(t_cursor >> 8,t_cursor);         // restore cursor
    return(0);
    } // end of function

/*************************************************************************
 *    Name   execute_test()                                              *
 *                                                                       *
```

```
*     Description:                                                   *
*     This routine causes each of the test routine specified        *
*     in the string to be executed in the order that they were      *
*     found. A check has already been made to verify that the       *
*     format and the test names are legal. Therefore no checking     *
*     is required.                                                   *
*                                                                   *
*       Input Arguments:    None                                    *
*                                                                   *
*       Output Arguments:   None                                    *
*                                                                   *
*       Local Arguments:    None                                    *
*                                                                   *
*       Functions Called:   None                                    *
*                                                                   *
********************************************************************/
void execute_test()
  {
  int i,k,done;
  char *pnt,*tx;
  if (p_log)  printer = 1;
  if (f_log)  file_act2 = 1;
  k = 0;                              // initialize pass count
  passes = 1;                         // set pass count
  done = 0;                           // reset done flag
  do   {                              // start the loop
    run_test();                       // run test suite
  cprintf( "\n\rEnd of pass #%d\n\r",passes);
  if ( test_key()) {
    k = (get_key() & 0xff);          // read the key
    if (k == 0x1b)   done++;
    }
  passes++;
  if (passes > pass_cnt && pass_cnt != 0) done++;
  } while (!done);
  printer = 0;
  file_act2 = 0;
  wait_press();
  } // end of function


/********************************************************************
*     run_test()                                                    *
*                                                                   *
*     Description:                                                   *
*     This routine evaluates the ascii string str1 from the start.   *
*     The format of the string is three for each test, the first two *
*     characters represent the test to execute, the third character *
*     is the space or null character, terminating the test string.   *
*                                                                   *
*                                                                   *
*       Input Arguments:    None                                    *
*                                                                   *
*       Output Arguments:   None                                    *
*                                                                   *
*       Local Arguments:    None                                    *
*                                                                   *
*       Functions Called:   None                                    *
*                                                                   *
********************************************************************/
void run_test()
  {
  int i;
  char *pnt,*tx;
  pnt = str1;                         // set pointer to string
  while (*pnt != 0 ) {                // until end of test
    tx = str2;                        //
    *tx++ = *pnt++;                   // copy test name to str2
    *tx++ = *pnt++;
    *tx = 0;
    pnt++;
    printf("%s ",str2);
    // search the table for a match. Already know that it
    // was found in the table. Match for the address
    for (i = 0; i < MAX_TEST; i++) {
     if (!strcmp(str2,test_table[i]))  {
```

```
do {
  error = 0;                          // reset error flag
  test_add = test_tab[i];             // get the address
  (*test_add)();                      // call the routine
  if (test_key()) {
      if (get_key() & 0xff == ESC ) break;  }
  } while (error == 3);
  break;
} /* end of the if statement */
      } /* end of for statement  */
      if (i== MAX_TEST) cprintf("Test not found\n\r");
  } /* end of while statement  */
} // end of function
/****************************************************************
*                                                              *
*     save_suite()                                             *
*                                                              *
*     Save the current suite into the previous suite table     *
*                                                              *
*         Input Arguments:    None                            *
*                                                              *
*         Output Arguments:   None                            *
*                                                              *
*         Local Arguments:    None                            *
*                                                              *
*         Functions Called:   None                            *
*                                                              *
****************************************************************/
void save_suite()
  {
  int i,j;
  for (i=4;i>0;i--)  {                 // make room in table
    for(j=0;j<62;j++)
        suites[i][j] = suites[i-1][j];
    } // end of for loop
  for(j=0;j<62;j++)   suites[0][j] = str1[j];
  suite_num = 0;

  } // end of function

/****************************************************************
*     The following routines are the dummy routines for the pick  *
*     and link diagnostic executive. The diagnostic programmer can *
*     substitute there particular test routine with the dummy     *
*     routines                                                  *
*                                                              *
****************************************************************/
void A1()
  {
  write_under_test( "Data Line Test\n\r");
//   data_line_test((long) 0x60000000,16);
  }
void A2()
  {
  write_under_test("ATS Test\n\r");
//   ats_test((long) 0x60000000,64);
  }

void A3()
  {
  write_under_test( "Marching Test\n\r");
//   marching_test((long) 0x60000000,64);
  }

void A4()
  {
  write_under_test( "Galloping Test\n\r");
//   galloping_test((long) 0x60000000,64);
  }

void B1()
  {
  cprintf( "Marching B Test\n\r");
//   marching_b_test((long) 0x60000000,64);
  }
```

```
void B2()
  {
  cprintf( "Data Path Test\n\r");
  }

void B3()
  {
   cprintf("Partial Data Path Test\n\r");
  }

void C1()
  {
  cprintf("Test Routine C1\n\r");
  }

void C2()
  {
  cprintf( "Test Routine C2\n\r");
  }

void C3()
  {
   cprintf( "Test Routine C3\n\r");
  }

void C4()
  {
  cprintf( "Test Routine C4\n\r");
  }

void C5()
  {
  cprintf( "Test Routine C5\n\r");
  }

void D1X()
  {
   cprintf("Test Routine D1\n\r");
   error_report(12,0x1234);
  }

/***********************************************************************
 *   Name                                                              *
 *   Description:                                                      *
 *   This routine will create the test table. the routines can        *
 *   be arranged in any manner that the tester wishes. You must       *
 *   coordinate the selected item from the menu to the proper         *
 *   entry into this table.                                           *
 *                                                                    *
 *       Input Arguments:    None                                     *
 *                                                                    *
 *       Output Arguments:   None                                     *
 *                                                                    *
 *       Local Arguments:    None                                     *
 *                                                                    *
 *       Functions Called:   None                                     *
 *                                                                    *
 ***********************************************************************/
void create_test_table()
    {
    test_tab[0]  = A1;
    test_tab[1]  = A2;
    test_tab[2]  = A3;
    test_tab[3]  = A4;
    test_tab[4]  = B1;
    test_tab[5]  = B2;
    test_tab[6]  = B3;
    test_tab[7]  = C1;
    test_tab[8]  = C2;
    test_tab[9]  = C3;
    test_tab[10] = C4;
    test_tab[11] = C5;
    test_tab[12] = D1X;
    }
```

Menu.c Source Code

```
/***************************************************************************
 *    Name       menu.c                                                    *
 *                                                                         *
 *    This executive program is a demonstration executive                  *
 *    program that allows the user to select options from                  *
 *    a menu and execute those options.                                    *
 *                                                                         *
 *                                                                         *
 ***************************************************************************/

#include  <conio.h>
#include  <stdio.h>
#include  <string.h>
#include  "..\pick\diag.h"
#include  "..\pick\data.h"

int    auto_mode;

#define   TW1   1            // Top Window defining size
#define   TW2   1
#define   TW3   80
#define   TW4   11

#define   BW1   1 // Bottom Window defining size
#define   BW2   12
#define   BW3   80
#define   BW4   24

extern   char drive_type[3][8];

FILE   *handle;

extern   seek_test1();
extern   seek_test2();
extern   format_test();
extern   read_test();
extern   write_test();
extern   display_log();
extern   set_log();
extern   set_error_log();
extern   display_error_log();
extern   display_log_file();
```

```
/********************************************************************
*                                                                   *
*    The following address pointer identify the number of menus     *
*    that may be displayed on the screen. To change the number      *
*    of menus, change the constant PAGES to the number of menus.    *
********************************************************************/
#define PAGES  4

int   (*page_add)(), (*page_table[PAGES])();

/*
    The following address pointer table will hold the address of
    the test routines. To change the number of test routines,
    change the constant TEST to the total number of tests.
*/
#define TEST  25
int   (*test_address)();
int   (*test_table[TEST])();
/********************************************************************
*   Name    main                                                    *
*                                                                   *
*   Description:                                                     *
*   This is the main entry point for the diagnsotic executive.      *
*                                                                   *
*   Input Argument:       int - argc      Command Line              *
*                         char - argv[]                             *
*                                                                   *
*   Output Arguments:     None                                      *
*                                                                   *
*   Local Arguments:      int   i,j,k,done                          *
*                                                                   *
*   Functions Called:     display_config()                          *
*                         open_window()                             *
*                         create_page_table()                       *
*                         create_test_table()                       *
*                         auto_mode_suite()                         *
*                         get_option()                              *
*                         dis_config()                              *
*                         window()                                  *
*                                                                   *
*                                                                   *
*   Component History:  Initial Entry                               *
*                                                                   *
********************************************************************/
void main(int argc,char *argv[])
    {
    int i,j,done,k;
    read_cnt = 0;
/*
    Check the command line arguments. If there are no arguments, then the
    program will execute the default test suite once the return to DOS.
*/
    for (i = 1; i < argc; i++) {
       if (!strcmp(argv[i], "/m"))          // check if menu mode
          mode = 0;
       if (!strncmp (argv[i], "/p=",3))     // get pass count
          pass_cnt = atol(argv[i]+3);
       if (!strcmp (argv[i],"/u"))          // check if user define
          user_flag = 1;
       if (!strcmp (argv[i], "/a"))         // check for alternate address
          alternate_add = 1;                // set alternate address
       } // end of for loop
    textattr(0x17);
    display_config();                       // diplay the configuration
    open_window(BW1,BW2,BW3,BW4,1,1,"");
    create_page_table();                    // set-up page table
    create_test_table();                    // set up test table
                                            // loop here forever and ever
/*
    check if non-menu mode. If so execute non menu,
    otherwise enter the menu mode.
*/
    if (mode == 1) {
        for (pass_cnt=0;pass_cnt<pass_cnt;pass_cnt++) {
window(BW1,BW2,BW3,BW4);            // set window inner box
```

```
        auto_mode_suite();              // execute auto mode
        display_config();               // update configuration
      }
        exit_diag();                    // return to DOS
        } // end of if (mode == 1)
/*
    Loop here forever, or until the exit to DOS option selected
*/
    for (;;) {
      textattr(0x17);
      option = get_option();            // get selected test routine
      if (p_log)  printer = 1;          // if output to line printer
      if (f_log)  file_act2 = 1;        // if output ti file
      k = 0;                            // initialize pass count
      done = 0;                         // reset done flag
      pass_cnt = 0;
      do  {
        once = 0;                       // accomplish once
        clrscr();                       // clear the screen
        test_address = test_table[option];  // Now execute that routine
        (*test_address)();              // NOW!!!!
        if (once) break;                // if execute once break
        cursor = get_cursor();          // save current cursor position
        dis_config();                   // update config information
        window(BW1+1,BW2+1,BW3-1,BW4-1);  // set window inner box
        pass_cnt++;                     // increment pass count
//      gotoxy(cursor >> 8,cursor);       // restore the cursor
        cprintf("End of pass #%d\n\r",pass_cnt);
        if ( test_key()) {              // test for ESC key
          k = (get_key() & 0xff);       // read the key
          if (k == 0x1b)  done++;       // flag done if ESC key
        }
        if (pass_cnt > passes) done++;  // check if pass count complete
        } while (!done);                // loop till done
      printer = 0;                      // reset pritner flag
      file_act2 = 0;                    // and file flag
      if (!once) wait_press();          // if not once wait for key press
      } //end of forever loop
    } // end of function
/*****************************************************************
*  Name        display_config()                                 *
*                                                               *
*  Description:                                                 *
*  This routine will display the configuration window.          *
*                                                               *
*  Input Argument:          None                                *
*                                                               *
*  Output Arguments:        None                                *
*                                                               *
*  Local Arguments:         None                                *
*                                                               *
*  Functions Called:        open_window()                       *
*                           gotoxy()                            *
*                           write_position()                    *
*                                                               *
*  Component History:    Initial Entry                          *
*                                                               *
*****************************************************************/
display_config()
    {
    open_window(TW1,TW2,TW3,TW4,25,1, "Diagnostic Configuration");
    write_position(3,3, "Drive Under Test      ");
    if (disk == 1)      cprintf( "A:");
    else                cprintf( "B:");
    gotoxy(3,4);
    cprintf("Last Access Sector      %x:%x:%x",head,track,sector);
    write_position(38,3 ,"Drive Type      ");
    cprintf( drive_type[type]);
    write_position(3,5 ,"Action on Error      ");
    if (error_mode == 0) cprintf( "Stop");
    if (error_mode == 1) cprintf( "Cont.");
    if (error_mode == 2) cprintf( "Loop");
    gotoxy(3,6);
    cprintf( "Pass Count            %d",pass_cnt);
    gotoxy(38,4);
```

```
    cprintf( "Total Read Access      %d",read_cnt);
    gotoxy(38,5);
    cprintf("Total Write Access      %d",write_cnt);
    gotoxy(3,7);
    cprintf( "Required Passes         %d",passes);
    gotoxy(38,6);
    cprintf( "Total Error Detected  %d",error_count);
    } // end of function
/**********************************************************************
*    get_option()                                                     *
*                                                                     *
*    Description:                                                     *
*    This routine will start by displaying the menu of the           *
*    current page selected. After displaying the menu, the           *
*    routine will wait for a function key to be pressed. Once         *
*    the fucntion key is pressed, the case statement will be         *
*    used to dispatch to the proper code.                            *
*                                                                     *
*    return    =   Return to calling routine with selected routine    *
*                                                                     *
*    I         =   Page up                                            *
*    Q         =   Page Down                                          *
*    P         =   Arrow Up                                           *
*    H         =   Arrow down                                         *
*                                                                     *
*    Input Argument:      None                                        *
*                                                                     *
*    Output Arguments:    Selected option number                     *
*                                                                     *
*    Local Arguments:     int  key                                    *
*                                                                     *
*    Functions Called:    get_key()                                   *
*                         arrow_up()                                  *
*                         arrow_down()                                *
*                                                                     *
*    Component History:   Initial Entry                               *
*                                                                     *
**********************************************************************/
get_option()
    {
    int key;
    option = 0;                         // Reset option number
    page_add = page_table[page_number]; // load page address
    (*page_add)();                      // enter proper page menu
    while (key != 0x1c0d) {             // loop until ENTER key
    key = get_key();                    // get the next key from keyboard
// determine the type of key function
    switch (key)                        // get next key
        {
        case CR:                        // if Carriage Return
        return(min+option);
        case PGUP:        // if Page up key
      if (page_number != 0) {
        page_number--;
        page_add = page_table[page_number];
        (*page_add)();
        option = 0;
        }
    break;
        case PGDN:                      // if page down key
      if (page_number != pages - 1) {
        page_number++;
        page_add = page_table[page_number];
        (*page_add)();
        option = 0;
        }
    break;
        case DN_ARR:                    // if arrow down key
    arrow_down();          // move the arrow down
    break;
        case UP_ARR:        // if arrow up key
    arrow_up();                // move the arrow up
    break;
        } // End of Case Statement
```

```
    } // End of While loop
  } // End of Function
/*******************************************************************
*    exit_diag()                                                   *
*                                                                  *
*    Description:                                                  *
*    This routine is used to exit the program and return to        *
*    DOS or the parent process. In either case, the window         *
*    will be reset to the full screen and the entire screen        *
*    will be erased.                                               *
*                                                                  *
*    Input Argument:      None                                     *
*                                                                  *
*    Output Arguments:    None                                     *
*                                                                  *
*    Local Arguments:     None                                     *
*                                                                  *
*    Functions Called:  exit()                                     *
*                                                                  *
*    Component History:   Initial Entry                            *
*                                                                  *
*******************************************************************/
exit_diag()
    {
    window(0,0,80,25);                  // select entire screen as window
    clrscr();                           // erase the screen
    exit(0);                            // exit to DOS
    } // end of function
/*******************************************************************
*    arrow_down()                                                  *
*                                                                  *
*    This function will Position the arrow display on the menu     *
*    down one additional line. Erase the arrow at current location *
*    and then re-write it one option down. If at the last option   *
*    on the menu disregard down arrow                              *
*                                                                  *
*    Input Argument:      None                                     *
*                                                                  *
*    Output Arguments:    None                                     *
*                                                                  *
*    Local Arguments:     None                                     *
*                                                                  *
*    Functions Called:   write_position()                          *
*                                                                  *
*    Component History:   Initial Entry                            *
*                                                                  *
*******************************************************************/
arrow_down()
    {
    // If already at bottom line can't go any further - return
    if (option+min < max) {
      option++;
      write_position(16,option+1, "         ");
      write_position(16,option+2, "------> ");
      } // end of the if statement
    } // end of the function


/*******************************************************************
*    arrow_up()                                                    *
*                                                                  *
*    Description:                                                  *
*    This function will move the arrow display on the menu up one  *
*    additional line. Erase the aoorw at the current line and then *
*    re-write it one option up. If at the top option, disregard the*
*    up arrow.                                                     *
*                                                                  *
*    Input Argument:      None                                     *
*                                                                  *
*    Output Arguments:    None                                     *
*                                                                  *
*    Local Arguments:     None                                     *
*                                                                  *
```

```
*  Functions Called:   write_position()                                *
*                                                                       *
*  Component History:   Initial Entry                                   *
*                                                                       *
***********************************************************************/
arrow_up()
       {
   // if already at top line can't go any further  - return
     if (option+min > min) {
       option--;
       write_position(16,option+3 ,"           ");
       write_position(16,option+2 ,"------> ");
     }  // end of the if statement
   }  // end of the fnction


/***********************************************************************
*  Name   error_menu                                                    *
*                                                                       *
*  Description:                                                         *
*  This routine will allow the user to select the options              *
*  for the error reporting. The routine will set up the                *
*  proper window, then display the proper selections on the            *
*  screen, and then allow th euser to select the option. Pressing       *
*  a '9' will cause the routine to re-establish the previously         *
*  selected window and exit the screen.                                *
*                                                                       *
*                                                                       *
*  Input Argument:     None                                             *
*                                                                       *
*  Output Arguments:   None                                             *
*                                                                       *
*  Local Arguments:    int  i,done                                      *
*                                                                       *
*  Functions Called:   get_cursor()                                     *
*                       open_window()                                   *
*                       write_position()                                *
*                                                                       *
*                                                                       *
*  Component History:   Initial Entry                                   *
*                                                                       *
***********************************************************************/
error_menu()
    {
    int i,done = 0;
    cursor = get_cursor();
    open_window(1,14,78,24,30,1, "Error Menu");
    ch = 0;
/*
    Loop in while statement until a '9' is pressed on the keyboard
*/
    while (ch != 0x39)
     {
     clrscr();
                              // clear the screen
     // display status of stop[ on error
     write_position(20,2, "1. Stop on Error     ");
     if (error_mode == 0)
        cprintf( "[Y]");
     else  cprintf( "[N]");
     // display status of continue on error
     write_position(20,3 ,"2. Continue on Error ");
     if (error_mode == 1)
        cprintf( "[Y]");
     else  cprintf( "[N]");
     // display status of loop on error
     write_position(20,4 ,"3. loop on Error     ");
     if (error_mode  == 2)
        cprintf( "[Y]");
     else  cprintf( "[N]");
     // display status of bell on error
     write_position(20,5 ,"4. Bell on Error     ");
     if (error_bell)
        cprintf( "[Y]");
     else  cprintf( "[N]");
```

```
    write_position(20,6 ,"9. Return to Main Menu");
    ch = (get_key() & 0xff);
    switch(ch)
      {
      case '1': error_mode = 0;
        break;
      case '2': error_mode = 1;
        break;
      case '3': error_mode = 2;
        break;
      case '4': error_bell = !error_bell;
      case '9': break;
      default: beep();                   //sound warning
        break;
      }
    } // end of while statement
    window(BW1+1,BW2+1,BW3-1,BW4-1);    // set window inner box
    once = 1;                           // we only do this once
    } // end of function
/*****************************************************************
 *    Name  page1                                                *
 *                                                               *
 *    Description:                                               *
 *    This is the Main Menu of the test program. Upon enter the  *
 *    program from the command line, this routine will be called.*
 *                                                               *
 *    Input Argument:     None                                   *
 *                                                               *
 *    Output Arguments:   None                                   *
 *                                                               *
 *    Local Arguments:    None                                   *
 *                                                               *
 *    Functions Called:   open_window()                          *
 *                        write_position()                       *
 *                        botton_line()                          *
 *                                                               *
 *    Component History:  Initial Entry                          *
 *                                                               *
 *****************************************************************/

#define Menu1_Min 0
#define Menu1_Max 3

page1()
    {
    pages = PAGES;
    open_window(BW1,BW2,BW3,BW4,28,1, "Main Diagnostic Menu");
    write_position(26,2, "AutoMatic Test Mode");
    write_position(26,3, "Diagnostic Configuration");
    write_position(26,4, "Individual Test");
    write_position(26,5, "Exit to DOS");
    write_position(16,2, "-------> ");
    min = Menu1_Min;
    max = Menu1_Max;
    bottom_line1();
    } // End of Function
/*****************************************************************
 *    Name  page2                                                *
 *                                                               *
 *    Description:                                               *
 *    This function will display the first sub-menu. After displaying *
 *    the menu, the minimum and maximum menu values will be set-up.   *
 *                                                               *
 *    Input Argument:     None                                   *
 *                                                               *
 *    Output Arguments:   None                                   *
 *                                                               *
 *    Local Arguments:    None                                   *
 *                                                               *
 *    Functions Called:   open_window()                          *
 *                        write_position()                       *
 *                        bottom_line()                          *
 *                                                               *
```

```
*   Component History: Initial Entry                                          *
*                                                                             *
******************************************************************************/
#define Menu2_Min  Menu1_Max + 1
#define Menu2_Max  Menu2_Min + 4

page2()
    {
    open_window(BW1,BW2,BW3,BW4,28,1, "Diagnostic Configuration");
    write_position(26,2, "Set Pass Count");
    write_position(26,3, "Hardware Configuration");
    write_position(26,4, "Logging");
    write_position(26,5, "Action on Error");
    write_position(26,6, "Return to Main Menu");
    write_position(16,2, "-------> ");
    min = Menu2_Min;
    max = Menu2_Max;
    bottom_line1();
    } // End of Function

/*****************************************************************************
*   Name    page3                                                           *
*                                                                           *
*   Description:                                                            *
*   This function will display the second sub-menu. After displaying        *
*   the menu, the minimum and maximum menu values will be set-up.           *
*                                                                           *
*                                                                           *
*   Input Argument:     None                                                *
*                                                                           *
*   Output Arguments:   None                                                *
*                                                                           *
*   Local Arguments:    None                                                *
*                                                                           *
*   Functions Called:   open_window()                                       *
*                        write_position()                                   *
*                        bottom_line()                                      *
*                                                                           *
*   Component History: Initial Entry                                        *
*                                                                           *
******************************************************************************/
#define Menu3_Min  Menu2_Max + 1
#define Menu3_Max  Menu3_Min + 5

page3()
    {
    open_window(1,12,79,24,28,1, " Individual Test Menu");
    write_position(26,2, "Forward/Backward Seek");
    write_position(26,3, "Hourglass Seek");
    write_position(26,4, "Format Track");
    write_position(26,5, "Read Sector");
    write_position(26,6, "Write Sector");
    write_position(26,7, "Return to Main Menu");
    write_position(16,2, "-------> ");
    min = Menu3_Min;
    max = Menu3_Max;
    bottom_line1();
    } // End of Function

/*****************************************************************************
*   Name    page4                                                           *
*                                                                           *
*   Description:                                                            *
*   This function will display the third sub-menu. After displaying         *
*   the menu, the minimum and maximum menu values will be set-up.           *
*                                                                           *
*                                                                           *
*   Input Argument:     None                                                *
*                                                                           *
*   Output Arguments:   None                                                *
*                                                                           *
*   Local Arguments:    None                                                *
*                                                                           *
*   Functions Called:   open_window()                                       *
*                        write_position()                                   *
```

```
*                      bottom_line()                              *
*                                                                 *
*  Component History: Initial Entry                               *
*                                                                 *
******************************************************************/
#define Menu4_Min  Menu3_Max + 1
#define Menu4_Max  Menu4_Min + 4

page4()
    {
    open_window(1,12,79,24,28,1, "Logging Menu");
    write_position(28,2, "Set Log ");
    write_position(28,3, "Display Log File");
    write_position(28,4, "Set Error Log");
    write_position(28,5, "Display Error Log");
    write_position(28,6, "Exit to DOS");
    write_position(16,2, "------> ");
    min = Menu4_Min;
    max = Menu4_Max;
    bottom_line1();
    } // End of function

/****************************************************************
*  Name   bottom_line1()                                        *
*                                                               *
*  Description:                                                 *
*  This routine will display the message at the bottom of the   *
*  screen. If on the first pare, it is assumed that the change  *
*  page message should appear.                                  *
*                                                               *
*  Input Argument:      None                                    *
*                                                               *
*  Output Arguments:    None                                    *
*                                                               *
*  Local Arguments:     None                                    *
*                                                               *
*  Functions Called:    write_position()                        *
*                                                               *
*  Component History:   Initial Entry                           *
*                                                               *
****************************************************************/
bottom_line1()
    {
    write_position(15,10,
(char far *) "Use up/down arrow to select your option");
    if (page_number)
 write_position(15,11,
    "Change Page selection, use PgDn/PgUp");
    } // End of Function

/****************************************************************
*  Name   create_page_table                                     *
*                                                               *
*  Description:                                                 *
*  This routine set up the address table. The address of each   *
*  routine that displays a menu will be entered here. If a page *
*  is added, you must add to the end of the table, You cannot   *
*  leave an element of the table entry. All enteries must be made. *
*  To delete a page you must delete from the end of the table.  *
*  Note: The main menu routine, page1, must always be placed in the *
*  first element of the table. page1 routine set the value of pages. *
*                                                               *
*  Input Argument:      None                                    *
*                                                               *
*  Output Arguments:    None                                    *
*                                                               *
*  Local Arguments:     None                                    *
*                                                               *
*  Functions Called:    None                                    *
*                                                               *
*  Component History:   Initial Entry                           *
*                                                               *
****************************************************************/
create_page_table()
```

```
    {
    page_table[0] = page1;                  // set page 1
    page_table[1] = page2;                  // page 2
    page_table[2] = page3;                  // page 3
    page_table[3] = page4;                  // and page 4
    // if you have more pages include them here to build the table
    } // End of Function
/***********************************************************************
 * Name   main_menu()                                                  *
 *                                                                     *
 * Description:                                                        *
 * This routine will sets up for the first page.                      *
 *                                                                     *
 *                                                                     *
 * Input Argument:      None                                          *
 *                                                                     *
 * Output Arguments:    None                                          *
 *                                                                     *
 * Local Arguments:     None                                          *
 *                                                                     *
 * Functions Called:    None                                          *
 *                                                                     *
 * Component History: Initial Entry                                   *
 *                                                                     *
 ***********************************************************************/
void main_menu()
    {
    page_number = 0;                        // select proper page
    option = 0;                             // set option to zero
    once = 1;
    } // End of function


/***********************************************************************
 * Name   auto_mode_suite                                              *
 *                                                                     *
 * Description:                                                        *
 * This routine is used to select a default test suite. Each          *
 * routine that is to be tested in the auto suite must be called      *
 * here. The tester must insert the test in the sequence that        *
 * they are to be tested.                                             *
 *                                                                     *
 * Input Argument:      None                                          *
 *                                                                     *
 * Output Arguments:    None                                          *
 *                                                                     *
 * Local Arguments:     None                                          *
 *                                                                     *
 * Functions Called:    Test routines                                 *
 *                                                                     *
 * Component History:   Initial Entry                                 *
 *                                                                     *
 ***********************************************************************/
auto_mode_suite()
    {
    auto_mode = 1;          // set auto mode
    clrscr();                               // clear the screen
    cprintf( "Automatic Test Sequence\n\r");
    seek_test1();
    seek_test2();
    read_test();
    write_test();
    auto_mode = 0;                          // reset auto mode
    } // End of function
/***********************************************************************
 *  Name:   Dis_config                                                 *
 *                                                                     *
 *  Description:                                                       *
 *  This routine will update the counters during test mode            *
 *                                                                     *
 *  Input Argument:     None                                          *
 *                                                                     *
 *  Output Arguments:   None                                          *
 *                                                                     *
 *  Local Arguments:    None                                          *
```

```
    *                                                                      *
    *  Functions Called:    window()                                       *
    *                        gotoxy()                                       *
    *                                                                       *
    *  Component History:    Initial Entry                                  *
    *                                                                       *
    ***********************************************************************/
    dis_config()
       {
       window(TW1+1,TW2+1,TW3-1,TW4-1);      // Set up the window
       gotoxy(3,4);
       cprintf( "Last Access Sector      %x:%x:%x",head,track,sector);
       gotoxy(38,3);
       cprintf( "Drive Type             ");
       cprintf("%s",drive_type[type]);
       gotoxy(3,6);
       cprintf( "Pass Count             %d",pass_cnt);
       gotoxy(38,6);
       cprintf("Total Error Detected  %d",error_count);
       } // end of function
    /***************************************************************************
    *    Name:    configuration()                                           *
    *                                                                       *
    *    Description:                                                       *
    *    This routine will allow the user to setup the system              *
    *    configuration. This includes pass count,  logging, and           *
    *    hardware configuration.                                            *
    *                                                                       *
    *    Input Argument:      None                                          *
    *                                                                       *
    *    Output Arguments:    None                                          *
    *                                                                       *
    *    Local Arguments:     None                                          *
    *                                                                       *
    *    Functions Called:    None                                          *
    *                                                                       *
    *    Component History:   Initial Entry                                 *
    *                                                                       *
    ***********************************************************************/
    void  configuration()
       {
       page_number = 1;                    // select proper page
       option = 0;                         // set option to zero
       once = 1;
       } // End of Function




    /***************************************************************************
    *    Name:  test_mode()                                                 *
    *                                                                       *
    *    Description:                                                       *
    *    This routine will allow the user to setup the system              *
    *    configuration. This includes pass count,  logging, and           *
    *    hardware configuration.                                            *
    *                                                                       *
    *    Input Argument:      None                                          *
    *                                                                       *
    *    Output Arguments:    None                                          *
    *                                                                       *
    *    Local Arguments:     None                                          *
    *                                                                       *
    *    Functions Called:    None                                          *
    *                                                                       *
    *    Component History:   Initial Entry                                 *
    *                                                                       *
    ***********************************************************************/
    void  test_mode()
       {
       page_number = 2;                    // set for individual test mode
       option = 0;                         // set options to zero
       once = 1;
       } // End of Function
```

```
/*****************************************************************
*    Name    pass_cnt()                                         *
*                                                               *
*   Description:                                                *
*   This routine will allow the user to enter the number of passes *
*   that they wish to execute. If a pass count of zero is entered, *
*   then the test will run indefinately.                        *
*                                                               *
*   Input Argument:                                             *
*                                                               *
*   Output Arguments:                                           *
*                                                               *
*   Local Arguments:                                            *
*                                                               *
*   Functions Called:       write_position()                   *
*                           display_config()                    *
*                                                               *
*   Component History:      Initial Entry                       *
*                                                               *
*****************************************************************/
set_pass_cnt()
    {
    clrscr();                          // clear the screen
    write_position(3,2, "Enter pass count: ");
    scanf("%d",&passes);               // Enter the pass count
    display_config();                  // update the display
    once = 1;                          // This is a once only routine
    } // End of Function

/*****************************************************************
*    Name    hardware_conf()                                    *
*                                                               *
*   Description:                                                *
*   This routine must be created by the diagnostic designed.    *
*   it is placed here to allow the reader to understand that    *
*   in some cases the tester must specify certain hardware      *
*   confiration, such as base I/O address, IRQ, and etc.        *
*                                                               *
*   Input Argument:        None                                 *
*                                                               *
*   Output Arguments:      None                                 *
*                                                               *
*   Local Arguments:       None                                 *
*                                                               *
*   Functions Called:      write_position()                     *
*                          wait_press()                         *
*                                                               *
*   Component History:     Initial Entry                        *
*                                                               *
*****************************************************************/
hardware_conf()
    {
    clrscr();                          // clear the screen
/*
    This is where the user is allowed to set up the hardware
    configuration. Code must be placed in here to allow for
    proper setup. Attempts should be made to select configuration
    from menus in the same fashion as selecting the test menus.
*/
    write_position(3,2, "Hardware Configuration Setup ");
    wait_press();                      // wait for keyboard input
    once = 1;                          // we only run it once
    } // End of function
/*****************************************************************
*    Name    logging_menu                                       *
*                                                               *
*   Description:                                                *
*   This routine set up to enter the logging menu.              *
*                                                               *
*   Input Argument:        None                                 *
*                                                               *
*   Output Arguments:      None                                 *
*                                                               *
```

```
 *   Local Arguments:     None                                            *
 *                                                                        *
 *   Functions Called:    None                                            *
 *                                                                        *
 *   Component History:   Initial Entry                                   *
 *                                                                        *
 ************************************************************************/
void  logging_menu()
   {
   page_number = 3;              // set for individual test mode
   option = 0;                   // set options to zero
   once = 1;                     // run it only once
   } // End of Function


/*************************************************************************
 *   Name    set_log_window
 *
 *   Description:
 *   This routine is used to set up a different window size.
 */
set_log_window()
   {
   window(25,15,60,23);


   } // end of function
/*************************************************************************
 *   Name    create_test_table                                           *
 *                                                                        *
 *   Description:                                                         *
 *   This routine will create the test table. the routines can           *
 *   be arranged in any manner that the tester wishes. You must          *
 *   coordinate the selected items from the menu to the proper           *
 *   entry into this table.                                              *
 *                                                                        *
 *   Input Argument:      None                                           *
 *                                                                        *
 *   Output Arguments:    None                                           *
 *                                                                        *
 *   Local Arguments:     None                                           *
 *                                                                        *
 *   Functions Called:    None                                           *
 *                                                                        *
 *   Component History:   Initial Entry                                  *
 *                                                                        *
 ************************************************************************/
create_test_table()
    {
    test_table[0]  = auto_mode_suite;
    test_table[1]  = configuration;
    test_table[2]  = test_mode;
    test_table[3]  = exit_diag;
    test_table[4]  = set_pass_cnt;
    test_table[5]  = hardware_conf;
    test_table[6]  = logging_menu;
    test_table[7]  = error_menu;
    test_table[8]  = main_menu;
    test_table[9]  = seek_test1;
    test_table[10] = seek_test2;
    test_table[11] = format_test;
    test_table[12] = read_test;
    test_table[13] = write_test;
    test_table[14] = main_menu;
    test_table[15] = set_log;
    test_table[16] = display_log_file;
    test_table[17] = set_error_log;
    test_table[18] = display_error_log;
    test_table[19] = configuration;
    } // End of function

//    END of File    //
```

Sade.c Source Code

```
/****************************************************************************
*    Name SADE.C                                                            *
*                                                                           *
*       This is the Stand Alone Diagnostic Executive                        *
*                                                                           *
****************************************************************************/

#define   MAX_TEST   20
#include   <dos.h>
#include   <stdio.h>
#include   <conio.h>
#include   <string.h>
#include   "..\pick\data.h"
#include   "proto.inc"


void   main(void);
void   execute_test(void);
void   select_test(void);

FILE     *handle;

union  REGS  ioregs;


/*
     Key code definitions
*/
#define F1         0x3b00
#define F2         0x3c00
#define F3         0x3d00
#define F4         0x3e00
#define F5         0x3f00
#define F6         0x4000
#define L_ARR      0x4d00
#define R_ARR      0x4b00
#define DN_ARR     0x5000
#define UP_ARR     0x4800
#define CR         0x1c0d
#define DEL        0xe08
#define ESC        0x1b


#define SW1    22
#define SW2     8
```

```
#define SW3   58
#define SW4   15

#define  WIDTH   80

extern char buffer[];
extern int done = 0,count1,forgr,backgr;

int  window1[30*8];
int  window2[40*8];
int  window3[80*25];


char selected_file[20];
int  error_flag;
int  pass_count;
char file_names[20][15];

//    Control window options
char  opt[6][12] = {"",
                 "Run      ",
                 "Select   ",
                 "Options  ",
                 "Log      ",
                 "Config   " };

int   tx[6] = {2,15,30,45,60 };
/************************************************************************
 *  Name   main                                                        *
 *                                                                     *
 *  Description:                                                       *
 *  This is the main entry point of the diagnsotic executive. The     *
 *  routine allows the user to select options from the main menu.     *
 *                                                                     *
 *                                                                     *
 *Input Arguments    None                                             *
 *                                                                     *
 *Output Arguments   None                                             *
 *                                                                     *
 *Local Arguments    None                                             *
 *                                                                     *
 *Functions called   clrscr  test_window                              *
 *                   control_window        get_key                    *
 *                   write_position write_reverse                     *
 *                   execute_test    select_test                      *
 *                   opt_menu        log_menu                         *
 *                   config_menu                                      *
 ************************************************************************/
void main()
    {
    clrscr();                           // clear the screen
    test_window();                      // create the test window
    textattr(0x17);                     // set the attribute
    control_window();                   // Initialize the screen
/*
    The following while loop will continue until the
    variable done become true.
*/
    while (!done) {
    key = get_key();                    // wait for a key stroke
    switch(key)  {                      // Action on the key stroke
    case L_ARR:                         // Left ARROW
        count++;
        switch (count)  {
  case 6:
    count = 1;
    write_position(60,2,opt[5]);
  case 1:
    write_reverse(2,2, opt[1]);
    break;
  case 2:          // case 2,3,4 and 5 all the same
  case 3:
  case 4:
  case 5:
    write_position(tx[count-2],2, opt[count-1]);
```

```
        write_reverse(tx[count-1],2, opt[count]);
        break;
  }  /* end of inner case statement */
break;
        case R_ARR:                    // RIGHT ARROW
    count--;
    if (count == 0)
    count = 5;
    switch (count)  {
    case 1:          // case 1,2,3 and 4 are the same
    case 2:
    case 3:
    case 4:
      write_position(tx[count],2, opt[count+1]);
      write_reverse(tx[count-1],2, opt[count]);
      break;
case 5:
      write_position(2,2, opt[1]);
    · write_reverse(60,2, opt[5]);
      break;
  }  /* end of inner case statement */
break;

        case 0x11b:
    done = 1;
    break;
        case CR:                       // Carriage Return
switch(count)  {
    case 1:
      execute_test();                // execute the suite
      break;
    case 2:
      select_test();                 // select test to execute
      break;
    case 3:
      opt_menu();                    // option menu
      break;
    case 4:
      log_menu();                    // log menu
      break;
    case 5:
      config_menu();
      break;
  }  /* end of inner switch statement */
        control_window();
        break;
        } /* end of outter case statenment  */
    } /* end of while statement */
    window(1,1,WIDTH,5);                 // full window
    clrscr();                            // clear the screen
    }


/****************************************************************************
 *    Name:    execute_test()                                               *
 *                                                                          *
 *    Description:                                                          *
 *                                                                          *
 *    This routine will cause the execution of the test suite               *
 *                                                                          *
 *                                                                          *
 *    Input Arguments    None                                               *
 *                                                                          *
 *    Output Arguments   None                                               *
 *                                                                          *
 *    Local Arguments    i and j                                            *
 *                                                                          *
 *    Functions called   load_exe test_window                              *
 ****************************************************************************/
void execute_test()
    {
    int i,j;
    window(0,5,78,20);                   // Setup work window
    // loop for all possible selection
    for (i=0;i<pnt;i++) {
```

```
      if (selected_file[i] == 1)
  j =0;
//         j = load_exe( file_names[i]);
    } // end of for loop
  test_window();                          // create the test window
  }
/*****************************************************************
 *   Name:    select_test()                                      *
 *                                                               *
 *   Desciption:                                                 *
 *   This routine will allow the user to select/ de-select a test *
 *   from the list of programs that are defined in the file prog.lst *
 *                                                               *
 *                                                               *
 *Input Arguments     None                                       *
 *                                                               *
 *Output Arguments    None                                       *
 *                                                               *
 *Local Arguments     int pnt,flag,i,j,ch                        *
 *                                                               *
 *Functions called    save_window()                             *
 *                          border()                             *
 *                          write_reverse()                      *
 *                          write_position()                     *
 *                          restore_window()                     *
 *                                                               *
 *****************************************************************/
#define  ST1  10
#define  ST2 3
#define  ST3  30
#define  ST4 4
void  select_test()
  {
  int pnt;
  int flag;
  int i,j,ch;
  //
  //   Clear all the selected file flags
  //
  for (i=0;i<20;i++)  selected_file[i] = 0;
  handle = fopen("prog.lst","r");    // open file to read
  if (handle == -1) {
      cprintf ( "Unable to open 'prog.lst'");
      get_key();
      return(-1);
      }
  //
  // clean the file_names array
  //
  pnt = 0;               // default to no entries
  for (i=0; i<20;i++) {                    // a maximum of 20 entries
    fgets(file_names[i],24,handle);        // read each file name
    pnt++;                                 // keep count of entries
    } // end of for loop
  fclose(handle);                          // close the file
// At this time all 20 file names have been loaded
// Now must get the number of EXEs and display there names
  pnt = 0;
  for(i=0;i<20;i++)
     {
     if (file_names[i][0] == 0) break;
     pnt++;
     }
  window(ST1,ST2,ST3,ST4+pnt+1);
  save_window(ST1,ST2,ST3,ST4+pnt+1, window1);
  border(ST1,ST2,ST3,ST4+pnt+1);
  window(ST1+1,ST2+1,ST3-1,ST4+pnt);
  for (i=0;i<pnt;i++)
     {
     if (selected_file[i] != 0) write_position(2,1+i,  " X ");
     else                       write_position(2,1+i,  "   ");
     cprintf( file_names[i]);
     } // end of display of files
  getch();
/*
```

```
    Now the window is open, the menu is displayed, we must allow
    the tester to move the selected option up and down
*/
  i = 0;
  j = pnt;
  ch = 0;
  while (ch != 0x11b)
    {
    if (selected_file[i] != 0) write_position(2,1+i,  " X ");
     else                       write_position(2,1+i,  "   ");

    write_reverse(5,1+i,  file_names[i]);
    write_position(5,1+j, file_names[j]);
    ch = get_key();
    switch (ch)
      {
      case DN_ARR:
    j = i;
    i++;
    if (i == pnt)  i = 0;
    break;
      case UP_ARR:
    j = i;
    i--;
    if (i<0) i = pnt - 1;
    break;
      case CR:
    selected_file[i] = !(selected_file[i]);
    break;
      } // end of the switch
    } // end of while loop
  restore_window( ST1,ST2,ST3,ST4,window1);
  }

/***********************************************************************
*    opt_menu()                                                        *
*                                                                      *
*    Description                                                       *
*    This function save the option window area, then opens the window. *
*    The option for this window are displayed and the user is able to  *
*    use the up and down arrows to select the desired option.          *
*                                                                      *
*                                                                      *
*Input Arguments       None                                           *
*                                                                      *
*Output Arguments      None                                           *
*                                                                      *
*Local Arguments       key   count                                    *
*                                                                      *
*Functions called      save_window()                                  *
*                         border()                                     *
*                              write_reverse()                         *
*                              write_position()                        *
*                              down_option()                           *
*                              up_option()                             *
*                              error_window()                          *
*                              restore_window()                        *
*                              get_pass_count()                        *
*                              gotoxy()                                 *
*                                                                      *
***********************************************************************/
char opt_msg[5][30] = {"Action on Error      ",
                "Test Pass Count     " };
#define OM1      30
#define OM2    4
#define OM3    60
#define OM4    8
opt_menu()
  {
  int key,count;
  count = 0;
  window(OM1,OM2,OM3,OM4);                    // open the window
  save_window(OM1,OM2,OM3,OM4, window1);// save it
  border(OM1,OM2,OM3,OM4);                    // make the border
  write_position(12,1,  "Mode");             // title of window
```

```
      window(OM1+1,OM2+1,OM3-1,OM4-1);      // reduce the window
      write_reverse (2,1,  opt_msg[0]);     // display the options
      write_position(2,2,  opt_msg[1]);
      cprintf("%d",pass_count);
      while (key != 0x11b) {                 // loop until ESC key
         key =get_key();                     // get the key
         switch (key) {
   case DN_ARR:                              // if down arrow
      count++;
      if (count > 1) count = 0;      // adjust for wrap
      down_option(count,2,opt_msg);;// display active option
      break;
   case UP_ARR:                              // if up arrow
      count--;
      if (count < 0) count = 1;      // adjust for wrap
      up_option(count,2,opt_msg);    // display active option
      break;
   case CR:
      window(SW1,SW2,SW3,SW4);       // set up new window
      save_window(SW1,SW2,SW3,SW4, window2);
      border(SW1,SW2,SW3,SW4);       // border it
      switch (count) {
       case 0:
         write_position(12,1,  "Error Menu");
         window(SW1+1,SW2+1,SW3-1,SW4-1);
         error_menu();
         window(SW1,SW2,SW3,SW4);
         restore_window(SW1,SW2,SW3,SW4, window2);
         break;
       case 1:
         write_position(12,1,  "Pass Count");
         window(SW1+1,SW2+1,SW3-1,SW4-1);
         get_pass_count();
         window(SW1,SW2,SW3,SW4);
         restore_window(SW1,SW2,SW3,SW4, window2);
         break;
      } // end of inner switch
   } // End of switch statement
         window(OM1+1,OM2+1,OM3-1,OM4-1);
         gotoxy(22,2);
         cprintf("%d",pass_count);
         } // end of while statement
   restore_window(OM1,OM2,OM3,OM4, window1);
   textattr(0x17);
   } // end of function

char conf_msg[4][30] = {"Save Configuration ",
                "Load Configuration ",
                "Change Directory   ",
                "Directory " };
#define  CM1  50
#define  CM2   4
#define  CM3  79
#define  CM4  10
/***************************************************************
*  Name   config_menu                                         *
*                                                             *
*  Description:                                               *
*  This function provides a configuration menu and allows the user *
*  to select options that are within the configuration menu. *
*                                                             *
*Input Arguments     None                                     *
*                                                             *
*Output Arguments    None                                     *
*                                                             *
*Local Arguments     key   count                              *
*                                                             *
*Functions called    save_window border                      *
*                     write_position write_reverse            *
*                     down_option     up_option               *
*                     save_configuration load_configuration   *
*                     restore_window                          *
***************************************************************/
config_menu()
   {
```

```
       int key,count;
       count = 0;
       window(CM1,CM2,CM3,CM4);
       save_window(CM1,CM2,CM3,CM4, window1);
       border(CM1,CM2,CM3-1,CM4);
       write_position(10,1,  "Configuration");
       window(CM1+1,CM2+1,CM3-1,CM4-1);
       write_reverse (2,1,   conf_msg[0]);
       write_position(2,2,   conf_msg[1]);
       write_position(2,3,   conf_msg[2]);
       write_position(2,4,   conf_msg[3]);
       while (key != 0x11b) {
          key =get_key();                    // get the next key entry
          switch (key) {
 case DN_ARR:                    // if down arrow
       count++;
       if (count > 3) count = 0;       // wrap if needed
       down_option(count,4,conf_msg); // uppdate menu
       break;
 case UP_ARR:                    // if up arrow
       count--;
       if (count < 0) count = 3;
       up_option(count,4,conf_msg);
       break;
 case CR:
       switch (count) {
          case 0:
            save_configuration();
            break;
          case 1:
            load_configuration();
            break;
          case 2:
            break;
          } // end of inner switch
 } // End of switch statement
          window(CM1+1,CM2+1,CM3-1,CM4-1);
          } // end of while statement
       restore_window(CM1,CM2,CM3,CM4, window1);
       textattr(0x17);
       } // end of function


char log_msg[3][30] = {"Set logging_Output",
                  "Set Error output",
                  "View File" };
/****************************************************************
 *    Name     log_menu()                                       *
 *                                                              *
 *    This option will allow the user to set the logging output for  *
 *    either the general output or eror logging. Output can be to a  *
 *    file, th eprinter, or to the screen. This option also lets the  *
 *    user view the log files. The log file must be opened to view it.  *
 *                                                              *
 *Input Arguments    None                                       *
 *                                                              *
 *Output Arguments   None                                       *
 *                                                              *
 *Local Arguments    key   count                                *
 *                                                              *
 *Functions called   save_window  border                        *
 *                    write_position write_recverse              *
 *                    down_option      up_option                 *
 *                    restore_window                             *
 ****************************************************************/
#define LM1   45
#define LM2    4
#define LM3   70
#define LM4    8
 log_menu()
   {
   int key,count;
   count = 0;
   window(LM1,LM2,LM3,LM4);
```

```
    save_window(LM1,LM2,LM3,LM4, window1);
    border(LM1,LM2,LM3-1,LM4);
    write_position(5,1,  "Logging Window");
    window(LM1+1,LM2+1,LM3-1,LM4-1);
    write_reverse(2,1,  "Set Logging Output");
    write_position(2,2,  "Set Error Output");
    write_position(2,3,  "View File");
    while (key != 0x11b) {
        key =get_key();
        switch (key) {
case DN_ARR:
        count++;
        if (count > 2) count = 0;
        down_option(count,3,log_msg);
        break;
case UP_ARR:
        count--;
        if (count < 0) count = 3;
        up_option(count,3,log_msg);
        break;
case CR:
        log_options(count);
} // End of switch statement
        window(LM1+1,LM2+1,LM3-1,LM4-1);
        } // end of while statement
    restore_window(LM1,LM2,LM3,LM4, window1);
    textattr(0x17);
    } // end of option
/*********************************************************************
 *  Name    log_options                                              *
 *                                                                   *
 *  This routine is used here to reduce the amount of code.          *
 *  The program simply set up the log menu window, save the current  *
 *  contents of the window, performs the proper operation, and the   *
 *  restores the original contents of the window and returns.        *
 *                                                                   *
 *  A single argument is passed to this routine. The value must be   *
 *  0, 1, 2. This argument represent the operation to perform.       *
 *                                                                   *
 *                                                                   *
 *Input Arguments      OPT                                           *
 *                                                                   *
 *Output Arguments     None                                          *
 *                                                                   *
 *Local Arguments      None                                          *
 *                                                                   *
 *Functions called     save_window  border                          *
 *                      set_log      set_error_log                   *
 *                      restore_window show_ascii_file               *
 *********************************************************************/

#define  LO1   20
#define  LO2    7
#define  LO3   60
#define  LO4   16
log_options(int opt)
    {
    switch (opt) {
      case 0:  window(LO1,LO2,LO3,LO4);
        save_window(LO1,LO2,LO3,LO4, window2);
        border(LO1,LO2,LO3,LO4);
        window(LO1+1,LO2+1,LO3-1,LO4-1);
        set_log();
        window(LO1,LO2,LO3,LO4);
        restore_window(LO1,LO2,LO3,LO4, window2);
        break;
      case 1:  window(LO1,LO2,LO3,LO4);
        save_window(LO1,LO2,LO3,LO4, window2);
        border(LO1,LO2,LO3,LO4);
        window(LO1+1,LO2+1,LO3-1,LO4-1);
        set_error_log();
        window(LO1,LO2,LO3,LO4);
        restore_window(LO1,LO2,LO3,LO4, window2);
        break;
      case 2:  show_ascii_file();
```

```
      break;
    } // end of switch
  } // end of function
/*****************************************************************************
 *   Name:    show_ascii_file()                                              *
 *                                                                           *
 *   Description:                                                            *
 *                                                                           *
 *   This routine will save the current small screen, open a second         *
 *   screen.                                                                 *
 *                                                                           *
 *Input Arguments    None                                                    *
 *                                                                           *
 *Output Arguments   None                                                    *
 *                                                                           *
 *Local Arguments    buffer[x]     file[x]    str1[x]                        *
 *                             exit        done       line                   *
 *                             error       i                                 *
 *                                                                           *
 *Functions called save_window border                                       *
 *                  write_position    wait_press                             *
 *                  restore_window                                           *
 *****************************************************************************/
show_ascii_file()
    {
    char buffer[257];
    char file[20],str1[90];
    int exit = 0,done,line,error,i;
    window(25,7,64,11);
    save_window((int far *) window2);
    clrscr();
    border(25,7,64-1,11);
    window(26,8,63,10);
    write_position(1,1,  "Enter the file name: ");
    gets(file);
    handle = fopen(  file,"r");
    if (handle == -1) {
      cprintf(  "\n\rUnable to open file");
      wait_press();
      exit = 1;
      }
    if (!exit) {
      window(0,3,WIDTH,24);
      save_window((int far *) window3);
      border(0,3,WIDTH-1,24);
      window(1,4,WIDTH-1,23);
      str1[0] = 'a';
      line = 0;
      while (str1[0] != 0) {
        fgets(str1,80,handle);
        if (str1[0] == 0)  break;              // end of file
        cprintf(  str1);
        line++;
        if (line > 10)  {
    wait_press();
  line = 0;  }
      }
      fclose(handle);
      if (error == -1)  cprintf(  "--Error in Reading File");
      else       cprintf(  "--End of file");
      wait_press();
      window(0,3,WIDTH,25);
      restore_window((int far *) window3);
      }
    window(25,7,64,11);
    restore_window((int far *) window2);
}


#define  TW1   1
#define  TW2   4
#define  TW3   80
#define  TW4   24
```

```
/****************************************************************
*  Name   test_window                                          *
*                                                              *
*  Description:                                                *
*  This function opens the test window for use                 *
*                                                              *
*  Input Arguments: None                                       *
*                                                              *
*  Output Arguments      None                                  *
*                                                              *
*  Local Arguments       None                                  *
*                                                              *
*  Functions called borderwrite_position                       *
****************************************************************/
test_window()
   {
   textattr(0x47);
   window(TW1,TW2,TW3,TW4);
   border(TW1,TW2,TW3-1,TW4);
   write_position(30,1,  "Test Selection Window");
   textattr(0x17);
   }

#define CW1  1
#define CW2  1
#define CW3  WIDTH
#define CW4  3
/****************************************************************
*  Name   control_window                                       *
*                                                              *
*  Description:                                                *
*  This routine opens the control window for output.           *
*                                                              *
*Input Arguments    None                                       *
*                                                              *
*Output Arguments   None                                       *
*                                                              *
*Local Arguments    None                                       *
*                                                              *
*Functions called  write_position       write_reverse          *
*                  border                                       *
****************************************************************/
control_window()
   {
   count = 1;
   window(CW1,CW2,CW3,CW4);
   border(CW1,CW2,CW3-1,CW4);
   write_position(30,1,  "Control Window");
   write_reverse(2,2,   opt[1]);
   write_position(15,2,  opt[2]);
   write_position(30,2,  opt[3]);
   write_position(45,2,  opt[4]);
   write_position(60,2,  opt[5]);
   }

/****************************************************************
*     Name   error_menu                                        *
*                                                              *
*  This routine will allow the user to select the options      *
*  for the error reporting. The routine will set up the        *
*  proper window, then display the proper selections on the    *
*  screen, and then allow th euser to select the option. Pressing *
*  a '9' will cause the routine to re-establish the previously *
* selected window and exit the screen.                         *
*                                                              *
*                                                              *
*Input Arguments    None                                       *
*                                                              *
*Output Arguments   None                                       *
*                                                              *
*Local Arguments    i  done                                    *
*                                                              *
*Functions called  write_position beep                         *
****************************************************************/
 error_menu()
```

```
    {
    int i,done = 0;
    char ch;
    ch = 0;
/*
    Loop in while statement until a '9' is pressed on the keyboard
*/
    while (ch != 0x39)
      {
      clrscr();                              // clear the screen
      // display status of stop[ on error
      write_position(5,2,  "1. Stop on Error       ");
      if (error_mode == 0)
        cprintf(  "[Y]");
      else cprintf(  "[N]");
      // display status of continue on error
      write_position(5,3,  "2. Continue on Error ");
      if (error_mode == 1)
        cprintf(  "[Y]");
      else cprintf(  "[N]");
      // display status of loop on error
      write_position(5,4,  "3. loop on Error       ");
      if (error_mode  == 2)
        cprintf(  "[Y]");
      else  cprintf(  "[N]");
      // display status of bell on error
      write_position(5,5,  "4. Bell on Error       ");
      if (error_bell)
        cprintf(  "[Y]");
      else  cprintf(  "[N]");
      write_position(5,6,  "9. Return to Main Menu");
      ch = (get_key() & 0xff);
      switch(ch)
        {
        case '1': error_mode = 0;
          break;
        case '2': error_mode = 1;
          break;
        case '3': error_mode = 2;
          break;
        case '4': error_bell = !error_bell;
        case '9': break;
        default:  beep();                    //sound warning
          break;
        }
      } // end of while statement
}
/********************************************************************
*   Name    get_pass_count                                         *
*                                                                  *
*   Description:                                                   *
*   This routine allows the user to enter the pass count           *
*                                                                  *
*Input Arguments     None                                          *
*                                                                  *
*Output Arguments    None                                          *
*                                                                  *
*Local Arguments     None                                          *
*                                                                  *
*Functions called    write_position                               *
********************************************************************/

get_pass_count()
  {
  clrscr();                    // clear the window
  write_position(5,3,  "Pass count = ");
  scanf("%d",&pass_count);                   // get the new pass count
  } // end of function


/********************************************************************
*    Name save_configuration                                       *
*                                                                  *
*    This routine saves the current script to a file. If the       *
*    file already exist, the script will be appended to the end     *
```

```
*    of the file.                                                    *
*                                                                    *
*Input Arguments    None                                             *
*                                                                    *
*Output Arguments   None                                             *
*                                                                    *
*Local Arguments    i j x y t_cursor                                 *
*                            file_name[x]   temp[x]                  *
*                                                                    *
*Functions called   save_window border                              *
*                           write_position          clrscr           *
*                           restore_window                           *
*********************************************************************/
#define SC1  18
#define SC2   7
#define SC3  54
#define SC4  14
save_configuration()
    {
    int i,j,x,y,t_cursor;
    char  ans;
    char file_name[20],temp[80];
    window(SC1,SC2,SC3,SC4);                    // new window
    save_window(SC1,SC2,SC3,SC4, window2); // save the window
    border(SC1,SC2,SC3,SC4);                     // draw border
    write_position(5,1,  "Save Configuration File");
    window(SC1+1,SC2+1,SC3-1,SC4-1);   // condense window
    clrscr();                             // clear the new window
    write_position(2,1,
     "Save the Configuration.(Y/N)");
    ans = get_key();                  // get answer
    if (ans == 'Y' || ans == 'y')     // if Yes
       {
       write_position(2,3,  "Enter the file name: ");
       gets(file_name);               // get the file name
       strcat(file_name,ext);         // add extension
       // open the file
       handle = fopen(  file_name,"r");
       // if unable to open file report an error
       if (handle == -1)
    {
    write_position(4,4,"Unable to open file");
    get_key();                 // wait for key
    return(0);                 // return to caller
    }
       // write string to the file
//     write_data(handle,48,  selected_file);
       fclose(handle);               // close the file
       }
    window(SC1,SC2,SC3,SC4);                   // new window
    restore_window(SC1,SC2,SC3,SC4, window2);
    }

/*******************************************************************
*    Name    load_configuration                                    *
*                                                                  *
*    This routine loads the script and execute the script file.    *
*    if the script file has more than one script, then each and    *
*    every script is loaded and executed.                          *
*    The routine returns a value of zero if the file was opened,    *
*    otherwise an error code will be returned.                     *
*                                                                  *
*                                                                  *
*Input Arguments    None                                           *
*                                                                  *
*Output Arguments   None                                           *
*                                                                  *
*Local Arguments    i j t_cursor    file_name[x]                   *
*                                                                  *
*Functions called   save_window border                            *
*                           write_position restore_window          *
*******************************************************************/
int  load_configuration()
    {
    int i,j,t_cursor;
```

```
      char file_name[20];
      window(SC1,SC2,SC3,SC4);                      // new window
      save_window(SC1,SC2,SC3,SC4, window2);     // save the window
      border(SC1,SC2,SC3,SC4);                    // draw border
      write_position(5,1,  "Load Configuration File");
      window(SC1+1,SC2+1,SC3-1,SC4-1);            // condense window
      clrscr();                                   // clear the screen
      write_position(3,2,    // requeszt file name
      "Name of file:");
      gets(file_name);                            // get file name
      strcat(file_name,ext);                      // add extension
      // open the file
      handle = fopen(  file_name,"r");
      // report any error during opening
      if (handle == -1)
         {
cprintf(  "Unable to open file");
get_key();                             // wait for key
return(1);                             // return to caller
         }
    // read config file
//     read_data(handle,48,  selected_file);
      fclose(handle);          // close the file
      window(SC1,SC2,SC3,SC4);                         // new window
      restore_window(SC1,SC2,SC3,SC4, window2); // restore window
      } // end of function
/******************************************************************
*    Name save_window                                            *
*                                                                *
*    Description:                                                *
*    This routine saves the window defined by the input arguments *
*    into the array defined in the input argument.               *
*                                                                *
*Input Arguments    cl  rl  c2  r2  win[x]                       *
*                                                                *
*Output Arguments   None                                         *
*                                                                *
*Local Arguments    i  j                                         *
*                                                                *
*Functions called   None                                         *
********************************************************************/
save_window(int c1,int r1,int c2,int r2,int *win)
   {
   int i,j;
   unsigned int far *buff;
   unsigned int far *bufx;
   buff = (int far *) 0xb8000000;
   for(i=r1-1;i<r2;i++) {
      bufx = buff + (80 * i) + c1-1;
      for(j=c1-1;j<c2;j++) {
*win++ = *bufx++;
} // end of inner for loop
      } // end of outter for loop
   } // end of function
/******************************************************************
*Name      restore_window                                        *
*                                                                *
*Description:                                                    *
*This routine re-paints the window area define with             *
*The first four arguments with the data in the array            *
*pointed to by the fifth argument.                              *
*                                                                *
*Input Arguments    cl  rl  c2  r2  win[x]                       *
*                                                                *
*Output Arguments   None                                         *
*                                                                *
*Local Arguments    i  j                                         *
*                                                                *
*Functions called   None                                         *
********************************************************************/
restore_window(int c1,int r1,int c2,int r2,int *win)
   {
int i,j;
   unsigned int far *buff;
   unsigned int far *bufx;
```

```
    buff = (int far *) 0xb8000000;
    for(i=r1-1;i<r2;i++) {
        bufx = buff + (80 * i) + c1 -1;
        for(j=c1-1;j<c2;j++) {
*bufx++ = *win++;
} // end of inner for loop
        } // end of outter for loop
    } // end of function


set_log_window()
  {

  }
```

Support Routines

```
/***********************************************************************
*    SUPPORT.C                                                         *
*                                                                      *
*    This module contains support routines that are used by all        *
*    of the diagnsotic executives. It is developed using Borland C++. *
*                                                                      *
*    Function that are in this module are:                             *
*                                                                      *
*1. get_key()                                                          *
*2. test_key(()                                                        *
*3. set_att()                                                          *
*4. border()                                                           *
*5. write_position()                                                   *
*6. get_cursor()                                                       *
*7. bottom_line()                                                      *
*8. wait_press()                                                       *
*9. get_decimal()                                                      *
*10 get_hex()                                                          *
*11 get_lhex()                                                         *
*12 write_reverse()                                                    *
*13 check_key()                                                        *
*14 down_option()                                                      *
*15 up_option()                                                        *
*16 get_val()                                                          *
*17 beep()                                                             *
*18 at_window()                                                        *
*19 set_window()                                                       *
*20 error_report()                                                     *
*21 write_under_test()                                                 *
*22 set_error_log()                                                    *
*23 set_log()                                                          *
*24 logging()                                                          *
*25 set_file()                                                         *
*26 display_log()                                                      *
*27 data_path()                                                        *
*28 partial_data_path()                                                *
*29 clear_buffer()                                                     *
*30 outreg()                                                           *
*31 inreg();                                                           *
*32 del_char();                                                        *
***********************************************************************/
```

```
#define  HOR    205
#define  VER    186

#include  <conio.h>
#include  <stdio.h>
#include  <string.h>
#include  <ctype.h>
#include "..\support\diag.h"
#include "..\support\data.h"
#include "..\support\proto.inc"


FILE   *error_handle;
FILE   *log_handle;
/*********************************************************************
*    get_key()                                                      *
*                                                                   *
*    Description                                                    *
*    This routine call the BIOS keyboard software interrupt to      *
*    read a key from the keyboard bufffer. If no key is present,    *
*    then the routine waits until a key is pressed.                 *
*                                                                   *
*    Input Argument:    None                                        *
*                                                                   *
*    Output Arguments:  Return Key code                             *
*                                                                   *
*    Local Arguments:   None                                        *
*                                                                   *
*    Functions Called:  None                                        *
*                                                                   *
*    Component History: Initial Entry                               *
*                                                                   *
*********************************************************************/
get_key()
  {
  asm {
    mov  ah,0              // set for read keyboard character
    int  16h }            // call the interrupt service
  return _AX;              // save key stroke
  } // end of function
/*********************************************************************
*    test_key()                                                     *
*                                                                   *
*    Description                                                    *
*    This routine call the keybaord software interrupt and checks   *
*    if a key has been pressed. If a key has been pressed, the routine*
*    returns a 1, otherwise it returns a 0.                         *
*                                                                   *
*    Input Argument:    None                                        *
*                                                                   *
*    Output Arguments:  Return Keyboard Status                      *
*                                                                   *
*    Local Arguments:   None                                        *
*                                                                   *
*    Functions Called:  None                                        *
*                                                                   *
*    Component History: Initial Entry                               *
*                                                                   *
*********************************************************************/
test_key()
  {
  asm {
mov  ah,1                  // set for read keyboard character
int  16h                   // call the interrupt service
mov  ah,0                  // force to no key present
jz   no_char               // br if no char
mov  ah,1 }                // otherwise we got a character
no_char: return _AH;              // save key stroke
  } // end of function
/*********************************************************************
*    Name    set_att                                                *
*                                                                   *
*    Description:                                                   *
*    This routine set the background color and the text color of    *
```

```
*    characters that will besent to the console          *
*                                                        *
*                                                        *
*  Input Argument:    backg, text                        *
*                                                        *
*  Output Arguments: None                                *
*                                                        *
*  Local Arguments:   None                               *
*                                                        *
*  Functions Called:  textcolor()                        *
*                      textbackground()                  *
*                                                        *
*  Component History: Initial Entry                      *
*                                                        *
***********************************************************/
void set_att(int backg,int text)
    {
    bg = backg;          // save background color
    fg = text;           // save text color
    textcolor(text);
    textbackground(bg);
    } // end of function
/*********************************************************
*  border()                                              *
*                                                        *
*  Description                                           *
*  This routine  places a border around the present selected window. *
*  The top and bottom rows, and ht eleft and right sides must be  *
*  passed to the routine. The is no check to verify that the values *
*   passed are legal.                                    *
*                                                        *
*  Input Argument:    left_col,top_row,right_col,bottom_row *
*                                                        *
*  Output Arguments: None                                *
*                                                        *
*  Local Arguments:   int i                              *
*                                                        *
*  Functions Called:  gotoxy()                           *
*                      putch()                           *
*                                                        *
*  Component History: Initial Entry                      *
*                                                        *
***********************************************************/
void border(int left_col,int top_row,int right_col,int bottom_row)
    {
    int i;
    clrscr();                          // clear the screen
    gotoxy(1,1);                       // position the cursor
    for (i = 1; i < right_col - left_col+1; i++)
        putch(HOR);                    // place bar across top row
    gotoxy(1,bottom_row - top_row+1 );
    for (i = 1; i < right_col - left_col+1; i++)
        putch(HOR);                    // place bar across bottom row
    for (i = 2;i < bottom_row - top_row + 1; i++) {
      gotoxy(right_col - left_col,i);
      putch(VER);                      // and on the left side
      gotoxy(1,i);
      putch(VER);                      // veritical bar on right side
      }
    // now place the four cornors on the screen
    gotoxy(1,1);
    putch(201);                        // set upper left corner
    gotoxy(right_col-left_col,1);
    putch(187);                        // lower left corner
    gotoxy(1,bottom_row-top_row+1);
    putch(200);                        // upper right corner
    gotoxy(right_col-left_col,bottom_row - top_row+1);
    putch(188);                        // lower right corner
    } // end of function
/*********************************************************
*  Name    write_position                                *
*                                                        *
*  Description:                                          *
*  This routine set the video in high intensity mode, then place *
*  the cursor to the specified row/column and display the message *
```

```
*                                                                    *
*  Input Argument:     None                                          *
*                                                                    *
*  Output Arguments:   None                                          *
*                                                                    *
*  Local Arguments:    None                                          *
*                                                                    *
*  Functions Called:   gotoxy()                                      *
*                                                                    *
*  Component History:  Initial Entry                                 *
*                                                                    *
*********************************************************************/
void write_position(int col,int row,char *text)
 {
 gotoxy(col,row);                    // set cursor position
 cprintf(text);                      // display the string
 }
/*********************************************************************
*  Name get_cursor                                                   *
*                                                                    *
*  Description:                                                      *
*  This routine read the current position of the cursor and returns *
*  that value to the calling routine as an integer                  *
*                                                                    *
*  Input Argument:     None                                          *
*                                                                    *
*  Output Arguments:   Cursor Location                               *
*                                                                    *
*  Local Arguments:    None                                          *
*                                                                    *
*  Functions Called:   wherex()                                      *
*                       wherey()                                     *
*                                                                    *
*  Component History:  Initial Entry                                 *
*                                                                    *
*********************************************************************/
get_cursor()
  {
  return( (wherex() << 8) +wherey());
  }


/*********************************************************************
*  Name      wait_press                                              *
*                                                                    *
*  Description:                                                      *
*  This routine will write the message "Press any key..." and then  *
*  wait for a character to be pressed on the keyboard.              *
*                                                                    *
*  Input Argument:     None                                          *
*                                                                    *
*  Output Arguments:   None                                          *
*                                                                    *
*  Local Arguments:    None                                          *
*                                                                    *
*  Functions Called:   bottom_line()                                 *
*                       get_key()                                    *
*                                                                    *
*  Component History:  Initial Entry                                 *
*                                                                    *
*********************************************************************/

void wait_press()
  {
  bottom_line("                        Press any key to continue...");
  get_key();
  clrscr();
  }

/*********************************************************************
*  Name    Get_decimal()                                            *
*                                                                    *
*  Description:                                                      *
*  This routine is used to enter a decimal value from the           *
*  keyboard.                                                         *
```

```
*                                                                    *
*  Input Argument:      Pointer to argument to enter                 *
*                                                                    *
*  Output Arguments:    None                                         *
*                                                                    *
*  Local Arguments:     digit                                        *
*                                                                    *
*  Functions Called:    get_key()            put_char()             *
*                                                                    *
*  Component History: Initial Entry                                  *
*                                                                    *
*********************************************************************/
void get_decimal(int *value)
    {
    char digit;
    int done = 0;
    *value = 0;                          // initialize the value
    while (!done) {                      // loop until illegal digit
        digit = get_key();               // get next key
        putch(digit);                    // display it
        // check if digit between 0 and 9
        if (digit > '0' - 1 & digit < '9' + 1)
    *value = *value * 10   + (digit - 0x30);
        else   done = 1;                 // prepare to exit function
        } // end of while loop
    } // end of fucntion

/*******************************************************************
*    Name    Get_hex()                                               *
*                                                                    *
*    Description:                                                    *
*    This routine will return a 16 bit hex integer value             *
*                                                                    *
*                                                                    *
*    Input Argument:      pointer to value                           *
*                         nibble count                               *
*                                                                    *
*    Output Arguments:    None                                       *
*                                                                    *
*    Local Arguments:     digit   c                                  *
*                                                                    *
*    Functions Called:    get_key()            putch()              *
*                toupper()                                           *
*                                                                    *
*    Component History: Initial Entry                                *
*                                                                    *
*********************************************************************/
void get_hex(int *value,int cnt)
    {
    char digit,c;
    int done = c = 0;
    *value = 0;                          // initialize the value
    while (!done) {                      // loop till done
digit = get_key();               // get key character
digit = toupper(digit);          // convert to upper case
putch(digit);                    // display character
// check if between 0 - 9 and A - F
if (digit > '0' - 1 & digit < '9' + 1)
    *value = *value * 0x10   + (digit - 0x30);
else if (digit > 'A' - 1 & digit < 'F' + 1)
    *value = *value * 0x10   + (digit - 0x37);
// if not prepare to exit
else   done = 1;
c++;
if (c == cnt) done = 1;
} // end of while loop
    } // end of function

/*******************************************************************
*    Name    Get_lhex()                                              *
*                                                                    *
*    Description:                                                    *
*    This routine will return a 16 bit hex integer value             *
*                                                                    *
*                                                                    *
```

```
*   Input Argument:    Pointer to argument                              *
*                                                                       *
*   Output Arguments:  None                                             *
*                                                                       *
*   Local Arguments:   digit   c     done                               *
*                                                                       *
*   Functions Called:  get_key()            toupper()                   *
*                       putch()                                         *
*                                                                       *
*   Component History: Initial Entry                                    *
*                                                                       *
*************************************************************************/
void get_lhex(long *value)
  {
  char digit,c;
  int done = c = 0;
  *value = 0;                            // intialize the value
  while (!done) {                        // loop till done
    digit = get_key();                   // get next char
    digit = toupper(digit);              // convert to upper case
    putch(digit);                        // display character
    // check ifbetween 0 and  9  and A - F
    if (digit > '0' - 1 & digit < '9' + 1)
  *value = *value * 0x10  + (digit - 0x30);
    else if (digit > 'A' - 1 & digit < 'F' + 1)
  *value = *value * 0x10  + (digit - 0x37);\
    // if not prepare to exit
    else   done = 1;
    c++;
    if (c == 8) done = 1;
    } // end of while loop
  } // end of function

/***********************************************************************
*   Name   write_reverse                                                *
*                                                                       *
*   Description:                                                        *
*   This routine write the specified string at teh row/column position* 
*   but in reverse video color.                                         *
*                                                                       *
*                                                                       *
*   Input Argument:    Row, Column ans ASCII string                     *
*                                                                       *
*   Output Arguments:  None                                             *
*                                                                       *
*   Local Arguments:   temp_bg,temp_fg                                  *
*                                                                       *
*   Functions Called:  write_position()                                 *
*                                                                       *
*   Component History: Initial Entry                                    *
*                                                                       *
*************************************************************************/
void write_reverse(int row,int col,char *str)
  {
  int temp_bg,temp_fg;
  temp_bg = bg;                          // save current background
  temp_fg = fg;                          // and the current foreground
  textattr((RED<<4) + LGRAY);
// if (!gr_board) textattr(0x8f);
  write_position(row,col, str);
  set_att(temp_bg,temp_fg);              // restore orginal colors
  textattr((CYAN<<4) + BLUE);            // set attributes
  }
/***********************************************************************
*   Name   check_key                                                    *
*                                                                       *
*   Description:                                                        *
*                                                                       *
*                                                                       *
*   Input Argument:    ASCII string                                     *
*                                                                       *
*   Output Arguments:  None                                             *
*                                                                       *
*   Local Arguments:   None                                             *
*                                                                       *
```

```
*   Functions Called:  down_option()           up_option()              *
*                                                                        *
*   Component History: Initial Entry                                     *
*                                                                        *
*************************************************************************/
void check_key(char opts[][30])
   {
   switch(key)  {                        // Action on the key stroke
case DN_ARR:                     // Down ARROW
   count++;                             // update counter
   if (count == max) count = 0;         // adjust for wrap
   down_option(count,max, &opts[0][0]); // update display
   break;
case UP_ARR:                     // UP ARROW
   count--;                             // update counter
   if (count < 0)  count = max-1;       // adjust for wrap
   up_option(count,max, &opts[0][0]); // update display
   break;
} // end of switch statement
   } // end of function

/*************************************************************************
*   name   down_option                                                   *
*                                                                        *
*   Description:                                                         *
*   This rouitne selects the next item in the menu. If at the last       *
*   item, it will sdlect the top item of the menu.                       *
*                                                                        *
*                                                                        *
*   Input Argument:     function count,  maximum option and              *
*                       an ASCII string                                  *
*                                                                        *
*   Output Arguments:  None                                              *
*                                                                        *
*   Local Arguments:   None                                              *
*                                                                        *
*   Functions Called:  write_position()      write_reverse()            *
*                                                                        *
*   Component History: Initial Entry                                     *
*                                                                        *
*************************************************************************/
void  down_option(int count, int max, char optx[][30])
   {
   write_reverse(2,1+count, optx[count]);
   if (count == 0) write_position(2,max, optx[max-1]);
   else            write_position(2,count, optx[count-1]);
   } // end of fucntion

/*************************************************************************
*   Name   up_option                                                     *
*                                                                        *
*   Description:                                                         *
*   This routine is called when the up arrow was entered. This routine*
*   select the menu item preceeeding the current menu item sleected.     *
*   If at the top item, it selects the bottom item.                      *
*                                                                        *
*                                                                        *
*   Input Argument:     count, maximum options and the string            *
*                                                                        *
*   Output Arguments:  None                                              *
*                                                                        *
*   Local Arguments:   None                                              *
*                                                                        *
*   Functions Called:  write_position()      write_reverse()            *
*                                                                        *
*   Component History: Initial Entry                                     *
*                                                                        *
*************************************************************************/

void  up_option(int count, int max, char optx[][30])
   {
   write_reverse(2,1+count, optx[count]);
   if (count == max-1) write_position(2,1, optx[0]);
   else                write_position(2,2+count, optx[count+1]);
   } // end of function
```

```
/*********************************************************************
 *  Name    bottom_line                                             *
 *                                                                  *
 *  description:                                                    *
 *  This routine opens a window that contains the bootom line       *
 *  of the screen. The background color is set for black and        *
 *  the forground color is set for light gray.                      *
 *                                                                  *
 *  Next the text string that is passed to the routine is           *
 *  written to the screen.                                          *
 *                                                                  *
 *  At present it is the responsiblity of the calling routine       *
 *  to re-establish the working window and attributes.              *
 *                                                                  *
 *  Input Argument:    ASCII String                                 *
 *                                                                  *
 *  Output Arguments:  None                                         *
 *                                                                  *
 *  Local Arguments:   None                                         *
 *                                                                  *
 *  Functions Called:  set_attr()                                   *
 *                                                                  *
 *  Component History: Initial Entry                                *
 *                                                                  *
 *********************************************************************/
void bottom_line(char *text)
   {
   set_att(BLACK,LGRAY);              // set text attributes
   window(1,24,80,25);                // create bottom line window
   clrscr();                          // erase the line
   cprintf("%s",text);                // write the text string
   set_att(BLUE,7);
   } // end of function

/*********************************************************************
 *  Name   get_val(int *)                                           *
 *                                                                  *
 *  Description:                                                    *
 *  This routine is used to enter a value. After the value is       *
 *  entered, it is then place into the argument pointed to          *
 *  by the calling routine.                                         *
 *                                                                  *
 *  Input Argument:    pointer value                                *
 *                                                                  *
 *  Output Arguments:  None                                         *
 *                                                                  *
 *  Local Arguments:   inp_string[6]                                *
 *                                                                  *
 *  Functions Called:  gotoxy()                                     *
 *                                                                  *
 *  Component History: Initial Entry                                *
 *                                                                  *
 *********************************************************************/

void get_val(int *pvar)
   {
   char inp_string[6];
   gotoxy(15*x + 30,y+2);             // position to coordinates
   textbackground(LIGHTGRAY);         // background color
   cprintf("      ");                 // clear the line
   textcolor(RED);                    // text to red
   gotoxy(15*x + 30,y+2);
   scanf("%ld",pvar);                 // input value
   textattr((CYAN<<4) + BLUE);        // set attributes
   gotoxy(15*x+30,y+2);               // reposition cursor
   cprintf("%5d ",*pvar);             // re-display value
   } // end of function
/*********************************************************************
 *  Name   beep                                                     *
 *                                                                  *
 *  Description:                                                    *
 *  This routine send a value of '7' to the console. In most consoles *
 *  this value will cause a beep  to occur.                         *
 *                                                                  *
```

```
*    Input Argument:     None                                              *
*                                                                          *
*    Output Arguments:   None                                              *
*                                                                          *
*    Local Arguments:    None                                              *
*                                                                          *
*    Functions Called:   open_window()                                     *
*                                                                          *
*    Component History: Initial Entry                                      *
****************************************************************************/
void beep()
   {
   putch(7);
   }
/***************************************************************************
*    Name   at_window                                                      *
*                                                                          *
*    Description:                                                          *
*    This routine opens the AT window.                                     *
*                                                                          *
*    Input Argument:     None                                              *
*                                                                          *
*    Output Arguments:   None                                              *
*                                                                          *
*    Local Arguments:    None                                              *
*                                                                          *
*    Functions Called:   border()           gotoxy()                       *
*                                                                          *
*    Component History: Initial Entry                                      *
****************************************************************************/
void at_window(char *str)
   {
   gettext(1,1,80,25,window2);          // save current window
   window(AT1,AT2,AT3,AT4);             // set up this window
   textattr((CYAN<<4) + BLUE);          // set attributes
   border(AT1,AT2,AT3-1,AT4);           // draw border
   gotoxy(20,1); cprintf(str);          // display window title
   window(AT1+1,AT2+1,AT3-1,AT4-1);
   }
/***************************************************************************
*    Name   set_window                                                     *
*                                                                          *
*    Descrioption:                                                         *
*    This routine opens the selected window for viewing.                   *
*                                                                          *
*    Input Argument:     Window Save flag                                  *
*                         Buffer to save the windows in                    *
*                         attribute of the window                          *
*                         Title of the window                              *
*                         the four connors of the window                   *
*                                                                          *
*    Output Arguments:   None                                              *
*                                                                          *
*    Local Arguments:    None                                              *
*                                                                          *
*    Functions Called:   border()           window()                       *
*                                                                          *
*    Component History: Initial Entry                                      *
****************************************************************************/
void   set_window(int s,int *win,int attr,char *str,int a1,int a2,
       int a3,int a4,int r)
   {
   if (s) gettext(a1,a2,a3,a4,win);     // save current window
   window(a1,a2,a3,a4);                 // set up this window
   textattr(attr);                      // set attributes
   border(a1,a2,a3-1,a4);               // draw border
   gotoxy(r,1); cprintf(str);           // display window title
   window(a1+1,a2+1,a3-1,a4-1);
   }
```

```
/*******************************************************************
 *  Name:  error_report(int,int)                                   *
 *                                                                 *
 *  Description:                                                   *
 *  This is the generic error report for the diagnostics. Upon enter *
 *  the routine a check will be made to see if the output is to a  *
 *  printer, screen, or a file                                     *
 *                                                                 *
 *  Upon completion, the integer printer will be resest to the orginal*
 *  value                                                          *
 *  Input Argument:     test # and error code                      *
 *                                                                 *
 *  Output Arguments:  None                                        *
 *                                                                 *
 *  Local Arguments:   temp1, temp2                                *
 *                                                                 *
 *  Functions Called:  write_error()                               *
 *                                                                 *
 *  Component History: Initial Entry                               *
 *                                                                 *
 *******************************************************************/
void error_report(int t,int code)
   {
   int temp1,temp2;
   temp1 = printer;                     // save orginal value
   temp2 = file_act1;
   if (p_error) printer = 1;            // check if output to printer
   if (f_error) file_act1 = 1;
   sprintf(str1,"Error Code = %x.%x\n\r",t,code);  // generic message
   write_error(str1);
   file_act1 = temp2;
   printer = temp1;                     // restore orginal value
   if (error_bell)  beep();             // ring the bell
   if (error_mode == 0)  wait_press();  // wait for key stroke
   error = error_mode + 1;
   }

/*******************************************************************
 *    write_under_test()                                           *
 *                                                                 *
 *    Description                                                  *
 *    This routine write a string of ASCII text in the test mode.  *
 *    If the c_log is set, the text is sent to the console.        *
 *    if the p_log is set, the text is sent to the printer.        *
 *    if the f_log is set, the text is sent to the file            *
 *                                                                 *
 *    Input Argument:    ASCII Message                             *
 *                                                                 *
 *    Output Arguments:  None                                      *
 *                                                                 *
 *    Local Arguments:   None                                      *
 *                                                                 *
 *    Functions Called:                                            *
 *                                                                 *
 *    Component History: Initial Entry                             *
 *                                                                 *
 *******************************************************************/
void  write_under_test(char *message)
   {
   cprintf("%d **",f_log);
   if (c_log) cprintf(message);
   if (f_log) fprintf(log_handle,message);
   if (p_log) fprintf(stdprn,message);
   } // end of function

/*******************************************************************
 *    write_error()                                                *
 *                                                                 *
 *    Description                                                  *
 *    This routine write a string of ASCII text in the test mode.  *
 *    If the c_error is set, the text is sent to the console.      *
 *    if the p_error is set, the text is sent to the printer.      *
 *    if the f_error is set, the text is sent to the file          *
 *                                                                 *
 *    Input Argument:    Error Message                             *
```

```
*                                                                        *
*   Output Arguments:  None                                              *
*                                                                        *
*   Local Arguments:   None                                              *
*                                                                        *
*   Functions Called:                                                    *
*                                                                        *
*   Component History: Initial Entry                                     *
*                                                                        *
**************************************************************************/
void write_error(char *message)
    {
    if (c_error) cprintf(message);
    if (f_error) fprintf(error_handle,message);
    if (p_error) fprintf(stdprn,message);
    } // end of function

/**************************************************************************
*    Name    set_error_log()                                             *
*                                                                        *
*   Description:                                                         *
*   This routine will allow the user to enter the name of the error      *
*   log file. If a file already exist by that name, the user will be     *
*   pompted. If the user answers No to the prompt, the routien will      *
*   exit without creating and opening the file.                          *
*                                                                        *
*   Otherwise, the file will be created and will exit this routine       *
*   with the file open.                                                  *
*                                                                        *
*   Output Arguments:  None                                              *
*                                                                        *
*   Local Arguments:   None                                              *
*                                                                        *
*   Functions Called:  logging()                                         *
*                                                                        *
*   Component History: Initial Entry                                     *
*                                                                        *
**************************************************************************/
void set_error_log()
    {
    set_log_window();
    logging(0,&c_error,&p_error,&f_error,&error_log_file);
    }

void set_log()
    {
    set_log_window();
    logging(1,&c_log,&p_log,&f_log,&log_file);
    }


void logging(int type,int *flag1,int *flag2,int *flag3,char *file)
    {
    char ch;
    clrscr();
    ch = 0;
    while (ch != '9') {
        write_position(2,1, "1 Console Toggle ");
        gotoxy(25,1);
        if (*flag1 == 0)        cprintf("OFF");
        else                    cprintf("ON ");
        write_position(2,2, "2 Printer Toggle ");
        gotoxy(25,2);
        if (*flag2 == 0)        cprintf("OFF");
        else                    cprintf( "ON ");
        write_position(2,3, "3 File Output    ");
        gotoxy(25,3);
        if (*flag3 == 0)        cprintf( "OFF");
        else                    cprintf( file);

        write_position(2,4, "9 Previous Screen");
        write_position(2,5, "Select ==> ");
        ch = get_key();
          switch (ch)
{
```

```
case '1':    *flag1 = (*flag1 ^ 1);
                break;
case '2':    *flag2 = (*flag2 ^ 1);
                break;
case '3':    *flag3 = (*flag3 ^ 1);
                if (*flag3)
                    set_file(file,type);
                break;
case '9':    break;
default:     beep();
                break;
} // end of switch statement
    } // end of while statement
  clrscr();
  once = 1;
  } // end of function
/**************************************************************************
 *  Name     set_file                                                     *
 *                                                                        *
 *  Description:                                                          *
 *  This routine request that the user enter the name of the logging      *
 *  file and then opens the file.                                         *
 *                                                                        *
 *                                                                        *
 *  Input Argument:    Log file pointer and type of file                  *
 *                                                                        *
 *  Output Arguments:  None                                               *
 *                                                                        *
 *  Local Arguments:   None                                               *
 *                                                                        *
 *  Functions Called:  wait_press()                                       *
 *                                                                        *
 *  Component History: Initial Entry                                      *
 *                                                                        *
 **************************************************************************/
void set_file(char *file,int type)
    {
  clrscr();
  write_position(1,1, "Enter the file name: ");
  gets(file);
  if (!type) {
    error_handle = fopen(file,"w+");
    if (error_handle == NULL) {
      cprintf("\n\rUnable to open file");
      wait_press(); }
      }
    else {
    log_handle = fopen(file,"w+");
    if (log_handle == NULL) {
      cprintf("\n\rUnable to open file");
      wait_press(); }
      }
  clrscr();
  }
/**************************************************************************
 *  Name display_log_file()                                               *
 *                                                                        *
 *   Description:                                                         *
 *   This routine will display of the log file from the beginning         *
 *   at the comletion of every 10 line there will be a pause allowing      *
 *   the read to read the text. After three seconds, the next ten line*
 *   will be displayed. If the read wishes to hold the current screen,*
 *   he must press the ESC key. to continue, press the ESC a second       *
 *   time.                                                                *
 *   Input Argument:    None                                              *
 *                                                                        *
 *   Output Arguments:  None                                              *
 *                                                                        *
 *   Local Arguments:   None                                              *
 *                                                                        *
 *   Functions Called:  wait_press( )                                     *
 *                                                                        *
 *   Component History: Initial Entry                                     *
 *                                                                        *
 **************************************************************************/
```

```
void display_log_file()
    {
    char  buffer[257];
    int done,line,error,i;
    once = 1;                      // one time only
    clrscr();                              // clear the screen
    if (log_handle == NULL) {              // if unable to open the file
       cprintf("Log file not open");       // report as an error
       wait_press();                       // wait for key press
       return;   }
    line = 0;
    done = 0;
    fseek(log_handle,0L,0);                // rewind the file
    while (!done) {                        // loop until blank line
       fgets(str1,80,log_handle);          // read next line
       if (str1[0] == 0) done = 1;         // end of file
       cprintf("%s\r",str1);               // display the line of text
       line++;
       if (line > 10)  {                   // allow ten lines then wait
    getch();
    line = 0;   }
       }
    if (error == -1)  cprintf("\n\r--Error in Reading File");
    else              cprintf( "\n\r--End of file");
    wait_press();
    }
/*************************************************************************
 *  Name display_log_file()                                             *
 *                                                                      *
 *  Description:                                                        *
 *  This routine will display of the error log file from the beginnin*
 *  at the comletion of every 10 line there will be a pause allowing  *
 *  the read to read the text. After three seconds, the next ten line*
 *  will be displayed. If the read wishes to hold the current screen, *
 *  he must press the ESC key. to continue, press the ESC a second    *
 *  time.                                                              *
 *  Input Argument:     None                                           *
 *                                                                      *
 *  Output Arguments:   None                                           *
 *                                                                      *
 *  Local Arguments:    None                                           *
 *                                                                      *
 *  Functions Called:   open_window()                                  *
 *                                                                      *
 *  Component History: Initial Entry                                   *
 *                                                                      *
 *************************************************************************/
void display_error_log()
    {
    char  buffer[257];
    int done,line,error,i;
    once = 1;                              // only once routine
    clrscr();                              // clear the screen
    if (error_handle == NULL) {            // if unable to open the file
       cprintf("Error file not open");     // report as an error
       wait_press();                       // wait for key press
       return;   }
    line = 0;
    done = 0;
    fseek(error_handle,0L,0);              // rewind the file
    while (!done) {                        // loop until blank line
       fgets(str1,80,error_handle);        // read next line
       if (str1[0] == 0) done = 1;         // end of file
       cprintf("%s\r",str1);               // display the line of text
       line++;
       if (line > 10)  {                   // allow ten lines then wait
    getch();
    line = 0;    }
       } // end of display
    if (error == -1)  cprintf("\n\r--Error in Reading File");
    else              cprintf( "\n\r--End of file");
    wait_press();
    } // end of function
```

```
/*************************************************************************
 *  Name:   data_path()                                                 *
 *                                                                      *
 *  Description:                                                        *
 *  This routine is the generic test routine for checkout of full      *
 *  I/O registers. First a walking zero will pass through a field       *
 *  of 1's. Second part of the test will be a walking one passing       *
 *  through a field of 0's                                              *
 *                                                                      *
 *  Input Argument:     None                                            *
 *                                                                      *
 *  Output Arguments:   None                                            *
 *                                                                      *
 *  Local Arguments:    None                                            *
 *                                                                      *
 *  Functions Called:   open_window()                                   *
 *                                                                      *
 *  Component History: Initial Entry                                    *
 *                                                                      *
 *************************************************************************/
int   input_value,output_value;

data_path(int reg ,int w )
    {
    int i;
    output_value = -2;           // value = 1111110
    for (i=0;i<w;i++) {
      outreg(reg,output_value);
      inreg(reg,&input_value);
      if (input_value != output_value)   return(-1);  // test failed
      output_value = (output_value << 1) + 1;
      }
    output_value = 1;
    for (i=0;i<w;i++) {
      outreg(reg,output_value);
      inreg(reg,&input_value);
      if (input_value != output_value)   return(-1);  // test failed
      output_value = (output_value << 1);
      }
    return 0;                                // return test passed
    } // end of function


partial_data_path(int reg ,int w , int bits)
    {
    int i,k;
    k=1;
    output_value = -2;           // value = 1111110
    for (i=0;i<w;i++) {
      if ((bits & k) != 0) {
        outreg(reg,output_value);
        inreg(reg,&input_value);
        input_value = (input_value | !(bits));
        if (input_value != output_value)   return(-1);  // test failed
        }
      k = (k << 1);
      output_value = (output_value << 1) + 1;
      }
    output_value = 1;
    for (i=0;i<w;i++) {
      if ((bits & output_value) != 0) {
        outreg(reg,output_value);
        inreg(reg,&input_value);
        input_value = (input_value | !(bits));
        if (input_value != output_value)   return(-1);  // test failed
        }
      output_value = (output_value << 1);
      }
    return  0;                               // return test passed
    }

void clear_buffer(char *pnt,int count)
    {
    int i;
```

```
      for(i=0;i<count;i++)   *pnt++ = 0;
      }

int   reg;

void outreg(int regist,int data)
  {
  outport(regist, data);
  }

void inreg(int regist,int *data)
  {
  *data = inport(regist);
  }
/***********************************************************************
*   Name   delete_char                                                 *
*                                                                      *
*   Description:                                                       *
*   This routine allows the user to delete a character from the command*
*   input stream.                                                      *
*                                                                      *
*                                                                      *
*   Input Argument:     None                                           *
*                                                                      *
*   Output Arguments:   None                                           *
*                                                                      *
*   Local Arguments:    None                                           *
*                                                                      *
*   Functions Called:   open_window()                                  *
*                                                                      *
*   Component History: Initial Entry                                   *
*                                                                      *
***********************************************************************/
void delete_char()
  {
  putch(0x8);                      // back up a character
  putch(0x20);                     // insert a space
  putch(0x8);                      // back up cursor again
  pnt--;                           // back up the pointer
  }

/***********************************************************************
*    open_window()                                                     *
*                                                                      *
*    Description:                                                      *
*    This routine defines the window, create a border around           *
*    the window, write the window title, and then reduces the          *
*    window size.                                                      *
*                                                                      *
*    Input Argument:    None                                           *
*                                                                      *
*    Output Arguments:  None                                           *
*                                                                      *
*    Local Arguments:   None                                           *
*                                                                      *
*    Functions Called:  border()         write_position               *
*                                                                      *
*    Component History: Initial Entry                                  *
*                                                                      *
***********************************************************************/
void open_window(int LC,int TL,int RC,int BL,int row,int col, char *message)
  {
  window(LC,TL,RC,BL);
  border(LC,TL,RC,BL);
  write_position(row,col,message);
  window(LC+1,TL+1,RC-3,BL-1);
  }
```

Keyboard Testing

The keyboard is the most common device for humans to input data into the computer. By pressing keys, an encoded representation of characters are sent to the computer via the keyboard controller.

This appendix introduces the keyboard, keyboard controller, and the hardware diagnostic tests that are used to test keyboard systems. Each level of the keyboard system has firmware. Tests must be developed to verify that the keyboard and keyboard controller are functional. The chances are that these tests will not be used for purposes other than to qualify the firmware.

E.1 The Keyboard Subsystem

The keyboard is external to the computer system, and it communicates with computer via serial communications. A keyboard controller, which is internal to the computer system, has the responsibility of maintaining two-way communication between the CPU and the keyboard. The following section presents an overview and block diagrams of the keyboard and the keyboard controller subsystems.

During the development stages, the firmware in each of the subsystems must be tested. This testing responsibility might fall on the diagnostic test engineer.

The keyboard is itself a small computer system. Figure E.1 is a block diagram of the keyboard. This block diagram displays CPU logic to read the key matrix, LEDs, a timer, an alarm control circuit, and serial communications to communicate to the host system. In many cases the keyboard has logic that supports a mouse.

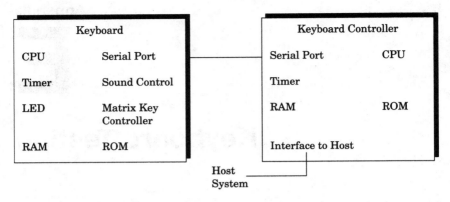

Figure E.1 Keyboard and controller block diagram.

The keyboard's ROM (firmware) contains diagnostic test routines. When power is applied, the firmware must cause the keyboard to execute a power-up diagnostic to verify that the hardware is working correctly. This diagnostic must be executed before the host controller is allowed to communicate with the keyboard.

E.2   Keyboard Power-Up Self-Test

Upon power-up, the firmware performs a self-test, which consists of a ROM CRC test, a RAM test, LED test, alarm test, timer test, and a serial port test. At the completion of the power-up diagnostic test, the normal operating mode of the keyboard will be entered.

E.3   The Keyboard Controller Test

The keyboard controller is also a computer, and it requires firmware to function. It also has RAM, ROM, a serial port, and an interface between the host CPU and itself. This CPU, like the keyboard CPU, must have a power-up diagnostic that checks out its part of the keyboard system.

This diagnostic is generally invoked at power-up, and it may also be invoked with special commands from the host CPU. The firmware in the keyboard controller has the ability to send commands to the keyboard, interface with the host system, and receive keystrokes from the keyboard.

E.4   Testing the Keyboard System

The power-up diagnostics test a major part of the keyboard subsystem. The diagnostic does not, however, check that the proper keys have been pressed or that the proper LEDs were lit when required. It also does not verify that the system is able to communicate properly from the CPU through the controller to the keyboard and back up to the CPU. There are many tests that can be performed on the keyboard that do not require manual intervention. However, to completely test the keyboard, including the aforementioned areas, manual intervention is required.

E.4.1 Scan code test

When a key is pressed on a keyboard, contact is made with a matrix of wires beneath the keypad. The point of contact uniquely determines which key has been pressed. The keyboard firmware then places a numeric code, called the *scan code*, into a local buffer to await transmission to the host. Upon receipt, the host, through its keyboard driver, translates the scan code into an ASCII or other code, which is more suitable for processing by most programming languages.

The scan code test routine verifies that the keys pressed return the proper scan codes to the host CPU. Generally, a layout of the keyboard is displayed on the screen. The tester must press the keys as displayed by the program. If the program is looking for the "A" key to be pressed, then the "A" key flashes on the keyboard display.

Once the scan code is read from the controller, the program compares the code read with what it was expecting. If the code is correct, then the program continues to the next key, otherwise an error is reported.

To summarize:

Step 1:	Initialize setup.
Step 2:	Set up display of keypad on screen.
Step 3:	Loop until all keys are tested.
Step 4:	Flash the next key to press.
Step 5:	Wait for key input.
Step 6:	Compare expected results.
Step 7:	Error if not correct.
Step 8:	Set key tested.
Step 9:	Prepare for next key.
Step 10:	Loop to Step 3 if more keys, else end.

E.4.2   Auto repeat key test

Auto repeat is a keyboard function that can detect a continuously pressed key and return scan codes as if the key had been pressed a number of times. The keyboard firmware detects when a key is pressed and when a key is released. If a scan code is returned to the keyboard controller when the key is pressed, then only one scan code would be returned. With auto repeat, as long as the key is pressed, a scan code is sent to the keyboard controller at timed intervals. In many cases, the host CPU may issue a command to the keyboard to set the time interval. The purpose of the auto repeat test is to verify that the keyboard is able to accept the auto repeat time interval command and send the scan codes at the proper interval.

The diagnostic should set up the proper time interval and then request the tester to press a key and hold the key until asked to release it. The time interval is generally a few seconds. The program counts the number of scan codes received and calculates the auto repeat time interval.

To summarize:

Step 1:	Initialize test setup.
Step 2:	Initialize keyboard.
Step 3:	Display message to press key and hold it, wait for key.
Step 4:	Start the timer.
Step 5:	Continue to read scan code.
Step 6:	Wait for 20 seconds.
Step 7:	Display message to release key.
Step 8:	Calculate the number of scan codes read.
Step 9:	If default value is OK, continue. Otherwise report the error.
Step 10:	Issue command to set new auto repeat value.
Step 11:	Repeat above exercise.
Step 12:	End of test.

E.4.3   Keyboard LED test

Most keyboard have LEDs controlled by an I/O port on the keyboard. A firmware function within the unit turns an individual LED on or off. The purpose of the LED test is to verify that each LED can be turned on and off. This also tests the keyboard firmware function.

This test should sequence through, setting each of the LEDs on. The tester should visually verify that the proper LEDs were turned on. After all the LEDs are turned on, the test should turn them off one at a time.

E.4.4   Keyboard echo test

One of the keyboard's diagnostic functions is the *echo character* command. The echo command informs the keyboard to transmit the last character sent back to the controller.

The keyboard echo test sends 256 echo characters to the keyboard and verifies that the proper responses were received. If an illegal character is received, an error is reported.

E.4.5   Click Test

The keyboard has the ability to sound an alarm. If the alarm is sounded at a very low level, it sounds like "click." Some keyboard have only one volume, but others have up to eight levels of click volume.

The click test routine must set all levels of the click so that the tester can listen and verify that these levels are correct. This can be done by setting the click volume level and then holding a key down. As long as the key is down, the key clicks should be audible.

The Fax Machine

The FAX machine is simply a computer system that transfers picture images over telephone lines. It includes a keypad, a small display, a printing device, a communication port, and a scanning device. The system provides the keypad so the operator can enter the telephone number and select special functions. The display provides visual feedback. The communication port allows connections via an internal modem to phone lines and another FAX machine. The printer device allows for printing of incoming data. The scanner digitizes the image of a page and, via the serial port, transmits the digitized image to a waiting FAX.

F.1 FAX Hardware

Figure F.1 is a block diagram of a FAX machine. In this figure, notice that there is a microprocessor, 4 MB of RAM, 64k of ROM, a serial communication interface, a keypad, a panel display, a scanner interface, and a printer interface. Notice the RS232 port marked "terminal." Under test conditions, an RS232 terminal may be attached for visual feedback, development, and debugging.

The power-up diagnostic resides in the ROM. After the power-up diagnostic is completed, and conditions are satisfied, the normal operational mode of the FAX machine is entered.

F.2 Diagnostic Requirements

When the prototype is ready to be checked out, there must be some form of a debugger program that requires minimal hardware to oper-

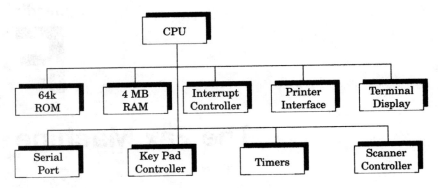

Figure F.1 Fax block diagram.

ate. The debugger allows the system to transmit and receive data via the RS232 port. This debugger must provide several features, as defined in Chap. 3.

F.2.1   Debugger

The debugger is a very important part of the development process. Once a working debugger has been developed, it is used by engineering to check out the fax system hardware. It is also used by the firmware group, or diagnostic group, as an aid in development part of the firmware and diagnostics, and by the software group in debugging the downloadable software.

During development of the debugger, you might find reasons to add features such as reading and writing to virtual memory, a function that converts from one base to another, a mini-calculator function, downloading of programs from external devices, and a function to watch certain memory locations.

F.2.2   Controller self-test

When power is applied to the system, program execution must determine if the power-up diagnostic tests are to be executed or if another mode of operation should begin. A jumper or key press may be used to inform the power-up process to enter a mode other than the normal power-up mode.

The diagnostic must start testing by checking out the components that other components depend upon; that is, by verifying that a basic subsystem is functioning at a level that allows the diagnostic to pass to the next component. The test program should start by testing any I/O register that must be set up before advancing into the diagnostic.

For instance, if a memory controller register must be tested and set up before the CPU is allowed to use the RAM, then the memory controller register must be tested first.

Next, the ROM checksum should be checked, followed by a test of RAM and any I/O registers. The clocks are used for various purposes and should be tested before testing any device that requires a clock signal.

Next, the UART should be tested. Generally, during the normal power-up test, the external loopback test is not performed. The external loopback test can be accomplished during a special field service mode test.

The final two tests are the *scanner test* and the *printer test*. Neither of these test constitute a full functional test. The functional tests are, once again, available in the field service test mode. A detailed description of the scanner and laser printer operation is provided in the following sections.

F.2.3 Laser printer operation

The laser printer is very much like a black-and-white TV. The data in each scan line is placed on the paper as it is pulled through the printer. When the scan line reaches the far side of the paper, a new scan line starts at the near side. This new scan line starts a little farther down the paper than the previous scan line. These scan lines continue until the paper is completely through the printer.

The scan lines contain data. In a 300×300 resolution printer, there are 300 data bits per inch. If a data bit is a one, then a black mark is placed on the paper; if a zero, no mark is placed on the paper. If the paper is 8 inches wide, there are 2400 dots or pixels per scan line.

There are 300 scan lines per inch, and in one inch of an 8 inch wide paper, there are 720,000 pixels. This is a substantial amount of data, and it must be transmitted at a very high rate of speed. If the system is only able to transmit 2200 bits of data before the end of the scan, the remaining bits of data may be lost or erroneously become part of the next scan line.

To maintain this data rate, data is placed into a high-speed FIFO (first-in/first-out) buffer by a DMA chip. The high-speed FIFO is able to provide a data shift register with the data at the proper speed.

F.2.4 Printer data interface testing

If a self-test routine is applied, the output of the data shift register is shifted into a register that the CPU is able to read. Then, the CPU can verify that the data being pumped out of the shift register and that the video scan signal is correct.

During this test, the CPU fills the FIFO with data and issues a clock pulse to the FIFO to shift out the next data byte. The CPU reads that data byte and saves it to the read buffer. At the completion of the shift of all data bytes, the read buffer can be compared to the write buffer. If the data matches, the FIFO and shift register work. This test should be performed without feeding paper through the printer.

To test at full speed, a predefined pattern must be generated. The data pattern must be transferred via DMA to the FIFO. The diagnostics start feeding paper. As the shift register extracts the data bytes from the FIFO, the DMA is filling the FIFO until the DMA detects that there is no more data.

F.2.5   Scanner operation

The scanner operation is very similar to the laser printer video data stream, but in reverse. The scanner starts a scan at the upper left corner of the paper, scans a single line, detecting if the pixel is a dot or a blank. If a dot, the data bit is marked as a one; if a blank, the data bit is marked as a zero. As each line is scanned, a high-speed shift register reads the data into memory. Each scan line has 2400 pixels (8 × 300).

Added test logic allows the video output stream to be applied to the input of the scanner input data. Therefore, a test in the video loopback mode can verify that the scanner and the laser can work properly when both scanning and printing.

F.2.6   Field service mode

The field service mode allows field service technicians to test the system in the customer's environment. The field service mode must provide the technician with diagnostic tests that could not be performed during the power-up diagnostic routine.

During the power-up process, certain key combinations instruct the fax firmware to enter this mode of operation. Once in the field service mode, the technician can select specific tests and execute them once or in a continuous loop.

Source Code Order Form

If you would like a diskette with all the source code presented in this book, complete the form below and send with a check for $25.00 (U.S. currency). Specify the diskette type.

Diskette size: ☐ 3½"   ☐ 5¼"

Name: _____

Address: _____

City: _____ State: _____ Zip: _____

Mail to:

Diagnostic Solutions
Ronald E. Howland
285 Central St.
Milford, MA   01757

Index

ABOUT THE AUTHOR

Ronald E. Howland is an independent diagnostic consultant engineer. He has more than 20 years of experience in computer diagnostics and holds an M.S. in computer science from Worcester Polytechnic Institute.